D0713071

Modern Poetry and Ethnography

Modern Poetry and Ethnography

Yeats, Frost, Warren, Heaney, and the Poet as Anthropologist

Sean Heuston

palgrave
macmillan

First published in 2011 by PALGRAVE MACMILLAN® in the United States—a division of St. Martin's Press LLC, 175 Fifth Avenue, New York, NY 10010.

Where this book is distributed in the UK, Europe, and the rest of the world, this is by Palgrave Macmillan, a division of Macmillan Publishers Limited, registered in England, company number 785998, of Houndmills, Basingstoke, Hampshire RG21 6XS.

Palgrave Macmillan is the global academic imprint of the above companies and has companies and representatives throughout the world.

Palgrave® and Macmillan® are registered trademarks in the United States, the United Kingdom, Europe and other countries.

ISBN: 978-0-230-11167-7

Library of Congress Cataloging-in-Publication Data is available from the Library of Congress.

A catalogue record of the book is available from the British Library.

Design by Scribe Inc.

First edition: December 2011

10 9 8 7 6 5 4 3 2 1

Transferred to Digital Printing in 2012

For my father, Joe Heuston,
and most of all for my wife, Kelly Heuston

After all, the boundaries between fiction and nonfiction, between literature and nonliterature and so forth are not laid up in heaven.

—Mikhail Bakhtin

I caught the sudden look of some dead master
Whom I had known, forgotten, half recalled
Both one and many; in the brown baked features
The eyes of a familiar compound ghost
Both intimate and unidentifiable.
So I assumed a double part, and cried
And heard another's voice cry: 'What! are *you* here?'
Although we were not. I was still the same,
Knowing myself yet being someone other—
And he a face still forming; yet the words sufficed
To compel the recognition they preceded.

. . .

. . . our concern was speech, and speech impelled us
To purify the dialect of the tribe . . .

—T. S. Eliot, "Little Gidding"

Contents

Acknowledgments

I owe great thanks to many people who helped me at various stages of this book's development. Mark Jarman, Vereen Bell, Michael Kreyling, Jay Clayton, Larry Griffin, Leonard Folgarait, and Anthony Wilson offered critical advice and support as my interests in modern poetry and ethnography developed. Noel Polk, Robert West, Jonathan Allison, Rachel Buxton, Marit MacArthur, Kristina Baumli, Rosanna Warren, John Burt, John Shelton Reed, and Dale Volberg Reed all provided valuable advice, information, and encouragement. Marjorie Perloff, Albert Gelpi, Herbert Lindenberger, Diane Middlebrook, Gilbert Sorrentino, Kevin Clark, Doug Keesey, Angie Estes, and Carol MacCurdy contributed less directly but no less profoundly by encouraging and shaping my work at earlier stages.

Numerous staff members at Bellaghy Bawn, the National Library of Ireland, the Rauner Special Collections Library at Dartmouth University, the Cecil H. Green Library at Stanford University, and the Jean and Alexander Heard Library at Vanderbilt University also provided support and advice as I worked on this project. Jonathan Jeffrey at Western Kentucky University and Matthew Bailey and Emma Butterfield of the National Portrait Gallery, London, helped me obtain permission to use the cover photographs of Robert Penn Warren and W. B. Yeats, while John Minihan graciously agreed to let me use his excellent photograph of Seamus Heaney.

My Citadel colleagues (particularly David Allen, Jim Hutchisson, Philip Leon, and Scott Lucas) provided excellent advice and encouragement in addition to serving as great examples. The Citadel and The Citadel Foundation provided invaluable support for my research, thanks in no small part to the efforts of Provost Sam Hines and Bo Moore, Dean of the School of Humanities and Social Sciences. Libby Walker provided excellent administrative support and a tremendous reserve of institutional wisdom. The staff members of The Citadel's Daniel Library were unfailingly helpful (particularly Debbe Causey, who dealt with what must have seemed like an endless series of interlibrary loan requests). My undergraduate students at Vanderbilt and my undergraduate and graduate students at The Citadel provided moments of inspiration and insightful comments while reminding me of how teaching and scholarship can and should work in tandem.

No acknowledgments would be complete without special thanks to my family, particularly my wife, Kelly Heuston; my father, Joe Heuston; my brother, Ian Heuston; and my grandparents, Joseph Walter Heuston and Rita Heuston. Charlie Heuston provided inimitable support and encouragement as well.

INTRODUCTION

"Stories about Stories, Views about Views"

Since Clifford Geertz emphasized the idea that writing is the common denominator of all forms of anthropology and the goal of all disciplinary anthropological activity, numerous scholars have written about the literariness of anthropology, but few have written about the anthropological aspects of literature. In a project such as this one, the first order of business should be to set out the terms by which the work proceeds. Unfortunately, in this particular case a certain amount of confusion about the terms in play is inevitable. Given this, the first priority seems to me to be an explanation of the reasons for the confusion. Geertz's emphasis on the production of texts as the *sine qua non* of anthropology helped precipitate what is commonly referred to as the linguistic turn in anthropology: Many anthropologists—influenced by Geertz and by postmodern critical theory—turned their attention to the processes of producing anthropological texts, most particularly to ethnography, the term at the center of this project.

In *The Predicament of Culture: Twentieth-Century Ethnography, Literature, and Art*, James Clifford defines ethnography as "a state of being in culture while looking at culture, a form of personal and collective self-fashioning."[1] This general definition of ethnography, along with the more basic definition of ethnography as writing about a culture or a cultural group, was the starting point for my consideration of literary texts as self-conscious ethnographic projects. Like Geertz, Clifford (whose suggestive writings about ethnographic authority were important to the genesis of this project) has contributed immeasurably to the prevailing confusion of terms that this introduction must acknowledge. One of the most important things to realize is that there is less than general acceptance of any one strict disciplinary sense of the terms *ethnography* and *anthropology*. Discussions of the ethnographicization of anthropology—a result of the linguistic turn—are common in social science publications, but such discussions have yet to produce anything like a general agreement about the limits of the terms or the practices those terms should represent.

Thus the confusion of terms is not my invention but a manifestation of ongoing controversies in the discipline itself. If at times in these chapters it is difficult to distinguish between ethnography and anthropology, if the terms appear not merely to overlap but to blur into one another, this is in large part because the terms are still subject to debate, overlapping and blurring in academic departments and the publications of their home discipline. Many theorists (Clifford, for one, but also a host of ethnographic theorists who have been influenced by Geertz and Clifford) work to destabilize and expand the definitions of the terms, while some have in mind a much more clearly defined and traditional set of disciplinary practices.

Although anthropology as an academic field recognizes that not all anthropology is ethnography (archaeology, for example, clearly is not), a common sentiment seems to be that, given Geertz's statement about the primacy of writing (a statement that has been broadly accepted by professional anthropologists worldwide), the distinction between anthropology and ethnography is no longer as important as it once was; however, there are anthropologists who criticize this mindset, in part because they believe it trivializes the discipline and reduces it to a sort of linguistic game. Some archaeologists, for example, have openly contemplated the future of their branch of anthropology. They seem to fear that contemporary anthropology has unwittingly helped ethnography mutate into the social-science equivalent of the Blob from the science fiction movies, and that this new ethnography will keep growing and growing and absorbing everything in its path. This sounds quite a bit like concerns about the proliferation of critical theory and cultural studies in academia. This type of widespread disciplinary uncertainty—or, alternately, these types of multiple conflicting certainties—should be familiar to those of us who hail from English departments, more than a few of whom have actively engaged in or have been inadvertently caught in similar contentious discussions about ubiquitous terms such as *postmodern* and *modern*—and for that matter, *literature* and *poetry*.

Arjun Appadurai sums up the feelings of many anthropologists and others in the social sciences in what Geertz has referred to as this era of "blurred genres":

> It is crucial to note that the high ground has been seized by English literature (as a discipline) in particular and by literary studies in general. This is the nexus where the word "theory," a rather prosaic term in many fields for many centuries, suddenly took on the sexy ring of a trend. For an anthropologist in the United States today, what is most striking about the last decade in the academy is the hijack of culture by literary studies . . . Social scientists look on in bewilderment as their colleagues in English and comparative literature talk (and fight) about matters

which until as recently as fifteen years ago would have seemed about as relevant to English departments as, say, quantum mechanics.[2]

Although at first Appadurai might seem hostile to a project such as mine, he goes on to point out a different sort of imbalance in the relationship between literary criticism and anthropology: "There has been much borrowing of literary models and metaphors in recent anthropology, but relatively little anthropology of literature . . . Fiction, like myth, is part of the conceptual repertoire of contemporary societies. Readers of novels and poems can be moved to intense action (as with *The Satanic Verses* of Salman Rushdie), and their authors often contribute to the construction of social and moral maps for their readers."[3]

Although this project does not purport to be a comprehensive anthropology of literature, it contributes to a series of recent scholarly publications that work to bridge sizeable gaps in the critical discourse similar to the one Appadurai identifies. Instead of exporting literary models and metaphors for use in anthropological discourse, in the pages that follow I primarily do the opposite, bringing the insights of ethnographic theory to bear on literature in order to produce new interpretations of four major modern poets: William Butler Yeats, Robert Frost, Robert Penn Warren, and Seamus Heaney.

Ethnographers such as Geertz have long acknowledged the influence of critical theory on their work and on the linguistic turn in anthropology. Part of what this entails is increased attention to ethnographies as fictions—not as *untrue* things, but as *made* things, as *fashioned* things, rather than simple reports of things as they are. By foregrounding the role of writing in anthropology, Geertz has encouraged anthropologists and those outside the discipline to think of ethnographic accounts as textual products constructed by authors, and to remain mindful that producing such accounts is always an inherently creative activity rather than a simple process of reflection, transcription, and reproduction. As Geertz puts it, "Things are, doubtless, whatever they are: what else could they be? But it is in accounts of them that we traffic, our informants', our colleagues', our forerunners', our own, and they are constructs. Stories about stories, views about views."[4]

A brief look at some of the issues under debate among contemporary ethnographers will make it easier to understand the concern about ethnography's expanding boundaries, and will also make it easier to understand the extent to which the relationship between contemporary ethnographic theory and literary or critical theory invites an approach such as mine. Lila Abu-Lughod advocates experimenting with narrative form and creating what she calls "narrative ethnographies of the particular," primarily autobiographical ethnographic accounts that could encompass several genres.[5]

Luke Eric Lassiter favors " 'collaborative' or 'reciprocal' ethnography," a model that explicitly seeks to resituate control and authority within the ongoing dialogue about the evolving ethnographic text itself rather than with the single-voiced author. In collaborative or reciprocal ethnography, dialogue is not just *represented* but sought at every point in the development of the ethnographic text. Collaborative ethnographers take the evolving text back to *identified* consultants (there are no anonymous voices unless directed otherwise by consultants) who offer critique, interpretation, and further dialogue. Consultant voices thus do not merely embellish that of the author; the consultants themselves actually collaborate in how the text is defined and written.[6]

Appadurai, Clifford, H. L. Goodall, George Marcus, and Steven Tyler are other prominent ethnographic theorists who similarly advocate experiments with form, structure, and genre in ethnographic writing. Some of these theorists have already attempted these kinds of experiments (albeit on a limited scale) and have further blurred the distinctions between ethnography and literature. For instance, Goodall opens *Writing the New Ethnography* with a poem about ethnographic theory and practice. Clifford and Marcus begin their groundbreaking study *Writing Culture* with a similar poem. Ivan Brady's *The Time at Darwin's Reef* expands this type of multigenre approach to ethnography throughout an entire monograph, combining poetry, prose, and even visual arts in a decidedly experimental and ambitious work of ethnography.

E. Valentine Daniel's "The Coolie," which appeared in the journal *Cultural Anthropology* in 2008, is an especially noteworthy example of experimental ethnography in that it almost entirely does away with disciplinary distinctions between poetry and ethnography. "The Coolie" is not an academic essay; rather, it is part of a longer poem Daniel wrote, a selection from what Daniel describes as an "'epic poem' about Tamil Labor on the plantations of Sri Lanka." Daniel claims that "by narrating the ethnohistory of the Tamil coolie in this form of verse, the certainties of prose are neither absent nor neutralized but are given a supportive and constraining role." In his introduction to the poem, Daniel calls "The Coolie" an "ethnohistorical poem" and explains its unusual aspects further:

After almost three decades of intermittent struggle . . . and failed attempts at writing a documentable and chronologized history, a few months ago, as I was attempting to construct a clear sentence with "sustainable" content, I found that the sentence took on a life of its own and settled into three tercets of iambic hexametrical, 12-syllabic lines in terza rima (aba, bcd, cda, . . .). I was writing in verse! An added bonus to this piece of serendipity came in the form of a discovery: there was a truth in verse that could not be conveyed in prose; a truth that was present at hand in oral history and ethnography that was made distant or secondary in prose. Social scientific prose does not merely overshadow or repress this affective truth in its secondary status but may even kill it. In the form of verse that I have chosen to narrate the ethnohistory of the Tamil coolie, the certainties of prose are neither absent nor neutralized but are given a supportive and constraining role. Whereas poesis is responsible for truth, prose keeps truth honest.[7]

"The Coolie" is remarkable for several reasons, among which are the fact that Daniel is a full professor in the Department of Anthropology at Columbia University, the fact that a prestigious academic journal printed the poem and Daniel's introduction, and the fact that the editors of the journal wrote of the piece in the "Editors' Overview," "Using verse to convey truths that prose cannot, Daniel draws out the coolie labor system." Not only do the editors express no reservations about this experimental text and its larger implications for their field of inquiry, they effectively endorse Daniel's claim by using his own words almost verbatim.[8]

Although Daniel's poem differs markedly from Lassiter's call for collaborative or reciprocal ethnography, they are both attempts to solve the representational and ethical problems of standard ethnography, attempts to achieve authentic representation by upending long-standing disciplinary protocols. According to Lassiter, "Collaborative ethnography is thus, in the end, a moral and ethical undertaking, one that ultimately privileges the discourse between consultant(s) and ethnographer over a disciplinary discourse."[9] Quetzil E. Castañeda similarly de-emphasizes disciplinary practices while emphasizing the creative aspects of ethnographic writing:

> It is not always or usually not at all very clear what doing ethnographic fieldwork really is or when one is doing it, especially when the research is primarily based in participant observation, informal interviewing, and other activities that are rarified and disciplinary versions of everyday practices—hanging out, talking, listening, remembering, engaging with people, asking questions, sharing stories and information about oneself and others. In other words, the invisibility of fieldwork as ethnography has precisely to do with the relationship of research practices to everyday life. The question of invisibility, whether in theatre or in ethnography, directs us . . . to questions of reality, realism, and fiction.[10]

Marcus concurs that "the positivist language that has defined anthropology in the academy is not supported by the kind of method that fieldwork is, especially after the publication of [Bronislaw] Malinowski's diaries in 1967."[11] Marcus also confirms the discipline-wide significance of the types of moral and ethical concerns evident in Lassiter's comments:

> If there has been a present central tendency within social and cultural anthropology amid all of its recent diverse curiosities and research pursuits, it has been the call for a public anthropology, an anthropology whose primary *raison d'être* and prestige lay in the direct and tangible contributions that it is making to certain

issues and events of the world . . . The desire for a public anthropology implies a discipline more concerned with its accountabilities, its ethics, and its obligations to diverse others in its research efforts than with a guild-like, enclosed preoccupation with debates, models, and theoretical traditions that drive it as a discipline.[12]

Much like the remarks of Lassiter and Castañeda, Marcus's statements clearly endorse experimental approaches to ethnography, many of which appear to emphasize one or more of the former concerns over traditional disciplinary practices.

The idea of ethnographers as creative author figures is by no means a postmodern invention. Rather, it figures prominently in the careers of some of the best-known anthropologists of the early-to-mid twentieth century. Eric Aronoff explains that "the rise of regional modernism in the 1920s and 1930s is also the period in which both literary criticism and anthropology attain their modern disciplinary identities . . . While critics have perceptively analyzed the various ways that literary artists have constructed this or that regional culture, and the aesthetic and/or political implications of those constructions, most have not recognized the way in which this literature participates in a raging interdisciplinary debate—involving anthropologists, artists, social scientists, and literary critics (to name a few)—over the idea of culture itself."[13] Aronoff points out that the influential anthropologist Edward Sapir (best known for his later work in linguistic anthropology) published reviews, critical essays, and poetry in major literary journals such as *The Dial* and *Poetry* during the 1920s.

The idea of the ethnographer as a creative author is also pervasive in the works of Malinowski, who is widely regarded as the father of twentieth-century ethnography. Marc Manganaro calls attention to the historical association between ethnography and literary art by way of Malinowski's own stated ambition: "In the years after 1922 anthropologists often performed dual roles as students of culture and artists . . . others, such as Malinowski, worked as anthropologists but conceived of themselves as author figures; both Clifford and George Stocking note Malinowski's claim that '[W. H. R.] Rivers is the Rider Haggard of anthropology; I shall be the Conrad.'"[14] Malinowski, long regarded as an exemplar of ethnographic practice and monograph production, functions as a representative figure of the discipline and interdisciplinarity. By insisting on Malinowski's self-conscious author function, Manganaro implicitly insists (and numerous contemporary anthropologists would agree) that such a complicated issue inheres in every act of ethnographic writing. A thoroughgoing exploration of what this might mean for anthropology and ethnography in the twenty-first century is beyond the scope of this project. What interests me primarily is what this could mean for literary study.

In his essay "A Transnational Poetics," Jahan Ramazani argues against the traditional conceptualization and compartmentalization of literatures as national in terms that bode especially well for ethnographic approaches to modern literature:

> Humanistic disciplines must draw artificial boundaries to delimit their object of study—nation, language, period, genre, and such—and so must allow for anomalies. But the "exceptions" to mononational narratives—modern "American," "British," "Irish" poetry—are so abundant that they should spur a reconsideration of the conceptual structure that continues to govern much critical production in the field . . . The citizenship of a poem by the migrants Yeats, Stein, Amy Lowell, Mina Loy, D. H. Lawrence, Ezra Pound, H. D., T. S. Eliot, Claude McKay, Robert Graves, Laura Riding, Langston Hughes, C. Day Lewis, William Empson, W. H. Auden, and Louis MacNeice, to mention only some of the most prominent examples before World War II, should not always be presupposed as "American," "British," "Irish," or "Jamaican" in advance.[15]

One could easily add Heaney to an updated version of Ramazani's list of names, and one could argue that Frost and Warren would belong on such a list were its emphasis to shift from nation to region. In any case, Ramazani's argument against simplistic national categorization of literature indicates the potential of ethnographic approaches to literature, in that such approaches tend to highlight complexities and examine hybrid elements of identity and influence closely instead of overlooking them.

I want to return to Appadurai's description of how scholars from university English departments have broadened the scope of what counts as scholarship within the profession by looking critically at culture in ways that have blurred distinctions between the subject matter of English departments and that of other branches of the humanities and the social sciences. I particularly want to focus on one statement quoted above: "There has been much borrowing of literary models and metaphors in recent anthropology, but relatively little anthropology of literature." Appadurai is correct that there has been little application of ethnographic theory to literature since the theory-induced linguistic turn, and most of that has concentrated on prose fiction rather than poetry. It appears that this is changing, because some literary critics have begun to notice ethnography's potential value to their work.

No study such as this one would be complete without an explanation of how its overall theoretical approach relates to recent scholarship and how this approach enables it to make critical connections that other scholarly methodologies thus far have not. A few provocative works that draw connections between literature and anthropology (including archaeology) have appeared in recent years. Christine Finn's *Past Poetic: Archaeology in the Poetry of W. B. Yeats and*

Seamus Heaney follows in the footsteps of Jon Stallworthy's essay "The Poet as Archaeologist: W. B. Yeats and Seamus Heaney." Although the archaeological approach of both critics provides significant insights into the works of Yeats and Heaney, ultimately it runs into the limits of archaeology as a generative mode of thinking for literary authorship. In focusing on artifacts and on analogies of excavation, an archaeological perspective largely screens out the poets' interactions with the living societies that are so important to their respective works and lives.

In Abdul JanMohamed's *The Death-Bound-Subject: Richard Wright's Archaeology of Death* and in his essay "Richard Wright as a Specular Border Intellectual: The Politics of Identification in Black Power," JanMohamed deals with a number of similar issues (including a problematic subject position, conflicted cultural allegiances, and textual production), but even these highly astute works would benefit from a deeper reading of ethnographic theory. Further engagement with the theoretical structures and the vocabulary of contemporary ethnography will enable critics to build on and go beyond critical works such as those produced by Stallworthy, Finn, JanMohamed, R. F. Foster, and Gregory Castle. Their uses of ethnographic and anthropological elements (much like Helen Vendler's conceptual use of anthropology, which I explain in the Heaney chapter) are admirable steps in a right critical direction, but there is much more ground left to cover.

Foster's masterful two-volume biography of Yeats details Yeats's interest and involvement in numerous aspects of Irish cultural issues throughout his career, and Foster's *The Irish Story: Telling Tales and Making It Up in Ireland* critiques the popular narratives of Irish history. Both works have been widely and rightly praised by critics, and both show Foster's keen eye for observing writers observing culture. A biography might not be the place for an intervention with narrative theory (though certainly other biographers have relied upon various critical theories, psychoanalytic theories being most common), but a thorough analysis of cultural narrative such as *The Irish Story* could make excellent use of an ethnographic perspective in its explanations of how various writers (including Yeats and Heaney) studied the culture in question, how they converted observations (and wishful thoughts, as Foster explains) into textual form, and how these artificial narratives became Irish history as it is commonly regarded.

Castle's *Modernism and the Celtic Revival* makes noteworthy moves toward incorporating ethnography into literary criticism, though its effectiveness in this is limited by the historical scope of the study and by an apparent lack of familiarity with recent developments in ethnography. I explain Yeats and ethnography not just within the Celtic Revival, but within a larger historical context stretching from the late nineteenth century to the present in order to examine the ways ethnography functions as a creative literary and critical element and the ways literary ethnography has developed alongside disciplinary ethnography and critical theory. Castle's title indicates the extent to which his project situates the Celtic Revival within the larger context of international literary modernism in what is an impressive work of scholarship. I concentrate more on ethnography and I focus on four major authors, favoring depth over breadth even while dealing with writers whose works cover well over a century of their respective subject cultures. This increased attention to ethnography leads to new insights about the divided and conflicted social positions of the four authors in question.

Beverly Skinner's essay "Sterling Brown: An Ethnographic Perspective" and her essay "Sterling Brown's Poetic Ethnography: A Black and Blues Ontology" provide additional rare examples of a literary critic using the lenses of ethnographic theory in order to see an author and his or her works in a new way. Skinner's incisive reading of Brown's work strikes me as potentially especially useful for critics who examine the works of other African American authors. That said, Castle, Skinner, and the other aforementioned critics do not adequately account for significant theoretical and practical developments in ethnography (such as the concepts of halfie ethnography and insider ethnography) that add a great deal to interpretations of the ethnographic elements of literary texts. This book is intended to bridge such gaps in the critical discourse and to show how much more can be done with ethnographic approaches to literature.

James Buzard's works *Disorienting Fiction: The Autoethnographic Work of Nineteenth-Century British Novels* and "On Auto-Ethnographic Authority" have called attention to the ethnographic elements of nineteenth-century British novels and to the similarities between modernist literary works (primarily prose) in Britain and elements of Mass Observation, a British research organization founded in 1937, which incorporated the observations of hundreds of untrained amateur volunteer observers in an attempt to create what the founders of the organization called an "anthropology of ourselves." Richard van Oort's "The Critic as Ethnographer" makes more ambitious claims about the growing connections between anthropology and literary criticism: "If humanity is defined as the culture-using animal, and if culture is defined as that object which invites symbolic interpretation, then it follows that literary studies stands at the center of an anthropology founded on these assumptions. For who is better trained than the literary critic in the exercise of searching for symbolic significance, of reading beyond the literal surface to see the deeper, more *sacred meaning* beneath?"[16] Van Oort goes on to explain Stephen Greenblatt's work and New Historicism more generally in terms of ethnography: "The new historicism is . . . truly an 'ethnography of the text,' its fieldwork conducted in the historical archive, which is carefully combed for instances of unfamiliarity and strangeness (for example, pamphlets on long-since-forgotten religious debates, transcripts from court cases, manuals on witch hunting, and so on)."[17] Several pages later, van Oort declares, "If literary critics can agree on one thing, it is that what takes primacy in the study of culture is the necessity of textual interpretation. Translated into a definition of the human, this premise becomes the basis of a literary anthropology or, as Greenblatt likes to put it, a cultural poetics."[18] Although I see the value of van Oort's analysis, particularly in terms of the way he explains strong similarities between ethnography and literary criticism, the approach I take in the four chapters that follow is significantly less metaphorical in its uses of terms such as *ethnography* and *anthropology*.

Yiorgos Anagnostou's comments about "metaethnography" also evince the growing interdisciplinary or cross-disciplinary awareness of the value of combining the insights of ethnography and literary criticism:

> Gently but insistently, metaethnography invites professional anthropologists and folklorists to embrace the critical readings of texts (autoethnographies, memoirs, novels, popular ethnographies, films, and documentaries) as a necessary component of the ethnographic project. Situating itself in conversation with anthropology, folklore, cultural studies, and literary studies, the metaethnographic perspective calls on ethnographic practitioners to expand their reading repertoire beyond the literatures of academic ethnographies and to engage with the vast textual field of diverse genres of social representation . . . If, from the point of view of ethnography-centered social sciences and humanities, the authors of nonprofessional ethnographies have been traditionally seen as ethnographic subjects, in my approach they are seen as makers of texts that I analyze as ethnographies.[19]

Anagnostou thus diminishes the distinctions between ethnography and literary criticism, in effect identifying literary criticism as part of the process of reading ethnographic texts and part of the process of the ethnographic project at the most basic levels.

Though persuasive, intriguing, and certainly insightful as far as it goes, the relatively small amount of scholarly work employing ethnographic approaches to literature largely serves to suggest the further expansive potential of ethnographic literary criticism. This is particularly true with regard to the potential for reading poetry via ethnographic approaches, because (as is often the case with emerging theoretical perspectives) most of the early work has concentrated on prose almost to the exclusion of poetry.

In the chapters that follow, I examine the works of Yeats, Frost, Warren, and Heaney in terms of ethnographic participant observation and ethnographic writing styles; by way of the works of anthropologists and contemporary ethnographic theorists and the works of literary critics, I consider the extent to which these four poets study and represent their respective cultures in their works via methods traditionally or recently associated with anthropology and ethnography. The persona of the writer has a great deal to do with this, which is why I distinguish between anthropology and ethnography in the previous sentence. Of the four, Yeats in particular requires consideration partly in terms of anthropology, specifically the early era of so-called armchair anthropology, rather than only in terms of ethnography, which demands participant observation as well as the presence of the ethnographic participant-observer within the text. I make this distinction in part to make it clear that I do not think this approach would work for all works of literature. That is, I do not think most literature is ethnographic. Although, for example, Alexander Pope and John Ashbery could be said to write about their respective cultures, their approaches to these cultures have little in common with the ethnographic practices of the twentieth century and the early twenty-first century.

The individual chapters that follow combine an emerging interdisciplinary theoretical approach with the more established pleasures and processes of close reading. They attempt a variety of approaches to the authors in question in order to consider the authors' works from a critical perspective that has yet to be thoroughly institutionalized. At times the chapters delve into works other than those for which the authors are most widely known in search of something like the undiscovered country of each poet's work and thought.

I vary my approaches somewhat in different chapters (though not so much in the Warren chapter and the Frost chapter, as I will explain below) in order to demonstrate different ways ethnographic literary criticism can be useful. For example, in the Heaney chapter I engage more extensively with other critics in order to demonstrate how an ethnographic approach addresses and builds on important elements of ongoing scholarly conversations, while in the Warren chapter I rely more on my own extended close readings (although I also deal with recent Warren criticism) in order to show how an ethnographic reading yields insights that other Warren criticism so far has not. The Yeats chapter's attention to textual manifestations of Yeats's mindset allows me to talk about Yeats's work and thought in a way that is somewhat different from the ways in which other critics have approached Yeats. This treatment of Yeats is more like the sort of wide-ranging idea- or theme-based criticism (as opposed to criticism that concentrates on extended close readings of a few literary texts) that figures so prominently in contemporary journals. I still do extensive close readings, but they are more in line with this sort of criticism, which tends to follow one idea or theme through a number of works or through an intellectual career instead of presenting an exhaustive explication of just about every aspect of, for instance, "Easter, 1916" (that is, an explication of aspects that do not seem to relate at all to ethnography).

Each chapter deals with differing models of ethnographic authority (Clifford's and those constructed by other theorists), often directly by explaining

Yeats, Frost, Warren, and Heaney in similar terms. Readers will encounter multiple instances of related critical moves and multiple appearances of certain quotations from important ethnographic theorists that frame the issues better than any other critical prose I have encountered. It is of course quite common for a critic to apply a particular methodology to one author's works and then move on to apply the same methodology to another author's works, especially when the critic is working with a new and developing methodology that does things other methodologies have not done. I do a good bit of this (repeating parts of my methodology by applying some of the same criteria and some of the same critical ideas more than once) throughout this project, particularly in the Warren chapter and the Frost chapter.

One of the reasons I have varied my approaches considerably in the Yeats chapter and the Heaney chapter is that I decided to make several of the same moves in the Frost chapter and the Warren chapter, though in the Frost chapter I look closely at ethnographic elements of Frost's work that relate to Frost's portrayals of masculinity in order to show how a particular version of masculinity is deeply intertwined with ethnographic aspects of Frost's writing. Because I am more or less inventing much of my methodology rather than following the lead of an established school of critics who have done the same sort of thing, I think it is helpful to make some of the same critical moves more than once in order to demonstrate that the first time was not a fluke and that the moves in question are useful in examinations of other texts as well. I explain this now in order to avoid creating confusion or a sense of déjà vu in readers later.

Geertz (who was an English major as an undergraduate at Antioch College) offers characteristically insightful advice in response to the increasingly interdisciplinary state of academic inquiry, advice that is simultaneously alert to the shifting intellectual terrain and unpretentious in its recognition of the risks and rewards of this kind of scholarly project: "Learning to exist in a world quite different from that which formed you is the condition, these days, of pursuing research you can on balance believe in and writing sentences you can more or less live with. Settling at a crossroads of controversy, artfully designed to make contentment difficult, is, it turns out, a very good way of doing that."[20]

CHAPTER 1

Off with the Fairies
Yeats, Ethnography, and Identifiction

Above all, [Yeats] was determined to present folk-stories as 'an ancient system of belief,' echoing the implications of anthropologists like E. B. Tylor and Frazer . . . WBY argued that psychical researchers and anthropologists were confronting the same reality.

—R. F. Foster, *W. B. Yeats: A Life*

It has gone without saying that W. B. Yeats was not a social scientist, at least not in the strict, disciplinary sense that literary critics have tended to assume must govern the modern social sciences. During a literary career that spanned over half a century, however, Yeats produced a great deal of commentary on Irish culture. Particularly since the beginning of the postcolonial theory boom in Irish Studies, Yeats's views of Irish culture have frequently been characterized as anything from wishful thinking to deliberate distortions of reality, often with the explicit charge that Yeats effectively reinforced the logic of colonial domination by imaginatively substituting an Anglo-Irish Protestant Ascendancy power structure in the place of the British colonial power structure. Applying the insights of contemporary ethnographic theory to Yeats's work on Irish culture will help balance the record and will make it clear that Yeats's approach to Irish cultural study resembles the prevailing ethnographic practices of his era far more than Yeats's critics have recognized thus far.

In his essay "The Ethnographic Self and the Personal Self," Edward M. Bruner refers to Susan Rodgers's statement that "many amateur ethnographers in many areas of the world are writing about their culture, and it would be useful for us 'to begin to collect such texts, interview their authors, and analyze such folk sociologies."[1] In his essay "A Tree That Stands Burning: Reclaiming a Point of View as from the Center," Robin Ridington summarizes James

Clifford's explanation of the difference between modern disciplinary ethnographic practices and earlier forms of ethnography: "By translating experience into textual form, Clifford wrote, 'ethnographic writing enacts a specific strategy of authority.' He suggested that 'a rather different economy of ethnographic knowledge prevailed . . . before [the discipline] had successfully established the norm of the university trained scholar testing and deriving theory from first-hand research."[2]

One can apply these remarks to Yeats's career-long ethnographic work, and can do so from both sides, so to speak. In the last two decades of the nineteenth century, Yeats began what we may now recognize as fieldwork among the peasants of the west of Ireland, accompanying Lady Augusta Gregory on excursions to record folklore, songs, and accounts of Irish culture by visiting the cottages of the west's rural residents. Insofar as Yeats and Gregory lacked any formal training, this was the sort of amateur ethnography Bruner and Rodgers discuss. Their view, however, extends only so much credit to amateur ethnographers. Bruner and Rodgers clearly regard *amateur* as the more important part of *amateur ethnographers*. Their view, bluntly put, is that *real* ethnographers (those with disciplinary know-how and appropriate credentials—identified as *us*) should interview these amateurs, subject them to professional scrutiny, and produce professional ethnographic accounts of the amateurs' ethnographic efforts.

The perspective expressed by Ridington and Clifford is entirely different in that it legitimates what Bruner and Rodgers regard as an inferior form of ethnographic inquiry. Ridington and Clifford remind readers that ethnography's current disciplinary requirements and practices are fairly recent inventions; that historically the boundaries separating ethnography from other forms of knowledge have been quite permeable when they have been there at all; and that "a rather different economy of ethnographic knowledge" did not exclude the findings and interpretations of amateur ethnographers or diminish them by treating them as mere native phenomena, fit objects for *real* (meaning *professional*) disciplinary inquiry.

In order to understand the importance of ethnographic elements in Yeats's thought and work, it is first necessary to consider Yeats's thought and work in more general terms. Derek Hand says of Yeats, "Oppositional readings of Yeats are a feature in almost all Yeatsian criticism, perhaps spurred on by the poet's own desire to take up marginal positions in his creative writing . . . however, reading Yeats in this fashion produces, or reproduces, a critical dead end. Neither Yeats in the past, nor those reading him in the present, are capable of moving beyond the either/or structure of established positions."[3] Hand seems to misunderstand Yeats's thought process (as well as the thought processes of a number of Yeats scholars) as a static opposition of binaries in which Yeats and his critics endlessly oppose irresistible intellectual forces with immovable intellectual objects. Hand largely concedes the inevitability of this sort of situation throughout his essay. He overlooks a crucial part of Yeats's thought process, however. Yeats is, as numerous critics have remarked, a dialectical thinker given to working through problems via an oppositional process rather than a more linear thought process. In failing to recognize the synthesis that often lies beyond Yeats's antithetical thoughts or statements, Hand surrenders too soon. Recognizing this aspect of Yeats's thought allows for a more accurate understanding of Yeats's seemingly paradoxical relationship with the still-evolving social science now known as ethnography.

This is not to say that simply thinking of Yeats in terms of dialectical reasoning suddenly renders his thought processes completely lucid. At times Yeats is a contradictory thinker in a way that is not redeemable by recourse to dialectics, a way that is somewhat Whitmanian in its acceptance of self-contradiction. As Brian Phillips notes of Yeats, "He seemed to believe with perfect conviction things he could not possibly have believed, and when they were proved wrong, to lay them aside with childlike equanimity, giving no sense of retreat, remaining blithely self-composed, preserving all his larger certainties."[4] Yeats seems at times to be an oscillating thinker, moving back and forth between contrary perspectives depending on the urgencies of the argument at hand, veering between outright contempt for empiricist knowledge or science and strategic uses of science, or something like it (the rhetorical force of science—partaking of the social power and prestige of science), in order to advance his claims and his Irish cultural agenda.

Readers who are familiar with Yeats's lifelong interest in the occult may suspect that this interest somehow makes it difficult, if not impossible, to think about Yeats and his work in ethnographic terms. In fact, this interest in the supernatural is at the heart of Yeats's ethnographic work and thought. Moreover, regardless of how odd it might seem to twenty-first-century readers, this fascination with the supernatural marks Yeats as a man of his era rather than as some lone crackpot. Seamus Deane says that "Yeats had no idea or attitude which was not part of the late-Romantic stock in trade. He was different in the fervour of his convictions, not in their form."[5] That this is so obviously an overstatement gives one a sense of the hostility with which some recent critics—particularly Irish postcolonial critics—have approached Yeats. Deane's remark is a reminder of the influence of the "poor silly Willie" view of Yeats, in which critics have tended to scoff at Yeats's promiscuous spirituality, emphasize his intellectual debts to English Romanticism, and argue that—because Yeats was addled by occult beliefs and a pernicious Englishness at both conscious and subconscious levels—Yeats and the authentic Ireland of his time fit together like a fish and a bicycle. Although the assertion that Yeats was very much a representative man of his age would seem to preclude this sort of scoffing at his now-unfashionable beliefs, this has not been the case; the scoffing has continued unabated by any sense that the beliefs of many contemporary critics and theorists might appear slightly ridiculous in a hundred years or so.

Yeats, it is well known, frequented séances, participated in Madame Blavatsky's Golden Dawn movement, believed fervently in reincarnation, and accorded a great deal of weight to Irish folk belief in spiritual manifestations and supernatural phenomena. Literary critics have appeared to be somewhat flummoxed by these aspects of Yeats's life, and most have avoided them altogether. What is often left out of discussions of Yeats's varied beliefs is that they were not entirely atypical in an era of revolt against determinism or scientism, and that such supernatural beliefs abounded in the polar opposite environments of Yeats's life. London and the west of Ireland were, it seems, both beset by fairies, spirits, and ghosts.

It is helpful to think of Yeats's beliefs against the background of what George Stocking describes as "the more general 'Victorian crisis of faith' to which Darwinism was a major contributing factor." Stocking identifies the prevalence of spiritualism in Victorian culture: "For some Victorians, the spiritualist movement was the post-Darwinian analogue to phrenology, providing a bridge back from a soulless secular meliorism toward the spiritual world they had lost."[6] Stocking explains that the renowned English anthropologist E. B. Tylor investigated spiritualist goings-on by attending séances and meeting with mediums. Also, Stocking adds, "For some Victorians spiritualism offered a surrogate for the emotional security provided by unquestioned religious belief."[7] In a discussion of resistance to the idea of evolution, Stocking says, "Although it reflected changes in the colonial situation and domestic ideological contexts of anthropology, the antievolutionary reaction was part of the more general 'revolt against positivism' in European social thought. It involved a reassertion of the role of 'irrational' factors in human social life, and a critique of the methodological and epistemological grounding of prevailing scientific determinisms."[8]

Observations by literary critics also help place Yeats's notorious irrationality in context. Quoting Yeats's "An Introduction for My Plays," Michael Valdez Moses says, "Yeats insists that Ireland's Celtic myths and Gaelic legends have a regenerative power not only for modern Anglo-Irish literature, but also for the whole of modern European literature. A return to ancient myth and ritual is the predictable 'reaction against the rationalism of the eighteenth century,' and 'the materialism of the nineteenth century.'" Moses also draws a surprising and insightful connection between Yeats and the value system of many of the contemporary critics who have been most hostile to him: "Despite his current reputation as a mere 'cultural reactionary,' Yeats nonetheless also oddly anticipates those postcolonial intellectuals and artists who defend the rights of minority cultures against the homogenizing threat of economic globalization and cultural imperialism."[9]

Like Moses, Russell McDonald draws attention to the context of Yeats's interest in Irish folk culture, particularly the extent to which Yeats thought of it as a corrective to modernity. As McDonald points out, "Thirty-five years after his formative experience collecting folklore in the west of Ireland with Lady Gregory, Yeats recalled in *Autobiographies* . . . 'when we passed the door of some peasant's cottage, we passed out of Europe as that word is understood.'"[10]

In an excellent essay that explains Yeats's work in terms of magical realism, Jonathan Allison makes an important series of claims and observations about Yeats's work, particularly the relationship between Yeats's cultural agenda and his treatment of supernatural elements of Irish folk culture in his work:

> Lyric poems using fantastic elements, shaped from indigenous folklore narratives, have the power to convey counter-cultural values and counter-imperialist descriptions of experience . . . supernatural events are recounted with matter-of-factness, as though they are expected. No rational explanation is offered, and there is no "hesitation" between rational and supernatural explanations. The rational is eschewed, the supernatural celebrated. This is anti-rationalist, anti-realist, and ultimately anti-imperial, a valorization of the magical pre-modern worldview of the Irish peasant, as that was understood by Anglo-Irish writers of the Revival period. Poetry such as this constitutes, perhaps, an attempt to re-write the story of the region and of "the nation." Using different paradigms from those used in the imperial British story . . . The process constitutes a form of counter-hegemonic magic, and of irrational Irishness, opposed to Anglo-Saxon administrative rationality.[11]

Allison is referring to poems such as "The Stolen Child," "The Wanderings of Oisin," and "The Hosting of the Sidhe," but his observations hold true for much of Yeats's other work (poetry and prose) as well.

Anagnostou further helps connect Yeats's work to relevant and divergent critical discourses, thereby drawing together three major strands in Yeats's writing: "Colonial discourse . . . saw the non-Western folk as an embodiment of inferior savagery, thus legitimizing their political and cultural subjugation. Romantic nationalism, on the other hand, saw peasants as the hearth of the national spirit, valorizing vernacular culture even as it excluded the folk from the institutions of high culture. In turn, folklore and anthropology, framed by those discourses and aspiring to scientific legitimacy, have represented the folk through an omniscient, authoritative ethnographer-narrator whose objectifying third-person authorial voice contained the plurality of subjective perspectives in the field."[12] In fact, in addition to seeing non-Western folk as inferior, and thus justly subjugated, colonial discourse saw some Western folk (such as the

Irish, particularly the rural Irish poor) the same way. Anagnostou's comments bring together colonial discourse, Romantic nationalist discourse, and ethnographic discourse, all three of which are crucial to Yeats's work and thought.

Arnold Krupat's commentary on the relationships between ethnography and literature will also help connect the broad social commentary provided by Stocking with a more specific examination of Yeats's ethnographic literary work. Krupat mentions a category of writing that falls somewhere between disciplinary professional ethnography and general creative writing: what I will call ethnographic fiction, a literary genre with ostensibly wider public appeal than the (developing) genres of professional ethnography. Here the example of Adolph Bandelier's novel *The Delight Makers*, published in 1890, serves as an important precursor. In his preface, Bandelier wrote that he "was prompted to perform the work by a conviction that however scientific works may tell the truth about the Indian, they exercise always a limited influence upon the general public; and to that public, in our country as well as abroad, the Indian has remained as good as unknown. By clothing sober facts in the garb of romance I have hoped to make the 'Truth about the Pueblo Indians' more accessible to the public in general."[13]

It is easy enough to see the similarities between works such as Bandelier's and Yeats's ethnographic literary projects. It is important to note, however, that Yeats's accounts of Irish culture typically do not appear in the guise of a unitary fictional narrative invented by an outsider (as Bandelier's novel clearly does), and therefore involve more determined truth claims. Krupat's analysis also invites a return to the subject of Yeats's oscillating habits of thought. In a discussion of "Franz Boas, whose name . . . is synonymous with the scientization of anthropology,"[14] Krupat explains a perplexing aspect of Boas's work, an aspect that is very similar to Yeats's oscillations:

> The famous Boasian hostility to theory and to laws . . . Boas also seems to have given many of his students and readers a strong impression that he was implacably opposed not only to theory but to all statements of phenomenal lawfulness, that for him anthropology was the sort of inquiry that best limits its view to the singularity or particularity of cultural phenomena. Nonetheless . . . one can also cite essays in which Boas asserts that the statement of general laws is, indeed, the ultimate aim of anthropology, as of any science. These latter assertions permit one to wonder whether there is not, at a deep level of Boas's thought, a commitment to sustaining contradiction, a refusal of closure as somehow a violation of the way things "really" are: a refusal, of course, that denies the possibility of science. This seems all the more likely when one considers that even in Boas's explicit remarks approving the possibility of scientific generalization, he insists again and again on impossible conditions for such generalization, for his contention is that laws will legitimately be "discovered" only when "all the 'facts' are in."[15]

Krupat asks, "Can such a conception be compatible with an anthropological *science*? Boas characteristically responds yes—and no?"[16] Krupat later declares, "It is a simple matter to quote Boas on both sides of what seem to me antithetical and—in the form in which they are stated—irreconcilable positions . . . Boas's 'attitude' is such as to offer firm support for both sides of a great many questions."[17] In short, poets are not the only contradictory thinkers. The contradictory aspects of Yeats's work do not in and of themselves mark his work as less serious or coherent than Boas's.

With this in mind, it becomes evident that reading Yeats's writings on Irish peasant culture in terms of ethnography makes a good deal of sense. Doing so, in fact, makes one aware of how many Yeats scholars have recognized the ethnographic or anthropological elements of his work but have passed over these elements with relatively little commentary or without naming the anthropological and ethnographic elements as such. R. F. Foster, the acclaimed Irish historian and author of the only authorized Yeats biography, says of Yeats, "He was a more stringent editor [of his ethnographic accounts] than is often realized. 'I have . . . written down accurately and candidly much that I have heard and seen, and, except by way of commentary, nothing that I have merely imagined.'" Foster is quick to point out that Yeats was not simply a man of science: "In connecting fairy belief with anthropological researches, he hinted at a scientific rationale; but more important, in his view, was its therapeutic function and literary inspiration."[18]

Deborah Fleming expands on this idea, pointing out the links between Yeats's notion of Ireland as a potential example for other nations and his interest in studying Irish culture: "For Yeats, Ireland was a revolutionary country precisely because it was traditional; it remained the only country left in Europe where aristocrat and peasant were able to defeat materialism. The true revolutionary in the modern world was a traditionalist."[19] Fleming's apparently paradoxical final sentence applies not only to Yeats's prioritization of and career-long interest in traditional forms of Irish culture; it also applies to the forms of his poems, which separate his work from the rising tide of free verse in the twentieth century. Although Fleming does not deal directly with ethnography, her assessment of Yeats's interest in Irish traditions contributes to an understanding of how motives beyond detached scientific curiosity figured into Yeats's ethnographic projects.

In order to understand the belief system underlying much of what Yeats thought about Irish culture, one must understand the Anglo-Irish antithesis, a concept Declan Kiberd explains in one of the italicized "interchapters" of his monumental *Inventing Ireland*. According to Kiberd's explanation of the Anglo-Irish antithesis (it is important to note that this hyphenated binary opposition should not be confused with the hyphenated hybridization implicit in discussions of Yeats's Anglo-Irish identity), Ireland functions as England's other, a country and a culture that supposedly embodies all that John Bull's island does not: "By Arnold's day, the image of Ireland as not-England had been well and truly formed. Victorian imperialists attributed to the Irish all those emotions and impulses which a harsh mercantilist code had led them to suppress in themselves. Thus, if John Bull was industrious and reliable, Paddy was held to be indolent and contrary; if the former was mature and rational, the latter must be unstable and emotional; if the English were adult and manly, the Irish must be childish and feminine."[20] Kiberd also points out the longevity of the Anglo-Irish antithesis, along with some of the tactical problems and contradictions it presented for Irish nationalists:

> It is remarkable, in retrospect, how durable such thinking proved, even among the Irish who fancied that they had exploded it. Many embraced the more insulting clichés of Anglo-Saxonist theory on condition that they could reinterpret each in a more positive light. The modern English, seeing themselves as secular, progressive and rational, had deemed the neighbouring islanders to be superstitious, backward and irrational. The strategy of the revivalists thus became clear: for bad words substitute good; for *backward* say *traditional*, for *irrational* suggest *emotional*. The positive aspect of this manoeuvre was that it permitted Irish people to take many images which were rejected by English society, occupy them, and make them their own: but the negative aspect was painfully obvious, in that the process left the English with the power of description and the Irish succumbing to the pictures which they had constructed . . . Sometimes in their progress the revivalists would seem to reinforce precisely those stereotypes which they had set out to dismantle: nevertheless, this was an inevitable, nationalist phase through which they and their country had to pass *en route* to liberation.[21]

Not all critics agree that accepting the terms of the Anglo-Irish antithesis was inherently self-defeating for Irish thinkers. Rached Khalifa, for example, reads Yeats's engagement with the Anglo-Irish antithesis as an example of reverse discourse, a series of rhetorical countermoves by which Yeats takes over the terms of the paradigm—originally freighted with assumptions about the relative inferiority of Irish culture and character as compared to English culture and character—and converts them to positive values: "His textualizing of Irish myths, say, tales of bewitching 'Sidhes' and of noble heroes and poets, should be interpreted as the poet's own counter-reading of the denigratory and stereotype-ridden colonial reading of Irish subjectivity and culture."[22]

Despite the plausibility of interpretations such as Khalifa's, much recent Yeats criticism has portrayed Yeats as deeply misguided in his cultural beliefs. Seamus Deane, one of the best-known critics of this sort, emphasizes the English invention of the Anglo-Irish antithesis by crediting Matthew Arnold with "introducing the 'Celtic' idea as a differentiating fact between Ireland and England. He managed to give this word (previously kept within the preserve of literary historians and antiquarians) a political resonance which it has not yet entirely lost."[23] This is a significant claim with respect to Yeats's ethnographic consciousness and with respect to ethnography in general because of the fact that, as Kiberd points out, Arnold had no in-depth, firsthand experience of Ireland. This fact drives home the importance of the shift in ethnographic practice that was underway during Yeats's lifetime. The era of so-called armchair anthropology—an era in which philosophizing, theorizing, and proclaiming things about cultures often went on unencumbered by any direct contact with the cultures or peoples in question—was drawing to a close, and ethnographic writing was increasingly (although not always completely) founded on the firsthand field experiences of the people who wrote the ethnographic accounts.

Deane emphasizes the influence of Arnold's dichotomous distinction between English culture and Irish culture, asserting that "even now it is difficult to overestimate the importance of Arnold's Oxford lectures, *The Study of Celtic Literature.*"[24] In the Oxford lectures (published in 1867), Arnold inaugurated an era of heightened interest in what is now called Irish Studies, ushering the subject matter into academic and social respectability even as he defined the antithetical terms by which the study of the subject would proceed.

Deane also faults Yeats for the class issues (sometimes latent and sometimes disturbingly explicit) that run through Yeats's work: "Much of what Yeats believed about the Irish peasantry, its past and its native literature, was formed by the literature produced by the more cultivated sections of the nineteenth-century landlord class. The paradox does not seem to have troubled him unduly."[25] Like Kiberd, Deane is one of the most prominent members of what David Krause has termed "the de-Yeatsification cabal," a group of contemporary Irish critics—most strongly influenced by postcolonial thought—who, according to Krause,

> insist on judging not only Yeats but all Irish poets according to a political ideology: the poet's work must first of all be relevant to contemporary Irish problems and particularly the historical situation of political unrest in Northern Ireland. A poet might be sympathetic toward the oppressed people in the North, but if his poems are not, even indirectly, related to that tragic grievance, they are suspect and irrelevant. It should be apparent that the patrician Yeats, with his arrogant Anglo-Irish prejudices and his anti-democratic views of the "filthy modern tide," is not acceptable to these critics, even though it should be evident that his poetry inevitably transcends his reactionary politics.[26]

It is possible to read the works of critics such as Deane and Kiberd in part as a necessary reaction—a sort of Bloomian anxiety-of-influence reaction against

Yeats, not unfounded, not without merit, and likely beneficial in the long run insofar as it allowed or allows Irish writers and critics to escape an Irish version of the situation Flannery O'Connor expressed when she described the danger and difficulty of writing Southern fiction after William Faulkner: "Nobody wants his mule and wagon stuck on the same track the Dixie Limited is roaring down."

Whether expressed as onrushing locomotive, looming mountain, long shadow, or any number of other presences, the potentially overwhelming fact of a singular immense figure in any literary landscape can make life and art and criticism difficult for many others, effectively defining the terms of the argument much in the way Arnold did. Thus, for quite some time, Yeats and Faulkner became the primary (if not the only) yardsticks by which subsequent generations of Irish and Southern writers were measured. Yeats's reputation at least had to contend with the legacy of Ireland's other legendary modernist writer, who cast what it is tempting to call the shadow of the Martello tower— not so grand a structure as Yeats's restored Norman keep Thoor Ballylee, but preferable to many Irish authors and critics for various reasons, some aesthetic and some political. Such authors and critics have, for some time now, cast a cold eye on Yeats and have often found him guilty of what amounts to being insufficiently James Joyce.

The reality of Yeats's mixed cultural inheritance is well established and important. In a larger discussion of transnational poetics, Jahan Ramazani sums up the intercultural complexities of Yeats's life and work about as succinctly as is possible: "Yeats is another poet whose life and work, despite his intermittent cultural nationalism, exceed the bounds of a nationalist disciplinary framework. Although usually tagged unambiguously Irish, he shuttled between England and Ireland, identified with both Irish nationalism and the Anglo-Irish Protestant Ascendancy, pined after an Irishwoman and married an Englishwoman, and collaborated with such South Asians as Tagore and Shri Purohit Swami. His writing hybridizes English and Irish genres, meters, and orthographies while also incorporating forms and motifs from East and South Asia."[27] Despite such complexities, it was perhaps inevitable that a self-identified Anglo-Irish poet such as Yeats would receive some rough treatment as Irish criticism became increasingly postcolonial and had to run to catch up to a national literature that had been postcolonial since 1916, the mid-to-late nineteenth century, or considerably earlier (depending on one's definition of postcolonial literature). A consideration of the ethnographic elements of Yeats's work and thought will build on the insights of postcolonial critics and contribute to a reappraisal of Yeats's relationship with and portrayals of Irish culture.

Although Yeats's ethnographic interests inform his poetry, they are most evident in his prose, which addresses them at greater length and in greater detail.

One could, for example, locate and explain the ethnographic elements in a poem such as "Meditations in Time of Civil War," but for the most part Yeats's poems do not foreground the figure of the ethnographic participant-observer in ways that reward extended close readings with ethnography in mind. Yeats's prose, on the other hand, repeatedly does just that. Yeats's fascination with ethnographic approaches to Irish culture is undoubtedly the reason that so many of the review essays he wrote for numerous publications in the late nineteenth century and the early twentieth century deal at length with books that are clearly ethnographic in orientation. These essays also show Yeats's oscillations of thought, along with his willingness to engage in the kind of obviously self-contradictory arguments that Krupat identifies as characteristic of Boas, even in his pursuit of ethnographic understanding and accurate accounts of authentic Irish culture. In one such essay, Yeats takes folklorist, novelist, and poet Emily Lawless to task for using a mental model or tactic that will be quite familiar to readers of Yeats's poetry and prose: "[Lawless] has accepted the commonplace conception of Irish character as a something charming, irresponsible, poetic, dreamy, untrustworthy, voluble, and rather despicable, and the commonplace conception of English character as a something prosaic, hard, trustworthy, silent, and altogether worshipful, and the result is a twofold slander. This bundle of half-truths made her . . . magnify a peasant type which exists here and there in Ireland, and mainly in the extreme west, into a type of the whole nation."[28] At bottom, Yeats objects to Lawless's reliance on or reflection of the Anglo-Irish antithesis. This objection is entirely puzzling in that at times Yeats subscribes wholeheartedly to the Anglo-Irish antithesis himself. Moreover, Lawless's treatment of west Ireland peasants sounds very much like Yeats's own treatments of similar inhabitants of the rural west, who came to stand—in Yeats's work and thought—for the essence of the nation.

Yeats displays this same sort of self-contradictory thinking, again directly in association with ethnographic accounts, in an 1889 review essay and a later reference to it—both contained in the Yeats Archives of the National Library of Ireland. The essay, printed in the *Scots Observer* and titled "Irish Wonders," is largely devoted to discrediting D. R. "M'Anally" (an Irish-American author) and his recently published renderings of Irish folk culture: "In his feeling for the old country there is a touch of genuine poetry. But the Ireland he loves is not the real Ireland: It is the false Ireland of sentiment."[29] Yeats continues his attack on what he identifies as M'Anally's suspect ethnographic methods and results, lacerating the author for vague references such as " 'a knowledgeable woman' of Colooney, Sligo. The matter discussed is a fairy ball, 'seen by her grandmother's aunt.' " Yeats goes on to quote a long description of the fairy ball rendered semiphonetically in order to represent the Irish accent of the native informant, and continues by declaring his own familiarity with the area in question: "The writer of this article [meaning Yeats himself], though he has not gathered folk tales in Coloomey, has done so within two miles of it . . . but never has he heard anything like this . . . By saying it was the poor 'knowledgeable woman's' grandmother's aunt that saw the fiddling [fairies], Mr. M'Anally means, we suppose, to suggest the old calumny that nobody but somebody's distant relation ever saw a spirit. There is probably not a village in Ireland where a fairy-seer or two may not be found."[30] Here Yeats exercises his own ethnographic authority, trumping the Irish-American author with his fieldwork and his local knowledge. (In fairness to Yeats, he also identifies a clear fabrication that casts the rest of the account into doubt: M'Anally reports that the woman in question was following a firefly; Yeats points out that there are no fireflies in Ireland.) This speaks to one of the problems surrounding ethnographic accounts—namely the difficulty of refuting or disproving an ethnographer's claims. Short of discovering an error such as inserting a nonnative species in a purportedly native account, how is it possible to prove that something did not happen, or that a native informant did not say something in particular?

Yeats regularly attempts to preempt such questions by way of appeals to one sort of cultural authority or another. At times, ironically enough, he even enlists the cultural authority of the English system that he intends for Ireland to oppose, as in a further rebuke of Mr. M'Anally: "He is wrong in saying that the Banshee never follows Irish families abroad. There are several recorded stories of its doing so. One, for instance, I forget where, of an Irish family settled in Canada who are still followed by their Banshee. And one of the most distinguished British anthropologists told me that he has not only heard, but seen it, in a Central American forest. It came to announce the death of his father, who had just died in England . . . He had since then twice seen and heard it in London."[31] Yeats is clearly buttressing his account of things by deploying the rhetoric of social prestige. That this rhetoric appears laughably unfounded only emphasizes the point. Although Yeats takes others to task for vague references, his own references here (as is often the case throughout his prose) are somewhat less than precise; likewise, his nameless name-dropping brings the prestige value of the prominent British anthropologist into the equation. In this, Yeats's story acquires a veneer of authority and scientific legitimacy, which would doubtless improve the odds that the account might be taken seriously by non-Irish readers.

The British anthropologist's experiences with the Banshee are, at this remove, both somewhat comical and quite practical in terms of promoting Yeats's cultural agenda. By exporting the Banshee to Canada and Central America, these accounts implicitly claim that this element of Irish folk culture has significance far beyond the island of Ireland. It is not clear from Yeats's account whether the English anthropologist had any family connection to Ireland whatsoever.

Regardless, by bringing the Irish Banshee to the seat of colonial power—turning the disquieted Irish spirit loose in London, apparently asserting that its power extends to people who are not even Irish—the account argues for and enacts a kind of victory of Irish folk culture over English logical positivism. Yeats's series of accounts implicitly argues for the broader relevance of Irish culture and, by extension, the relevance of Irish ethnography: If Irish folk beliefs have power or presence beyond Ireland, they are important and they merit serious study.

Surprisingly, in an essay that appears in the same National Library of Ireland manuscript archive folder Yeats cites M'Anally (who has by this point recovered the missing letter in his last name—here he is "McAnally") as a reliable source in an attack on another book on Irish culture. Shortly after attacking McAnally in print, partly in this very same periodical—*Leisure Hour*—Yeats directly and publicly contradicts himself by holding the Irish-American author up as an exemplar of ethnographic accuracy.

Yeats also asserts his own ethnographic authority in the long ethnographic sections of the 1901 essay "Magic," in which he relates several accounts of Irish peasants' beliefs in and encounters with supernatural phenomena, as well as his own experiences talking with such peasants and conducting personal research into such phenomena by way of séances. Although a brief summary such as this is sufficient to establish the general ethnographic interests of the essay, it is only through closer attention to specific word choices that the basic mechanisms of Yeats's rhetoric of authority become visible. Yeats establishes his ethnographic authority in part by taking it for granted. He presents himself as an expert who has done extensive field work, and who therefore has the ability to refute the accounts of others because of his special firsthand knowledge of the local culture: "I myself could find in one district in Galway but one man who had not seen what I can but call spirits, and he was in his dotage. 'There is no man mowing a meadow but sees them at one time or another,' said a man in a different district."[32] Yeats also strengthens his position by way of repeated references to his personal experiences, such as "I once saw,"[33] and repeated references to his field notes, such as "I find in my diary."[34] These kinds of rhetorical moves effectively establish Yeats's ethnographic authority, allowing him to explain Irish culture to outsiders (and, to a certain extent, to Ireland itself): "[Irish] peasants still believe in their ancient gods who gather in the raths or forts . . . and they believe . . . that the most and best of their dead are among them. The ancient gods, or spirits, styled 'The Others' by the peasants take most children who die. They prefer the young but they take the old also. They prefer the good and pious, and do not like the old and cross people. The 'living' often meet the 'others' and recognize among them friends and neighbours."[35] This statement is an example of what Edward Callan (quoting W. H. Auden's elegy for Yeats) calls the "Irish vessel" Yeats—an example of Yeats's writing that presents him as a container of essential Irishness that readers may imbibe. A quotation from Yeats's "A General Introduction for my Work" presents an extreme manifestation of the self-effacement inherent in this element of Yeats's work: "Talk to me of originality and I will turn on you with rage. I am a crowd, I am a lonely man, I am nothing."[36]

Although Callan does not make any move toward ethnography, this aspect of Yeats's accounts of Irish culture clearly has a strong relationship to his ongoing negotiation of his position as an Irish cultural authority. The longer example above reminds readers that Yeats was interested in establishing his cultural authority both within Ireland and with a wider, non-Irish reading public. The explanation of the word *rath* is superfluous for Irish readers; it is a direct concession to the needs of non-Irish readers, who are unlikely to have encountered the term.

The significance of the Irish vessel aspect of Yeats's work becomes more evident through a comparison to the aspect of Yeats's work that displays (either directly or via references to notes and diaries) the particulars of Yeats's firsthand experiences studying Irish culture. Unlike Yeats's aforementioned references to his personal experiences and his field notebooks, this Irish vessel account of Irish peasant belief downplays the presence of the observing, recording nonnative presence. The ethnographer effectively becomes invisible or at least transparent in this account. In accordance with Yeats's statement above, the ethnographic voice is not that of an individual, but rather that of a disembodied spokesperson for the crowd; it serves as a delivery system for an explanation of cultural beliefs as cultural facts.

Yeats's early prose collection *The Celtic Twilight* (1893) also downplays the distinctions between natives and an observing ethnographic other, but via a different set of narrative strategies, as Yeats's introduction makes clear: "I have . . . written down accurately and candidly much that I have heard and seen, and, except by way of commentary, nothing that I have merely imagined. I have, however, been at no pains to separate my own beliefs from those of the peasantry, but have rather let my men and women, dhouls and faeries, go their way unoffended or defended by any argument of mine."[37] One of the results of this approach is that *The Celtic Twilight* repeatedly presents belief in fairies as a fundamental aspect of Irish life by way of statements that ostensibly report the experiences of Irish peasants and sound very much as if Yeats himself uncritically accepts them as accurate. This leads to moments when Yeats speaks with a kind of self-assurance and willingness that, given the circumstances, appears presumptuous by today's standards: "No matter what one doubts, one never doubts the faeries, for, as the man with the Mohawk Indian [tattooed] on his arm said to me, 'they stand to reason.' Even the official mind does not escape this faith."[38]

Much of *The Celtic Twilight* is composed of narratives that, as Yeats's afore-mentioned comments suggest, are difficult to distinguish as Yeats's own or as faithful transcriptions of the accounts of Irish peasants. Most could be either, insofar as they leave out first person pronouns and instead report what happened to someone else (inevitably unidentified by any substantive information) in a series of limited-omniscience narratives. A section called "The Old Town" is a notable exception to this tendency. Writing in 1902, in what is clearly his own narrative voice (as opposed to the mediated voice of a peasant or a crowd), Yeats described an event that he thought might have been a firsthand encounter with Irish fairies: "I fell, one night some fifteen years ago, into what seemed the power of faery. I had gone with a young man and his sister—friends and relations of my own—to pick stories out of an old countryman; and we were coming home talking over what he had told us . . . I cannot think that what we saw was an imagination of the waking mind." Yeats goes on to describe seeing a series of inexplicable bright spots of light moving across the road, on the horizon, and across a nearby river. He strengthens his account by mentioning that "after that for some days came other sights and sounds, not to me but to the girl, her brother, and the servants. Now it was a bright light, now it was letters of fire that vanished before they could be read, now it was a heavy foot moving about in the seemingly empty house."[39]

This is significant as a moment when Yeats attempts to extend his ethnographic authority beyond that of an authoritative collector of peasant beliefs and experiences, thereby staking a claim to some firsthand knowledge of fairy phenomena. Regardless of whether he intended to tell nothing but the truth, the means by which he does this are questionable. By this point in *The Celtic Twilight*, Yeats has already blurred the lines between his narrative persona and the mediated voices of Irish peasants. He explains this above as a form of truth-telling, a narrative technique apparently intended to present readers with some unvarnished truth that they will evaluate on its own merits. Although it seems to set things at the readers' feet, this maneuver also transfers total narrative power to the author, whose narrative voice encompasses or appropriates all the other speaking voices because of the lack of distinction between them and because the Irish peasants, with the notable exception of the man with the Mohawk tattoo, are not identified in anything but very vague terms. Because the girl, her brother, and the servants remain anonymous (Yeats does not even provide the kinds of clues that would likely let biographers discover their identities), Yeats's account of their experiences carries much of the rhetorical force of a disciplinary ethnographic account but without the kinds of particulars that would verify or strongly suggest its adherence to the related experiences of particular people.

Yeats's relationship to the issue of ethnographic voice appears even more perplexing in light of a bizarre account he presents in his essay "Per Amica

Silentia Lunae": "Once, twenty years ago, I seemed to awake from sleep to find my body rigid, and to hear a strange voice speaking these words through my lips as through lips of stone: 'We make an image of him who sleeps and it is not him who sleeps, and we call it Emmanuel.'"[40] That the name Emmanuel means "God with us" (Matt. 1:23) makes this passage even more difficult to interpret with regard to Yeats's positions as a spokesman for Irish culture. Here the idea of voice takes a very different turn, away from the basic notion that at least the individual man who speaks speaks for himself, regardless of whether readers grant such an individual's authority to speak for a cultural group.

R. B. Kershner's provocative essay "Yeats/Bakhtin/Orality/Dyslexia" presents a compelling argument that Yeats often thought of himself as a conduit for words that were not his own, whether the source was some mysterious power or Irish peasants:

> Yeats informed George Moore that it was only from the peasants that "one could learn to write, their speech being living speech, flowing out of the habits of their lives, struck out of life itself." Indeed, at times Yeats presents himself as simply the transcriber of peasant narrative and wisdom. Speaking of his uncle's illiterate servant Mary Battle, Yeats observes, "much of my *Celtic Twilight* is but her daily speech." For Yeats, the speech of the peasantry provided access to genuine Irish folk culture, which was of value both in itself and also as a poetic buttress for the Nationalist movement . . . Still . . . an interest in folk materials by no means guarantees that a poet will enter into genuine dialogue with the "folk voice." In Yeats, it is precisely this dialogue that gives much of the strength to his lyrics. In lyrics such as "Down by the Salley Gardens," Yeats himself found it impossible to distinguish the folk source from his own contribution.[41]

In a surprising critical move, Kershner explains Yeats's complex relationship with poetic voice in terms of his dyslexia (undiagnosed in Yeats's lifetime, but now generally accepted by Yeats scholars, thanks in part to maddeningly inconsistent spelling in Yeats's handwritten notes, letters, and manuscripts), which Kershner explains taught Yeats to prioritize the spoken word over written forms of speech, and also in terms of disembodied voices:

> Even his own voice, or the voices in his head, seemed to come from elsewhere. Once he began writing, he composed aloud, sometimes—to his embarrassment— unconsciously and in public. One of the more bizarre manifestations of his obsession with the spoken word is that, from childhood onward, he quite literally heard "'the voice of conscience.' 'From that day the voice had come to me at moments of crisis, but now it is a voice in my head that is sudden and startling. It does not tell me what to do, but often reproves me.'"[42]

This type of experience is difficult to explain, and it clearly moves away from the social-science model of cultural investigation and explanation. Nevertheless, this sort of thing is not without similarities to aspects of ethnographic theory, albeit to theories that are often considered rather radical. In Edith Turner's essay "Experience and Poetics in Anthropological Writing," for example, Turner writes approvingly of "an emotional intuiting of another's feelings—resulting in not only polyphony or heteroglossia, the speech of different protagonists, but polypsychy, as one might say—the use of one's own spirit to intuit their different spirits (different from psychology, the word-science of the mind)."[43] This is not to claim that all—or even most—ethnographers would readily accept claims such as Yeats's or Turner's; it is an indication that thoughts or experiences such as Yeats's do not create an unbridgeable gap between Yeats and ethnographic theory. Indeed, Kershner (whose essay does not deal specifically with cultural inquiry) lapses into the terminology of ethnography in describing Yeats's work: "Reading Yeats is like listening to an oral informant in that information must be processed additively and linearly, rather than in the hierarchical way in which we can read sentences of ordinary prose. More precisely, it is like listening to a speaker who uses the artifices of rhetoric—those tricks of balance and parallelism . . . in ways that continually frustrate a reader's desire for syntactic logic."[44] Despite Kershner's observations about Yeats's own prose, Yeats frequently insists on standard logic in his comments about the prose of others, particularly when accounts of Irish culture are involved. His attacks on the ethnographic publications of McAnally and Lawless exemplify this tendency, which also manifests itself in Yeats's comments on the works of Lady Gregory.

At Gregory's request, Yeats wrote essays and explanatory notes for Gregory's *Visions and Beliefs in the West of Ireland* (1920), a book on which Yeats and Gregory collaborated extensively, doing fieldwork together and taking down verbatim notes of conversations with residents of the west Ireland villages they visited. Gregory was sufficiently aware of the collaborative nature of the fieldwork that she delayed the publication of the book for some time in order to give Yeats time to contribute two lengthy ethnographic essays ("Swedenborg, Mediums, and the Desolate Places" and "Witches and Wizards and Irish Folk-Lore") and to complete his extensive notes for the volume. These essays and notes demonstrate both the depth of Yeats's ethnographic interest in Irish peasant life and an attention to detail that would surprise the numerous critics who have (inadvertently reproducing the terms of the Anglo-Irish antithesis) characterized Yeats as a dreamy idealist with little patience for hard facts.

In identifying and explaining peasant beliefs, such as "Tir-na-n-og, the country of the young, the paradise of the ancient Irish . . . sometimes described as under the earth, sometimes all about us, and sometimes as an enchanted island," and relating peasant accounts of supernatural phenomena, such as "supernatural strength is often spoken of by the people as a sign of faery power,"[45] Yeats creates clear distinctions between his ethnographic self and the individuals who express these beliefs to him. The vagueness of Yeats's accounts—that is, the fact that they typically do not identify native informants by name—seems less problematic, and certainly less unusual, in light of George Stocking's identification of this type of vagueness as a common trait of early ethnography, particularly the kinds of nineteenth-century ethnographic accounts that would have exerted the greatest influence on Yeats's sense of how cultural inquiry should proceed: "Much of its data had been collected in loosely descriptive natural history or purely anecdotal terms ('a gentleman in Bombay assures me . . .')."[46]

Yeats's glosses of peasant beliefs do not differ significantly from the kind of thing one would expect to find in ethnographic accounts at least up until the middle of the twentieth century. Yeats condenses and summarizes elements of the subject culture's belief system, as indeed any ethnographer must do in order to smooth data into a coherent and relatively concise narrative. A few pages later, however, one of Yeats's explanatory notes indicates that he paid attention to the details of the native informants' accounts to a greater degree than critics have often assumed: "In my record of this conversation [reported by Gregory in one of her essays] I find a sentence that has dropped out in Lady Gregory's. The old man used these words: 'And I took down a fork from the rafters and asked her was it a broom and she said it was,' and it was that answer that proved her in the power of the faeries. She was 'suggestible' and probably in a state of trance."[47] Shortly after his inclusion of the missing sentence, Yeats adds a different kind of explanatory remark: "I have been several times told that a great [supernatural] battle for the potatoes preceded the great famine. What decays with us seems to come out, as it were, on the other side of the picture and is spirits' property."[48] This passage typifies the easy shift from reporting native accounts ("I have been several times told") to stating the beliefs contained in accounts as simple facts without recourse to native informants—that is, stating beliefs in a way that makes them seem to be Yeats's own, or at least beliefs Yeats shares. This type of characteristic shift has no doubt contributed to the critical tendency to think of Yeats as gullible, and perhaps a bit ridiculous, and to disregard much of what he claimed about Irish culture. Such a dismissive critical move is more difficult to justify when one realizes the extent to which Yeats apparently acted in good faith as a mouthpiece for rural subjects. This is not to say that every cultural comment he made over the course of his lengthy public career should now qualify as accurate reporting, but it is important to recognize the fact that a number of his claims apparently should, insofar as they follow the kinds of procedures that characterized the ethnographic practices of the day.

Neither Yeats's correction of Gregory's apparent oversight nor the fact that Gregory effectively let Yeats have the last word on their work by appending his notes to her accounts should be taken as evidence that Gregory and Yeats considered Yeats to be the superior authority on Irish ethnographic matters. Foster says of Lady Gregory's role in the early ethnographic expeditions she and Yeats undertook, "Her ability to talk to people was essential; language apart [Yeats spoke no Irish], he found it difficult to understand the local accent, and his stylish black clothes meant he was mistaken for a proselytizing clergyman."[49] This explanation of Gregory's influence—an explanation that conjures up an image of Yeats as somewhat less than masterful—prompts consideration of the ways in which Yeats maintained and reinforced his ethnographic authority. One of the methods by which Yeats did this reminds readers that the critical attacks of the de-Yeatsification cabal are not without merit. These Irish postcolonial scholars have repeatedly asserted that Yeats (if I may paraphrase Declan Kiberd's terms) invented Ireland much more than he reported on it or expressed its authentic elements. Whatever reservations one may have about the political biases of these arguments, it is clear that Yeats stretched the truth considerably when it came to establishing his ethnographic authority, particularly in his representations of his own background.

The National Library of Ireland's Yeats Collection contains a clipping of an essay called "Tales from the Twilight" (published in *Scots Observer*, March 1, 1890) in which Yeats refers to "Innismurray, an island near my own district." By "my own district" Yeats clearly means County Sligo,[50] but this reference is willfully misleading. Although Yeats spent time in Sligo as a child and a young man, and although he could certainly claim strong family connections to the area, a reference to Sligo as Yeats's district conveniently glosses over the significantly greater amounts of time Yeats spent in Dublin and (worst of all in the eyes of postcolonial critics) in London. Through narrative sleight of hand, Yeats transforms himself into a source of native knowledge rather than remaining merely an interpreter or recorder of such knowledge. In the same essay, Yeats exercises this authority, sighing that a recent book on Irish folklore is insufficiently precise: "The districts seldom specified and the dates of discovery never. I heartily wish they had been better and more scientifically treated."[51]

Yeats extends this claim to a form of ethnographic authority based in part on his affiliation with the subject culture in another document in the NLI Yeats Collection, a typescript draft of "The Irish Dramatic Movement: A Letter to the Students at a California School":

> Lady Gregory had spent most of her life between two great houses in South Galway, while Synge had wandered over half Europe with his fiddle, and I had gone to and fro between Dublin and London. Yet Synge and I—like Lady Gregory—were people of the country; I because of my childhood and youth in Sligo, he because of his in Wicklow. We had gone, all three, from cottage to cottage, collecting stories and hearing songs, and we thought that in these we had discovered that portion of the living mind of Ireland that was most beautiful and

distinguished, and we wished to bring what we had discovered to Dublin, where, it seemed to us, the popular mind had grown harsh and ugly.[52]

This is the kind of passage that tends to make postcolonial Irish critics apoplectic, in large part because of the way Yeats bends terms and truth to suit his needs. From this account, it would be reasonable to infer that Yeats's childhood and youth had been spent entirely in Sligo, but in fact this was far from the case. Collapsing the real distinctions between all three authors and the rural residents or peasants implies that there is no difference between (in Americanized terms) country people and country club people.

Although thus far I have explained a number of similarities between Yeats's ethnographic consciousness and the theories or practices of ethnography as an evolving and contested discipline, Yeats's maneuverings in pursuit of increased ethnographic authority compel a break from this pattern for a time. In at least one important way, Yeats goes against the prevailing ethnographic practices of his day. As Bruner explains, traditional ethnography discouraged its practitioners from blurring the distinctions between the ethnographer and the subject culture: "The distancing of ethnographic subject from native object was essential to an older model of ethnography, for how else could we be the impersonal authoritative voice empowered to represent the Other? If we were too much like them, if both we and they had active voices, then the distinction between the ethnographer as theorizing being and the informant as passive data would dissolve. Traditional ethnography required a sharp separation between subject and object if it was to retain its authoritative voice."[53] Yeats, it is clear, had little interest in maintaining critical distance from Irish culture. He was at pains to do the opposite. It would be a mistake to confuse Yeats's work with any of the contemporary theoretical models of ethnography that later chapters of this book will explain in greater detail, but Yeats's unconventional (for his time) positioning of himself merits a brief comparison with some of these models. "Insider ethnography" became increasingly common and increasingly important to the discipline during the last few decades of the twentieth century. As the term suggests, insider ethnography involves a member of a certain group writing an ethnographic account of that group (a Navajo woman writing about Navajo women, for example). "Halfie ethnography" is similar to insider ethnography in that it involves an ethnographer with some claim to affiliation with the cultural group in question, but in halfie ethnography the ethnographer's identity is typically divided between the culture under study and another culture.

Although these contemporary models of ethnographic inquiry are useful counterpoints to the more traditional model of ethnographic critical distance, Yeats does not fit neatly into any one of them. Yeats's work is not native insider ethnography of the sort that would become increasingly common and important throughout the twentieth century. Still, Yeats asserts some sort of insider status, often going against the facts of his biography in his attempts to forge an authoritative ethnographic persona. Not exactly that of a native, not exactly that of a halfie (because, as Foster's explanation of Yeats's reliance on Gregory's help makes clear, Yeats clearly did not belong to the rural peasant culture he studied), Yeats's insider status was itself as much of a fiction as anything he wrote.

A remark of Yeats's in his essay "J. M. Synge and the Ireland of his Time" makes it clear that Yeats was very much aware of the difference cultural insider status could make in one's perception of a culture (particularly with respect to a politically charged country such as Ireland): "A zealous Irishman, especially if he lives much out of Ireland, spends his time in a never-ending argument about Oliver Cromwell, the Danes, the penal laws, the Rebellion of 1798, the famine, the Irish peasant, and ends by substituting a traditional casuistry for a country."[54] Although in the essay Yeats speaks from his customary perspective of cultural authority, and although he apparently does not intend for these remarks to apply to him, they do. That Yeats was a zealous Irishman is unquestioned, as is the fact that he lived much out of Ireland. What is still potentially questionable—although a number of postcolonial Irish Studies scholars seem to be satisfied that they have established Yeats's guilt—is the extent to which Yeats's accounts of Irish culture were derived from the kinds of native sources that postcolonial thought is supposed to privilege, and the extent to which these accounts should be regarded as the substitutions of a traditional casuistry for a country.

Yeats seems to invite closer scrutiny of his claims by asserting that certain elements of the Celtic character do not square with the fidelity to facts that readers typically expect in ethnographic accounts. Even given Yeats's status as a writer of poetry, drama, and prose fiction, readers of his era had certain expectations about the truth-claim status of direct ethnographic accounts, particularly when such accounts concerned a culture as historically fraught with political problems as Ireland's. In his essay "The Celtic Element in Literature," Yeats responds to Ernest Renan's *The Poetry of the Celtic Races* and, quoting Matthew Arnold, agrees that the Celtic imagination is a "reaction against the despotism of fact."[55] Relating this remark to Yeats's ethnographic accounts produces an awareness of one of their minor paradoxes. On one hand, Yeats tends to insist on the veracity or accuracy of his accounts of peasant accounts of their beliefs and experiences; on the other hand, Yeats's insistence on the literal existence of supernatural phenomena may itself be read as a powerful and perplexing strategy of resistance against the despotism of fact.

Later in the same essay, there is a strange break from Yeats's usual insistence on apparent ethnographic accuracy. Referring to "a proverb a friend has heard in the Highlands of Scotland," Yeats identifies the friend in a footnote and also de-emphasizes the importance of accuracy: "William Sharp, who probably invented the proverb, but, invented or not, it remains true."[56] This is an unusual moment, but it perhaps is not indicative of a major contradiction in Yeats's ethnographic thought. It seems that Yeats might be distinguishing between truth versus authentic origin as a way to appraise the value of the apocryphal proverb. Yeats presumably did not have a problem with this in part because he agreed with the sentiment and in part because the account of the proverb (complete with the possibility of recent nonnative origin) does not present itself as a strict or accurate ethnographic account in the way Yeats's own accounts often do.

Although the bulk of Yeats's ethnographic writing deals directly with one type of fieldwork or another—that is, with what Yeats frames as actual research-minded encounters with actual Irish people—his late miscellany *On the Boiler* contains an interesting example of a divergence from this pattern, an example of what might most accurately be called (with a certain measure of skepticism) ethnographic architecture criticism. Yeats interprets the façade of the Mansion House in Dublin as an index to Irish culture: "All Catholic Ireland, as it was before the National University and a victory in the field that had swept the penal laws out of its bones, swells in that pretentious front. Old historic bricks and window-panes obliterated and destroyed, its porch invented when England was elaborating the architecture and interior decoration of the gin-palace."[57] This strange confluence of architecture criticism and ethnographic generalization is not an index to Yeats's thought, or indeed to much of anything. Rather, it is a potential reminder that even when Yeats swerved from the kinds of observations that most literary scholars would associate with disciplinary ethnography, he often went no farther afield than modern ethnographers have gone. In this case, the analog is Clifford Geertz's famous essay on the Balinese cockfight, in which Geertz makes sweeping cultural generalizations based on the cockfight and his subsequent flight from the authorities who raid it. Geertz claims quite seriously that he found in the cockfight and his escape from the police raid the key to understanding Balinese culture, a claim that seems as much a stretch as Yeats's reading of the Mansion House.

Shortly thereafter, Yeats presents an account of popular thought that reminds readers of the distance between his perspectives (shifting though they were) and the typical perspective of the modern ethnographer, who most often remains wary of his or her own potential ethnocentricity and seeks to minimize any status differences between ethnographer and natives in order to counteract any sense that the observer is morally or otherwise superior to the people being studied: "Try to be popular and you think another man's thought, sink into that slow, slothful, inanimate, semi-hypocritical thinking Dante symbolized by hoods and cloaks of lead."[58] Yeats also expresses a bluntly undemocratic opinion of the value of compulsory public education: "It seems probable that many men in Irish public life should not have been taught to read and write, and would not have been in any country before the middle of the nineteenth century."[59]

This is a long way from the presumptive liberal egalitarianism of much modern ethnography, but it gets closer; although here it sounds as if Yeats is being flatly undemocratic (which he was certainly capable of being), in fact, a few lines later he makes it clear that he is actually privileging (perhaps romanticizing) the rural inhabitants of Ireland's west, the very people he studied: "Our representative system has given Ireland to the incompetent. There are no districts in County Galway of any size without a Catholic curate, a young shopkeeper, a land-owner, a sawyer, with enough general knowledge to make a good library committee."

Later in the same essay, Yeats performs a semi-ethnographic series of rhetorical maneuvers that once again put forth his ideas about the core of Irish cultural identity. Because of the way Yeats positions himself with regard to his subject matter—Irish cultural identity—it is extremely difficult, perhaps impossible, to separate unfounded or romanticized essentialist elements from elements that Yeats observed, experienced, or perhaps created (although *created* might seem to belong in the previous category, there is a special sense in which it does not):

> I was six years in the Irish Senate. I am not ignorant of politics elsewhere, and on other grounds I have some right to speak. I say to those that shall rule here: If ever Ireland again seems molten wax, reverse the process of revolution. Do not try to pour Ireland into any political system. Think first how many able men with public minds the country has, how many it can hope to have in the near future, and mould your system upon those men. It does not matter how you get them, but get them. Republics, Kingdoms, Soviets, Corporate States, Parliaments, are trash, as Victor Hugo said of something else, "not worth one blade of grass that God gives for the nest of the linnet." These men, whether six or six thousand, are the core of Ireland, are Ireland itself.[60]

As is often the case, literature comes into the equation and contributes to Yeats's construction of cultural authority. Making vague literary references, as he habitually did throughout his career, perhaps helped establish his authority among many readers, especially by contrasting his self-asserted erudition with the supposed relative lack thereof in the Ireland of his time (although subsequent generations of editors and scholars have enjoyed pointing out how frequently Yeats misread or misquoted his sources, and how often he effectively Yeats-ified them—made them fit his larger argument or goals—by way of his selective memory or his interpretations).

His years in the Irish Senate gave him an unusual perspective, especially because he was not an elected official. Yeats served his term as a senator after being appointed for what amounted to meritorious public Irishness, and so was not subject to worries about reelection. He was, paradoxically, more free to be a representative of Irish culture—the reason for his appointment—because he did not have to worry about representing specific Irish voters back in some home district. Yeats's assertion that "on other grounds I have some right to speak" is particularly interesting in that it manifests Yeats's sense of his own cultural authority, his sense of his prominence in Irish society by virtue of his notoriety (and, by this time, his Nobel Prize). In a late letter to G. R. Barnes of the BBC, Yeats expresses his preference for working in Ireland in terms of the effects of his cultural authority: "I like working here because I am not afraid of anybody, and most people are afraid of me. It is the reverse in London."[61]

Elsewhere in *On the Boiler*, Yeats uses another of his characteristic devices: the vague scientific reference, cousin to the vague literary reference and similarly useful to Yeats in terms of asserting cultural authority. He asserts that "though well-known specialists are convinced that the principal European nations are degenerating in body and mind, their evidence remains almost unknown because a politician and newspaper that gave it adequate exposition would lose, the one his constituency, the other its circulation."[62] The claim about newspapers losing circulation seems simply wrong, especially if one considers the demonstrated historical (and continuing) eagerness of the Irish press (especially in the first decades of Ireland's independence) to trumpet the problems of England. Yeats presumably did not mean to include Ireland among this supposedly deteriorating lot, because he did not think of Ireland as a principal European nation and neither did the other European nations at the time.

One of the paradoxes of Yeats criticism is that while some critics have attacked Yeats's claims to cultural authority and emphasized his intellectual debts to England, other critics, drawn in by the gravitational pull of Yeats's accounts of Irish culture, have essentially confused Yeats with Ireland itself. Critics have routinely conflated Yeats's mind or thought with the mind or thought of his era in Ireland—sometimes approvingly, sometimes not. An ethnography-minded reading of Yeats engages this critical discourse by substituting, as often as possible, references to ethnographic theories and practices in place of more diffuse notions of Yeats embodying, exemplifying, or forging the uncreated conscience of the Ireland of his time. Ronald Schleifer points out an early instance of the critical confusion of Yeats with Ireland:

> Eliot came to praise Yeats after his death and described in his work another version of the mythical method, a kind of "impersonality" of the lyric poet "who," Eliot writes, "out of intense and personal experience, is able to express a general truth; retaining all the particularity of his experience, to make it a general symbol." "In becoming more Irish," he says of Yeats, "he became at the same time universal." This is high praise indeed; and by the end of Eliot's essay, he himself is

mythologizing Yeats, marking him as "one of those few whose history is the history of their own time, who are part of the consciousness of an age which cannot be understood without them."[63]

Moreover, as Adam Trexler points out, in "Ulysses, Order, and Myth" Eliot calls James Joyce "a 'scientist.'" But in the same paragraph Eliot claims the (scientific) method was "first adumbrated by Yeats."[64] This claim carries all the more intellectual weight because Trexler establishes that Eliot's knowledge of anthropology and social science in general was extensive: "Eliot's graduate work focused on the philosophy of the social sciences" and "Throughout the 1910s, Eliot reviewed works of anthropology and other social sciences for *The New Statesman* and *The Monist*. If anything, Eliot had more institutional authority to comment on anthropological methodology than literature."[65]

The greater clarity and contextualization provided by Trexler notwithstanding, the sort of mystification inherent in the Eliot passage quoted by Schleifer likely would have pleased Yeats, and though it would appear unlikely to sit well with many contemporary scholars, recent Yeats criticism abounds with critical pronouncements that similarly confuse Yeats with Ireland. Kershner points out J. Hillis Miller's assertion that the voice of Yeats's poetry is "not personal at all but another voice, universal, anonymous, depersonalizing, a voice speaking through the poet. It is the voice of human experience generally, of literary and philosophical tradition. It is the voice ultimately of 'nothing,' of that no one and no place from which the desolate winds blow in 'Nineteen Hundred and Nineteen.'" Kershner then astutely points out an important distinction obscured by Miller: "But a voice that becomes a decentered plurality is not the voice of nothing."[66]

It would be easier to make sense of the tendency to confuse Yeats with Ireland if it were a critical phenomenon generated by and confined to non-Irish critics, who might be forgiven for seeking a convenient standard of Irishness upon which to base the rest of our analyses. The fact, however, is that this confusion of the poet with the nation is by no means confined to those of us who must always approach Irish literature with the acknowledgement that we are, after all, cultural outsiders. The official statement of congratulations from the Irish Senate on Yeats's 1923 Nobel Prize provides an excellent example. One sentence in particular stands out as an expression of Yeats's immense stature within Irish culture, reminding contemporary readers that this stature is not some *ex post facto* construction of more recent literary scholars: "Our civilisation will be assessed on the name of Senator Yeats."[67]

Surprisingly, even the postcolonial critics who have taken Yeats to task so vigorously have demonstrated the influence of this kind of thought. Kiberd says in a discussion of Yeats's relationship to what Kiberd calls "the national longing for form" that characterized Ireland in the first decades of the twentieth century, "In such a self-charged context, nation-building can be achieved by the simple expedient of writing one's autobiography; and autobiography in Ireland becomes, in effect, the autobiography of Ireland."[68] Although Kiberd never uses the word, it is easy enough to recognize in his comments familiar strands of ethnographic thought. Such strands contribute to the Gordian knot of Yeats criticism: the great tangle of Yeats's multiple complex relationships to Ireland and Irish culture, including the extent to which he described Irish culture; the extent to which he embodied it; and the extent to which Ireland somehow internalized his creative accounts so that they achieved greater accuracy after the fact. (This is the special sense of *created* mentioned above.)

Although Kiberd's statement is somewhat surprising, it does not diminish the tendency among Irish postcolonial writers to portray Yeats as generally disconnected from Irish culture and entirely too convinced of his own cultural authority. Paul Muldoon's well-known lines that make fun of Yeats's question to himself in "Man and The Echo" ("Did that play of mine send out / Certain men the English shot?"—a question Muldoon apparently regards as ridiculously self-important) are a good example of this tendency: "If Yeats had saved his pencil lead / would certain men have stayed in bed?"[69] Richard Rankin Russell, one of the critics who has opposed this tendency, quotes Denis Donoghue at length in a passage that offers a rejoinder to those who have found Yeats's sense of his own cultural influence somewhat laughable:

> I concede that Yeats himself felt some misgiving, in his last years, on the question of his responsibility. When he wondered, in "Man and the Echo," whether that play of his *Cathleen ni Houlihan*, sent out "certain men the English shot," he was not taking his work with excessive gravity . . . It is entirely possible that some members of the audience at *Cathleen ni Houlihan* felt impelled to take up arms in a nationalist cause already well established. As David Lloyd has remarked, Yeats's writing . . . played an extraordinary part in forging in Ireland "a mode of subjectivity apt to find its political and ethical realization in sacrifice to the nation they believe is yet to be." Many young men and women in Northern Ireland are still prepared to make that sacrifice to the nation they believe is yet to be.

Russell also points out that the disclosure in 2000 of " 'listening posts' which dot the western British coast and were used up until recently for the sole purpose of hearing phone conversations in Dublin and elsewhere in the Republic demonstrates that imperial attitudes linger."[70]

Akhil Gupta explains some of the reasons for this type of confusion (though he does not mention Yeats or Ireland), and also points out problems that may arise from it, by drawing on Frederic Jameson's argument about the inseparability of nationality from third world texts in general:

Jameson . . . argues that all third world texts are necessarily *national* allegories. His reasoning is that what is particular to literary production in the third world is that it is always shaped by the experience of colonialism and imperialism. The binary opposition between a first and a third world embedded in the three worlds theory leads to the overvalorization of nationalist ideology; indeed, since the third world is constituted through the singular experience of colonialism and imperialism, there is nothing to narrate but the "national" experience. The problem with employing a monologic ideology such as "third worldism" is that it encapsulates all narratives of identity within the master narratives of imperialism and nationalism. It thus serves to foreclose a richer understanding of location and identity that would account for the relationships of subjects to multiple collectivities.[71]

Even a cursory examination of Irish history in the twentieth century yields examples of the processes Gupta and Jameson describe, including one issue that simultaneously touches on the two critics' comments about nationalist texts, discourses, and practices: the long-standing Irish language policy, mandating Irish language study in schools, Irish language proficiency for civil service job applicants, and street signs lettered in both English and Irish.

Khalifa's assessment of Yeats aligns Yeats with the kind of monologic narrative formation Gupta describes. In doing so, however, Khalifa overlooks an important aspect of Yeats's thought, which further recourse to Gupta will clarify. Khalifa compares Yeats's ethnographic work with the more diversity-oriented work of Ernest Renan (to whom Yeats responds in his essay "The Celtic Element in Literature") in order to present a simplistic reading of Yeats's understanding of and interest in Irish culture: "Renan sees 'ethnographic mixture' as a founding principle of national identity . . . Yeats, on the other hand, is imperturbably convinced that unity and not diversity, singularity rather than plurality, must make up the essence of a nation. Renan departs from homogeneity to demonstrate and validate a nation's heterogeneity, whereas Yeats prioritizes national unity, organic wholeness, to account for a well-consolidated national identity."[72] Gupta also offers an insightful explanation of how a viewpoint such as Jameson's may be imposed on the texts of a newly liberated third-world nation (or, presumably, to a lesser extent one in which rising anticolonial sentiment has not yet led to liberation) from within the country's borders as well as from without by critics such as Jameson: "One of the first things that new nation-states do is to write the history of the 'nation' (itself an entity consolidated during or after colonial rule) stretching into the distant past." After a thorough elaboration of this point, Gupta explains the processes of newly formed nationalist culture in a way that illuminates Yeats's relationship with Ireland as well as the ways in which confusing Yeats with Ireland might have been beneficial to Irish nationalist agendas. This explanation also indicates one of the problems with Khalifa's account of Yeats's thought:

The other way in which newly independent nation-states attempted to protect their fragile sovereignty was by aggressively employing nationalist discourses and practices *within* the country. Nationalism as a distinctively modern cultural form attempts to create a new kind of spatial and mythopoetic metanarrative, one that simultaneously homogenizes the varying narratives of community while, paradoxically, accentuating their difference. Taking an implicitly omniscient perspective, a national narrative seeks to define the nation, to construct its (typically continuous and uninterrupted) narrative past in an assertion of legitimacy and precedent for the practices of the narrative present—its own relation of the "national" story most especially.[73]

Gupta's commentary speaks to a crucial element of Yeats's ethnographic thought in pointing out the paradoxical way that insisting on a unitary narrative of community—in Yeats's case by prioritizing rural western Irish culture—accentuates nonconforming elements of the nation. Although Gupta does not have Yeats in mind, following the logic of this distinction effectively disproves Khalifa's claims. Khalifa overlooks the fact that throughout his literary career Yeats remained quite conscious of something other than homogeneity in Irish culture: Protestant Anglo-Irish identity.

Foster explains that far from being an identity category endowed with elements of cultural superiority or privilege, "the isolation, or marginalization, of the Southern Irish Protestant had been mercilessly highlighted since the 1830s—by the geographical breakdown demonstrated by religious censuses, as well as by less concrete demonstrations and threats."[74] Foster also emphasizes the importance of this marginalized status to Yeats: "It does not seem frivolous or irrelevant to locate Yeats in this context—Protestant marginalization—as much as in the world of international occultism, Indian mysticism, and London bohemianism: for it antedated these influences on him, as did his interest in supernaturalism."[75] Foster, like Kiberd in *Inventing Ireland*, persuasively argues that Yeats's valorization of Anglo-Irish Protestant Ascendancy identity was a reaction against that group's actual diminished and marginalized status rather than an accurate expression of the group's cultural prominence in the Ireland of his time.

Gupta's paradox both suggests an approach to Yeats's thought and recalls my assertion near the beginning of this essay that Yeats's thought was at times not so much dialectical as contradictory. *Paradoxical* is, it seems to me, a much better adjective in that it denotes the possibility that two things may be contradictory *and* that they may both still be correct, a nuance that *contradictory* fails to express. Paradox, then, should be the term to apply to certain aspects of Yeats's thought and life, especially those that relate to his simultaneous fidelity to authentic Irish national identity and to minority Anglo-Irish Protestant identity, the basic Irishness and relevance of which were increasingly in question with every step Ireland took toward legislative and cultural independence.

Seamus Heaney uses an excerpt from Yeats's *Autobiographies* as an epigraph to his poetic sequence "Singing School" (the title of which is an allusion to Yeats's "Sailing to Byzantium" and the first section of which is dedicated to Seamus Deane): "He [a stable boy] had a book of Orange rhymes, and the days when we read them together in the hay-loft gave me the pleasure of rhyme for the first time. Later on I can remember being told, when there was a rumour of a Fenian rising, that rifles were being handed out to the Orangemen; and presently, when I began to dream of my future life, I thought I would like to die fighting the Fenians."[76] This recollection of the boyhood dream of fighting with the Protestant Orangemen against the Catholic nationalist Fenians is an extreme example of Yeats's identification with Ireland's Protestant minority, and a surprising reminder that, as Foster points out, that identification preceded Yeats's affiliation with various other movements and schools of thought.

Although Yeats was prone to assertions that Anglo-Irish Protestant identity did not separate individuals from Irish culture—the aforementioned passage in which Yeats describes himself, Gregory, and Synge as people of the country, thereby obliterating religious, class, and geographical distinctions, exemplifies this tendency—the balance between his loyalties became increasingly difficult to negotiate after Ireland became the first colony to free itself from the grip of England's imperial power. In an independent Ireland that was overwhelmingly Catholic, the center of Yeats's paradox could not hold; although Yeats never abandoned the oppositional identity categories of the paradox, their contradictions became increasingly apparent.

Since long before Ireland's independence, Yeats had periodically made statements about men of genius at first not fitting in with their home cultures—a sentiment expressed by innumerable artists in societies worldwide. (It is worth remembering that this sentiment also holds true for James Joyce: In spite of his status as the exemplary modern Irish writer—at least in the minds of many contemporary critics of Irish literature, many of whom regard Joyce as a liberating postcolonial literary presence—Joyce was not at all broadly accepted by the Ireland of his time. His works were generally considered obscene and were widely banned.) In an independent Ireland, however, this sense of being separated from society by his genius began to give way in Yeats to a sense of being increasingly marginalized as an Anglo-Irish Protestant by Ireland's sheer numerical majority of Catholics. Yeats's views on this treatment of Ireland's Protestant minority and his insistence on their cultural significance are evident in his address to the Irish Senate during the debate on abolishing divorce in Ireland:

> I think it tragic that within three years of this country gaining its independence we should be discussing a measure which a minority of this nation considers to be grossly oppressive. I am proud to consider myself a typical man of that minority. We against whom you have done this thing are no petty people. We are one of the great stocks of Europe. We are the people of Burke; we are the people of Grattan; we are the people of Swift, the people of Emmett, the people of Parnell. We have created the most of the modern literature of this country. We have created the best of its political intelligence.[77]

Here, the paradox has not disintegrated, but it shows signs of great strain. This is at once an argument for Irish Protestant distinctiveness and an assertion that Irish Protestants are part of the core of Irish cultural identity and achievement.

As I mentioned early in this chapter, Yeats's ethnographic consciousness manifests itself in greater detail and at greater length in his prose. His poetry shows the mark of this ethnographic consciousness, but it does so in ways that are less conducive to close reading. Unlike Robert Penn Warren and Heaney, Yeats generally does not invite ethnographic readings by presenting himself or a persona as an ethnographic participant-observer moving within the poem. Yeats's poems refer to ethnographic pursuits and reflect the results of those pursuits; they do not present extended narrative accounts of the growth of an ethnographic poet's mind so much as they periodically express the kind of ethnographic consciousness of Ireland that Yeats gradually developed.

The early poem "The Hosting of the Sidhe"—from *The Wind Among the Reeds* (1899)—expresses an important element of Yeats's ethnographic Irish consciousness in its treatment of the fairy Sidhe. By placing the supernatural spirit riders in the Irish landscape and quoting their speech, the poem indicates their supposed reality and their cultural significance. The poem also refers to the Irish folk belief in fairy enchantment ("Niamh calling *Away, come away*") and abduction, a belief that was of great interest to Yeats. The issue of mortals being abducted by fairies or enchanted and lured away recurs in Yeats poems such as "The Song of Wandering Aengus," "The Stolen Child," and the epoch-making long poem *"The Wanderings of Oisin,"* which many critics identify as the seminal work of the Irish Renaissance.

Ethnographic commentary, rather than the sort of reflection of ethnographic consciousness discussed above, appears in some of Yeats's best-known poems, particularly the three famous date-titled poems of political crisis. "September 1913," the earliest of the three, expresses a sweeping ethnographic assessment of Irish culture, and does so via a narrative device not typically associated with ethnographic texts: The poem's famous repeated declaration "Romantic Ireland's dead and gone, / It's with O'Leary in the grave" sums up what Yeats identifies as the essential difference between the modern Irish society of the day and an earlier era symbolized by the presence of Fenian leader John O'Leary. The gist of the poem is that twentieth-century Irish society has surrendered to English mercantilism, thus renouncing its heritage and turning its back on the Irish half of the Anglo-Irish antithesis:

> What need you, being come to sense,
> But fumble in a greasy till
> And add the halfpence to the pence
> And prayer to shivering prayer, until
> You have dried the marrow from the bone;
> For men were born to pray and save;
> Romantic Ireland's dead and gone,
> It's with O'Leary in the grave.[78]

The bitter, witheringly snide tone of the poem underscores Yeats's disappointment at what he perceives as the triumph of two major evils over authentic Irish culture. One is England; the other is the Catholic Church. The narrative device Yeats uses to deliver his critique is unusual primarily in its direct address to the people of the culture in question. In other words, the *you* of the poem is the individual modern Irish person as a representative of modern Irish society or a collective Irish *you*. The poem declares that even if Ireland's nationalist martyrs could reappear and stand before modern Irish society, modern Irish society would misunderstand the reasons for the martyrs' acts, apparently misinterpreting them in terms of sexual passion: "You'd cry, 'Some woman's yellow hair / Has maddened every mother's son.'"[79] Yeats's acid ethnographic appraisal is that twentieth-century Irish society would not even understand the kind of patriotic passion that led previous generations of Irish nationalists to exile or execution.

The 1916 Easter Rising proved Yeats wrong, of course. As "Easter, 1916" makes clear, the events of the Rising inaugurated a fundamental change in Irish culture, a violent return to the nationalist ideals of the Romantic Ireland that "September 1913" mourns. Once again, pronoun use is at the heart of Yeats's cultural critique, beginning with the poem's famous opening lines "I have met them at close of day / Coming with vivid faces / From counter or desk among grey / Eighteenth-century houses," a pre-Rising situation that contributed to the speaker "Being certain that they and I / But lived where motley is worn: / All changed, changed utterly: / A terrible beauty is born."[80] The poem's accounts of individuals must be read as representative of Irish culture, placed as they are against the revolutionary backdrop of the Rising. The poem's famous refrain makes it clear that the individuals are all changed, and that Ireland is as well. (The remark that "England may keep faith / For all that is done and said" is a reference to England's 1914 resolution of home rule for Ireland, a resolution that was simultaneously suspended because of World War I and thus was not in effect in 1916.)

By "Nineteen Hundred and Nineteen," Yeats's interpretation of Irish culture had taken on a bitterness beyond even that of "September 1913" and had developed a sense of great potential squandered. As in "Easter, 1916," Yeats includes himself in the society by repeatedly attaching *we* to his cultural descriptions; these descriptions, though not as explicitly referential as those in Yeats's prose writings, are intense renderings of the state of Irish society at the time:

> Now days are dragon-ridden, the nightmare
> Rides upon sleep; a drunken soldiery
> Can leave the mother, murdered at her door,
> To crawl in her own blood, and go scot-free;
> The night can sweat with terror as before
> We pieced our thoughts together into philosophy,
> And planned to bring the world under a rule,
> Who are but weasels fighting in a hole.[81]

That these lines refer to actual social unrest is well known; 1919 was a time of frequent skirmishes between Irish nationalists and the English forces that were still in control of Ireland. What is less obvious is that Yeats himself connected the poem to his career-long ethnographic interests not only in terms of the commentary on the state of the Irish people, but in terms of his reference to the supernatural folk beliefs that were the subject of much of his ethnographic prose. Yeats appended a note to this effect: "The country people see at times certain apparitions whom they name now 'fallen angels,' now 'ancient inhabitants of the country,' and describe as riding at whiles 'with flowers upon the heads of the horses.' I have assumed in the sixth poem ["Nineteen Hundred and Nineteen"] that these horsemen, now that the times worsen, give way to worse."[82]

Yeats's persistent interest in distinctly Irish supernatural phenomena calls to mind a pejorative phrase common in Ireland today—*off with the fairies*—a phrase that approximates the way a number of recent critics have regarded Yeats and also resonates with Yeats's career-long interest in the supernatural folk beliefs that gave rise to the phrase. The phrase functions in contemporary Irish conversation not as an expression of literal belief in the supernatural, but as an ironic reference to the folk beliefs of previous generations: The phrase is sometimes a good-natured put-down, an indication that the person labeled as *off with the fairies* is not being logical and that he or she is talking nonsense or behaving strangely; the phrase is also sometimes used in a poignant way to refer to the mental degeneration of people with Alzheimer's disease. One of Yeats's lengthy notes to *Visions and Beliefs in the West of Ireland* indicates his fascination with the Irish folk belief in fairy abduction:

The most puzzling thing in Irish folk-lore is the number of countrymen and countrywomen who are "away". A man or woman or child will suddenly take to the bed, and from that on, perhaps for a few weeks, perhaps for a lifetime, will be at times unconscious, in a state of dream, in trance, as we say. According to the peasant theory, these persons are, during these times, with the faeries, riding through the country, eating or dancing, or suckling children. They may even, in that other world, marry, bring forth, and beget, and may when cured of their trances mourn for the loss of their children in faery. This state usually commences with their being "touched" or "struck" by a spirit. The country people do not say that the soul is away and the body in the bed, as a spiritist would, but that the body and soul have been taken and somebody or something put in their place so bewitched that we do not know the difference.[83]

Yeats's references to "countrymen and countrywomen" simultaneously gesture toward rural Irish people and forge a linguistic link between rural identity and national identity, an assertion of essential Irishness that surely did not escape Yeats. The quotation marks around *away* are a subtle ethnographic touch; they present the word as an authentic expression of the belief, and they also seem to distance Yeats from the belief somewhat. Yeats's reference to "a spiritist" is—like his earlier translation of the word *rath* for the benefit of non-Irish readers—a means of identification with a wider, non-Irish audience, in this case an audience that would be familiar with the idea of a more generic form of contact with the supernatural and hence more at home with the idea of a spiritist. In this passage, Yeats's use of the first-person plural pronoun is especially noteworthy, both in its importance to this passage and in its significance for Yeats's ethnographic thought in general: "as we say" and "so bewitched that we do not know the distance" identify Yeats with this wider, non-Irish (presumably largely English) readership rather than with Irish readers who would likely have no need of the explanatory touches Yeats provides.

In order to explain the local methods of trying to remedy fairy abduction, Yeats makes an appeal to a kind of cultural relativism, thereby engaging once again with the developing rhetoric of ethnographic thought both on a local level and on a global level:

The missionaries expel them [the fairy substitutes] in the name of Christ, but the Chinese exorcists adopt a method familiar to the west of Ireland—tortures or threats of torture. They will light tapers which they stick upon the fingers. They wish to make the body uncomfortable for its tenant. As they believe in the division of body and soul they are not likely to go too far. A man did actually burn his wife to death, in Tipperary a few years ago, and is no doubt still in prison for it. My uncle, George Pollexfen, had an old servant, Mary Battle, and when she spoke of the case to me, she described that man as very superstitious. I asked what she meant by that and she explained that everybody knew that you must only threaten, for whatever injury you did to the changeling the faeries would do to the living person they had carried away. In fact mankind and spiritkind have each their hostage. These explanatory myths are not a speculative but a practical wisdom. And one can count, perhaps, when they are rightly remembered, upon their preventing the more gross practical errors. The Tipperary witch-burner only half knew his own belief. "I stand here in the door," said Mary Battle, "and I hear them singing over there in the field, but I have never given in to them yet." And by "giving in" I understand her to mean losing her head.[84]

This passage exemplifies important aspects of Yeats's ethnographic practice, some of which figure prominently in standard modern ethnography: indications of doubt; a privileged relationship with a native informant; sidelong references to other cultures (to establish a sort of moral equivalence between cultures in order to avoid creating the impression of a freak culture or an aberrant society); and the explanation or interpretation of a local belief system as a sort of text. Yeats reads the system and explains it in a nonliteral way the local believers presumably would not. Note also the Yeatsian cultural nationalism, the implicit moral in Yeats's explanation of where the man went wrong: If the man had known his culture more thoroughly, we are to believe, the tragedy would have been averted. There is also some ambiguity about the *them* in the field, although it is apparently the fairies Mary Battle heard singing. By framing her comment the way he does, Yeats makes it clear that he does not regard simply believing in fairies (or hearing them sing) to be equivalent to losing one's head.

John Paul Riquelme addresses the disconcerting question of Yeats's belief in Irish supernatural incidents and tales and suggests something of a middle way between the critical extremes of outright rejection and wholesale acceptance: "The question arose concerning the extent to which Yeats believed in the authenticity of the Celtic myths that inform his writing . . . Yeats finds an alternative for aspects of British culture that are inauthentic for the Irish. He discovered and collected Irish myths and folk narratives, rather than simply inventing them, but they emerge explicitly as figures, rather than found, unchanging realities, in his later poetry . . . David Shumway claims that 'Yeats found' authenticity 'in Celtic mythology.' Although that may have been the case early in his career, Yeats's writings include prominently a fully modernist version of authenticity."[85] Riquelme's assertion of a "modernist version of authenticity" does not diminish the authenticity in question so much as it emphasizes the inclusion of authentic elements in a larger modernist context. Such a treatment of supernatural elements and beliefs was not unusual in the anthropological discourse of the time period. Trexler explains how Frazer interprets "the identity of unknown gods" (meaning gods previously unknown to Frazer, gods of societies being studied): "Each god becomes a 'fact': an account of irrationality (whether actually irrational, misunderstood or culturally divergent) that can be concretely located in a historical period and geographic location. It is precisely the misunderstanding of the savage that is valuable—Frazer is after 'superstition.' "[86] Yeats would have chosen words other than *savage* and *misunderstanding*, to be sure, but Trexler's gloss of Frazer relates to significant elements of Yeats's work, not least Yeats's treatment of supernatural Irish elements as facts. That Yeats was not at all hostile to irrationality gives a different implication to "a 'fact': an account of irrationality." In fact, as Moses says, such a positive view of supernatural elements, ethnographic facts, and irrationality is consistent with Yeats's larger pattern of thought: "In his cultural criticism Yeats called for a simultaneous repudiation of modernity (which he understood to be characterized by rationalism, materialism, commercialism, science, mechanical philosophy, liberalism, secularism, and the rise of the middle class), and a rejection of British imperial rule (which was the engine by which modernity had reached Ireland)."[87] Moses provides further explanation of the persistent connection between antimodern and anti-imperial elements in Yeats's worldview with a simple historical reminder that nevertheless may surprise readers who are unfamiliar with the details of Irish history: "In 1906 . . . all Irish subjects were still [theoretically] bound by their allegiance to an English king (a matter of intense debate and a contributing cause of civil strife after 1921 because the citizens of the Irish Free State had to swear an oath to the British Crown under the terms of the 1921 Anglo-Irish Treaty)."[88] Well aware of the historical and political background, Foster ascribes an almost imperialist motivation to Yeats's interest in Irish fairies, explains how the supernatural could function to legitimate Yeats's claims to Irish cultural authority and identity, and reminds readers of the historical connection between ethnographic pursuits and occult studies:

> Yeats remade an Irish identity in his work and life. In the process he reclaimed Ireland for himself, his family and his tradition. He began by asserting a claim on the land, particularly the Sligo land, through its people: the discovery of folklore and fairy belief. Difficulties arose: he could, for instance, be attacked as incapable of interpreting Ireland religiously, as he was a *Protestant* mystic. But folklore and anthropological interests, besides being often connected in the 1890s with theosophical or occult investigations, opened a way into nationalism via national tradition (as Scott and others had shown long before). It could also demonstrate the links between Yeatses, Pollexfens and the "real" Irish people around them.[89]

Although this explanation of some of the functions of Yeats's ethnographic interest in Irish supernatural phenomena is entirely convincing and, I believe, entirely correct, Foster then commits a rare misstep, asserting that "it was necessary for Yeats passionately to adhere to the idea that Sligo people did believe in fairies and talked about them all the time. So they did, of course—to children, as Lily Yeats remembered. The difference was that her brother expected to go on being talked to about them."[90] Foster follows this with an endnote reference to a reference in Yeats's sister Lily's scrapbook, a mention of household servants telling the children supernatural stories.

Although Foster's tone suggests that right-minded County Sligo adults did not believe in fairies, his partially paraphrased endnote quotation of Lily's remarks indicates nothing of the sort: "The Merville servants 'played a big part in our lives. They were so friendly and wise and knew so intimately angels, saints, banshees and fairies.'"[91] These remarks make no suggestion that the adults thought of the stories as untrue or as juvenile fare. Note that *saints* serves as a reminder that sincere belief in the supernatural was and is not entirely uncommon among adults. A grim reference to an aforementioned event involving earnest belief in fairies proves, in fact, that being off with the fairies could in Yeats's time mean something very different than its contemporary meaning— something very different than a term of ridicule that could accurately be directed at Yeats for his fascination with fairy phenomena—and that it could be deadly serious in the most literal sense.

Yeats's reference to the Tipperary man who burned his wife to death prompts a brief editorial note by William H. O'Donnell: "Michael Cleary was convicted of manslaughter in July 1895 and sentenced to twenty years of penal servitude for burning his wife, Bridget, to death, thinking that she was a fairy changeling. Convicted with him were her father, her aunt, four of her cousins, and two other neighbors."[92] Bridget Cleary's tragic death, which Angela Bourke's *The Burning of Bridget Cleary* examines in great detail, should certainly be recognized as more than simply a convenient piece of supporting evidence, but I refer to it here because of its relevance to Yeats. The gruesome facts of the event and the simple number of people convicted along with Michael Cleary testify to the persistence and seriousness of belief in fairy abduction in the Ireland of Yeats's time. In hindsight, this seems an extreme example of what we might think of as cultural division. The belief system of some rural Irish people ran headlong into the judicial system of turn-of-the-century Ireland, with the result being criminal convictions for the participants in Bridget Cleary's killing. Although as a British colonial holding at the time Ireland had its justice system imposed from without, there has of course been nothing like an accommodation of this kind of belief in the government or laws of independent Ireland.

In Yeats's general explanation of fairy abduction, the pronoun identification allies Yeats with a more cosmopolitan readership rather than with the people he describes or with Irish citizens in general. Yeats used similar maneuvers frequently, from signing essays he wrote for newspapers in Ireland and America "your Celt in London" to more specific identifications with the people of the west of Ireland, particularly Sligo. As is evident from these examples and from aforementioned cases of Yeats presenting drastically different versions of himself, Yeats's identifications with cultural groups and identity categories shifted according to the ethnographic self he wanted to present in a given argument and the kind of ethnographic authority he wanted to establish. I propose to call these ethnographic rhetorical maneuvers *identifictions*, a term that, in its similarity to *identification*, comprehends the fictionality of Yeats's ethnographic identifications and the subtlety with which he constructed them.

Ethnographic identifiction is a relatively unrecognized and unstudied component of Yeats's cultural authority. The tendency in recent years, especially among postcolonial critics, has been to discredit Yeats broadly by emphasizing aspects of his background and his thought that make him seem a colonial agent in Irish drag. This has for some time been the critical counterpart to the confusion of Yeats with Ireland. Yeats's Anglo-Irish Protestant ascendancy identifications, his periodic bursts of frustration and outright disgust with the Irish public, and his fascination with elements of fascism have drawn the most hostile critical attention, and not without reason. Further attention to Yeats's identifictions will contribute to the ongoing conversation about Yeats's roles in Irish culture by calling attention to an oversight in this postcolonial criticism of Yeats. Focusing more on the extent to which Yeats attempted to ground his views in actual Irish cultural beliefs—many of which he studied and recorded in accordance with the prevailing ethnographic practices of the day—will balance the postcolonial attacks on Yeats by the de-Yeatsification cabal and future postcolonial critics. I say *balance* rather than *refute* because the issues raised by such critics should not be disregarded, nor should my approach be misread as a simplistic apology for Yeats, who at times invented what he could not discover,[93] and at times expressed antidemocratic, crypto-fascist opinions that are impossible for any contemporary critic, no matter how sympathetic, to explain away.

CHAPTER 2

The Virtue of Fact and the Truth of Fiction

Frost and Literary Ethnography

I choose to be a plain New Hampshire farmer
With an income in cash of say a thousand
(From say a publisher in New York City).

—Robert Frost, "New Hampshire"

Whereas Yeats scholars have made much of the extent to which Yeats was not a representative figure (demographically or otherwise) of the Ireland of his time, relatively few scholars have paid this type of attention to Robert Frost. In part because of his own self-promotion; in part because there has been neither a concerted attempt to cast the rural New England of the late nineteenth century and the early to mid-twentieth century as postcolonial nor a turn to a New England–based identity politics; and in part because Frost's homespun persona did not appeal greatly to many critics of modern poetry,[1] Frost's protective coloring of rural New England identity has too often gone unrecognized.

Reading through the lenses of ethnographic theory enables a reader to reconceive the relationship between Frost and the culture region with which most people associate him so strongly. Among academic critics and nonacademic readers alike, the most common notion of Robert Frost is that of the crusty Yankee farmer. Other significant aspects of Frost's life (for instance, that he was a Harvard undergraduate, a Dartmouth undergraduate, a classical scholar, and—perhaps most surprising—a native Californian) tend to get overlooked or pushed aside.

John Kemp's excellent *Robert Frost and New England* was the first critical book to examine this aspect of Frost's life and work at length, and Kemp's remains the only book-length examination of the subject. Considering Frost's work in light of ethnographic theory expands on this kind of work and takes it beyond the limits of Kemp's valuable study. Unlike Kemp's work, the emerging methodology of ethnographic literary criticism offers numerous ways to connect Frost to a larger field of discourse, including scholarly conversations that go beyond the traditional disciplinary boundaries of English departments. This chapter focuses on Frost's earlier books for two general reasons. A literary career spanning eight decades is too vast to encompass in a project of this length. Moreover, Frost's ethnographic tendencies diminished with the years; as his career went on, he tended to write more and more as a cultural insider, more and more pithily, and less and less with sustained attention to the kinds of cultural particulars that reward ethnographic literary criticism.

James Clifford's *The Predicament of Culture: Twentieth-Century Ethnography, Literature, and Art* makes a number of analytical moves that (although Clifford does not mention Frost) will allow readers and critics to examine Frost's poetry as creative ethnography. This chapter will move back and forth between Frost's work and Clifford's critical work, juxtaposing Frost's work and Clifford's comments on the interrelationships between ethnography and literature, reinterpreting the comments of earlier Frost critics (especially Kemp), and recognizing the similarities between various paradigms of ethnography and Frost's approaches to two particular American cultural issues. This will call attention to the extent to which Frost's poetry both analyzes and constructs versions of his rural New England subject culture and the extent to which ethnographic theory offers useful new insights on Frost's work and thought. The literary-ethnographic model will also highlight Frost's complex narrative identity as a poet in and of rural New England, an identity that shifted significantly (and in ways that would likely strike most contemporary readers as surprising) during the first decades of his literary career. This approach will particularly enable readers to focus on two topics Frost examines and reexamines through much of his work: industrial market capitalism and the roles of men in society. This thematic concentration of ethnographic attention agrees with the literary-ethnographic models advanced by Clifford, who writes, "The ethnographic modernist searches for the universal in the local, the whole in the part,"[2] concentrating on a particular culture in a particular area, just as Frost concentrates on rural New England.

The observations about ethnographic representations of particular urban localities that Akhil Gupta and James Ferguson offer in their essay "Culture, Power, Place: Ethnography at the End of an Era" serve as useful reference points for a consideration of Frost's career-long project of constructing and representing versions of rural New England culture:

The urban ghetto . . . is transformed into a unique "locality," a "third world at home." [Kristin] Koptiuch points out that the "third world" is "a *name*, a representation, not a place" that can be geographically mapped as distinct from the "first world." The irony is that this place, made by struggles waged by forces of transnational capital, the state, and the residents of the barrio, then becomes a site for ethnographic constructions of "authentic" ways of life, to be recorded by folklorists. By pointing to anthropologists' and reporters' complicity in constructing representations of authentic localities (which thereby become suitable places to do "fieldwork"), Koptiuch highlights the fact that the establishment of spatial meanings—the making of spaces into places—is always implicated in hegemonic configurations of power.[3]

Although Gupta, Ferguson, and Koptiuch have in mind urban spaces, these observations also apply to Frost's rural New England (and to Robert Penn Warren's South, although contemporary Southern scholars would likely note that in the case of the South, geographical mapping of a third world as opposed to the presumptive first world of the North has in fact been quite common, notwithstanding the fact that Americans would no longer attribute much significance to the Mason-Dixon Line. Nowadays the Deep South might be the demarcated place, with a formerly Southern state such as Maryland no longer included, and with parts of Virginia, Texas, and Florida—and perhaps metropolitan areas such as Atlanta and Charlotte—marked as disputed territory).

In the case of Frost's New England, a territorial model from Ireland is most helpful: the pale, as in *beyond the pale*, the colonial British concept of a sphere of civilized urban influence, beyond which savage otherness ran unchecked. In the late nineteenth and early twentieth century view of rural life in America, Boston functioned as the pale of New England civilization. Aside from a handful of resort areas, the hinterlands of Vermont and New Hampshire had not yet been appointed as tourist destinations for the urban northeast. That is, at the time America did not primarily associate rural New England with bed and breakfast inns and foliage sightseeing tours. Instead (as in much of Frost's early poetry), the prevailing notion of rural New England was not unlike that of the South: Despite the existence of isolated retreats for weary urbanites (such as Asheville, North Carolina; the hot springs areas in Arkansas; and a few vacation communities in rural New England), the backwoods regions of both areas were popularly conceived of as third worlds at home, places where poverty, disease, incest, and insanity flourished.

A few examples from Frost scholars will demonstrate that such scholars have registered this sense of a distinctly nonidyllic rural New England and the impact of this cultural notion on the ways critics and readers experienced Frost's work. Kemp notes that "John Gould Fletcher . . . has attributed Amy Lowell's admiration for the poet of New England to her impression that he represented not merely a regional world, but a fascinatingly alien and unapproachable one: 'Frost stood in her mind for unfamiliar New England, not the New England of the cultivated and the affluent, among whom she had always lived, but the remote, shy, hermit-like New England of . . . the backwoods farmer.'[4] Jeffrey S. Cramer points out a parenthetical comment of Frost's about Amy Lowell in his essay "On Emerson," which indicates that although Lowell (who was a dyed-in-the-wool New Englander—albeit an urban New Englander—as well as a prominent critic and poet), accepted Frost's portrayals of New Hampshire people and life as accurate, she did not find these things particularly appealing in person: " 'I have left New Hampshire,' she told me. Why in the world? She couldn't stand the people. What's the matter with the people? 'Read your own books and find out.' "[5]

Maria Farland relates Frost's work to "a prevalent cultural preoccupation with rural degeneration—a concern with rural depopulation and defects that reached its zenith in the 1925 Eugenics Survey of Vermont."[6] Farland quotes from Adna Ferrin Weber's 1899 *The Growth of Cities in the Nineteenth Century: A Study in Statistics* to prove a surprising point about the pseudoscientific belief in the inferiority of rural people:

> Some went so far as to claim that city dwellers were an entirely different race, bio-logically speaking: "Migration cityward produces a distinct race—the dolicoce-phalic or long-heads, as distinguished from the brachycephelaic or round heads, who remain in the rural districts" (Weber 441). Sociologist Edward Ross [in his 1905 *Foundations of Sociology*] echoed the sentiment: "The city is a magnet for the more venturesome, and it draws to it more of the long-skulled race than of the broad-skulled race" (364). If rural populations needed "uplift" or improvement, it was in part because they were seen as a "lower" or less developed race, whose skulls bore the marks of their inferiority.[7]

Andrew Lakritz makes a related point about how Frost's poetry presents not an idyllic rendering of New England rural life as an escape from urban hustle and bustle but rather a series of troubling visions of rural life that reflect some of the prevailing notions and some of the prevailing realities of rural New England at the time: "Frost's poetry is a scattering of structures ruined and about to be ruined: fences of stone and wood, houses, clear-cut forests, communities and farms, woodpiles rotting in the forest, marriages, and even the frail human body. In part this wreckage and ruin scattered across the Frostian landscape is a testa-ment to the state of things in New England during the years Frost was writing, after the failure of the industrial base and the closing of mills and milltowns, as well as the decay of farming as a viable economic activity in the stony and cold Northeast."[8] Gupta and Ferguson's discussion of "bifocality" (a concept explored in detail by John Durham Peters) serves as further useful background for a discussion of ethnographic elements of Frost's work and thought and also provides a way to link the realistic particulars of Frost's rural narratives with a consciousness of social preconceptions about rural New England: "one way to characterize modernity is to see it as the condition of 'bifocality,' in which social actors simultaneously experience the local and the global, possessing both 'near-sight' and 'far-sight.' Bifocality is made possible by processes of social representation that first became widespread in the eighteenth century: newspapers, novels, statistics, encyclopedias, dictionaries, and panoramas. Peters points out that both novels and statistics represent invisible social totalities, the one by narrative, the other by aggregation."[9] This is true of poems, especially of narrative poems, as well as novels and statistics. Furthermore, a collection of poems (whether in a single volume, an edition of selected poems, a larger edition of collected poems, or an even larger edition of complete poems, perhaps including variant versions) shares characteristics that Peters attributes to statistics as well as characteristics he attributes to novels: Poems may represent segments of society through aggregation, through an accumulation of scores or hundreds of representations, as well as through narrative development, as is the case with the rural New England of Frost's poetry.

Frost's prose remarks concerning vernacular language indicate an awareness of himself as a collector of linguistic data, as if moving among the residents of rural New England were a kind of ethnographic fieldwork. I mean *fieldwork* not in the sense usually associated with Frost because of his depictions of agricultural labor but as the collection of anthropological or ethnographic data. Frost's interest in sentence sounds and his desire to incorporate vernacular language into literature led him, ears first, into this fieldwork. In a well-known 1915 letter to William Braithwaite, Frost says, "My conscious interest in people was at first no more than an almost technical interest in their speech."[10] Later in the same letter Frost refers to his ethnographic literary fieldwork in describing his project and indicates that such an approach to literature is in some sense necessary: "We must go out into the vernacular for tones that haven't been brought to book."[11]

David Sanders quotes from this letter (including the lesser-known sentence about Frost being interested in his rural New England neighbors for more than just their tones of speech) and explains its significance in terms that highlight ethnographic aspects of Frost's work, although Sanders never mentions ethnography specifically:

> "It would seem absurd to say it (and you mustn't quote me as saying it) but I suppose . . . that my conscious interest in people was at first no more than an almost technical interest in their speech—in what I used to call their sentence sounds— the sound of sense . . . There came a day ten years ago when I . . . made the discovery

in doing The Death of the Hired Man that I was interested in neighbors for more than merely their tones of speech—and always had been." By placing this discovery in 1905, when he drafted the earliest *North of Boston* poems, Frost makes it a cornerstone of the volume itself. Later he would say that the realization that "I was after poetry that talked" had "changed the whole course of my writing" and would even call it "providential." Aided by so weighty a term, Frost implies that, since any vernacular is rooted in its culture, a poetry that "talked" could never be a purely technical achievement. A poetry that "talked" would not only sound like conversation. It would really say something—something human, basic, and significant. Seeking a poetry that talked in the accents of his Derry neighbors gave Frost a way both to test and to convey such realities. In addition to evoking a specific culture in which to ground the human conflicts which he wished to explore, the search gave Frost a language free of false refinements in which anything inauthentic would prove weak or untrue.[12]

Sanders also explains other important aspects of *North of Boston* that show the significance of the ethnographic elements of Frost's work and thought:

> Frost's concern for his human subjects and his wish to make them known is implicit in the book's dedication to [his wife] Elinor—"to E.M.F. This Book of People"—and by the other titles that he considered for the volume: *New Englanders, New England Hill Folk*, or the one originally listed by his London publisher M. L. Nutt, *Farm Servants and Other People*. It may seem curious that, in the end, Frost chose a title that does not mention these people directly. Yet, as in so much of Frost's work, this reticence is eloquent. Like the book's language, the words "north of Boston" say something about its people not only by pointing to the region and culture that have shaped their lives, but by making clear what they are not. Posed against "Boston," with its history and urbanity, what lies "north" is simply out there, provincial and exposed . . . With just a little help from his dedication, Frost's title trusts the poems to bring his people to our notice, just as he has trusted their language to shape his poetic voice, and just as the poems, with their sparing narration, trust so largely to the speech of the characters themselves.[13]

Clifford's model of ethnography recognizes the elements of ethnographic consciousness in some literary works and encourages a broad understanding of ethnographic practices that encompasses literary approaches such as Frost's: "Modern ethnography appears in several forms, traditional and innovative. As an academic practice it cannot be separated from anthropology. Seen more generally, it is simply diverse ways of thinking and writing about culture from a standpoint of participant observation. In this expanded sense a poet like [William Carlos] Williams is an ethnographer." Ethnography, for Clifford, is "a state of being in culture while looking at culture, a form of personal and collective self-fashioning."[14] Frost devoted as much time and energy to self-fashioning as any modern poet and continually identified himself as being in and (less consistently) of rural New England culture. Frost's self-conscious cultivation of this persona is evident in his repeated comments about growing "Yankier and Yankier," as well as his frequent references to his years as a farmer.

Frost's identification of himself with what serve as the native people of his poems—the people for whom rural New England is home—complicates his status as an ethnographic observer. Despite ethnographers "mastering the vernacular and undergoing a personal learning experience comparable to an initiation," Clifford observes that traditional ethnographers "did not speak as cultural insiders but retained the natural scientist's documentary observational stance." In fact, absorption into the subject culture was actively discouraged and considered professionally counterproductive because "intuitive, excessively personal understanding . . . could not confer scientific authority."[15] Frost writes from a position that is inherently more complex than the traditional ethnographic participant-observer model. Frost, in fact, acts in his poems as both participant-observer and native informant, effectively feeding his own opinions and interpretations into the ongoing polyphonic discourse of the characters. Instead of keeping a traditional aesthetic or ethnographic distance, Frost injects himself into the action of the poems and speaks with the very sort of intuitive personal understanding that traditional ethnography disallows.

Kemp points out the fact that the typical narrative persona of Frost's early poems differs greatly from the rural Yankee insider America came to know Frost as in his later years as a literary celebrity. Though there were Yankee types in some of Frost's poems, Kemp explains, the types were not to be confused with the narrative voice:

> Yankee stereotypes had been important in several of Frost's [early] poems . . . But the persona in such poems was a neutral character who stood apart, observing recognizable Yankees like the cantankerous field hand in "The Code," the frustrated wife in "A Servant to Servants," the tight-lipped farmer in "Mending Wall," and the wry, quizzical one in "The Mountain." The few speakers directly associated with farming in the early poems (for example in "Storm Fear," "Mowing," "The Tuft of Flowers," and "After Apple-Picking") show little affinity with the conventional New England farmer, displaying aesthetic sensibilities, tendencies toward irresolution, and a metaphysical curiosity—all of which differentiated them from stereotypical local figures.[16]

Kemp describes Frost's early persona in terms that come remarkably close to the vocabulary of contemporary ethnographic theory, emphasizing Frost's marginal or liminal status in the culture region and driving home the point that Frost did not at that time speak with the voice of a native or a cultural insider:

As Frost developed his first extended treatment of New England, he did not attempt to write in the person of the Yankee farmer. He drew instead on his own experience as an outsider in Derry. *North of Boston* portrays rural life, but it also evokes a specific observer located in the regional setting, who seems to wonder whether he belongs there. Because of his role as observer, he stands somewhat apart from those he studies, and he finds himself susceptible to feelings of isolation and alienation. By conveying these feelings, Frost achieved an artistic depth and complexity often lacking in regional literature, and he transcended the predictability and chauvinism that afflict many New England authors.[17]

. . .

[Frost's poems create] exceptionally vivid portraits of New England by using observers who function as intermediaries between the reading audience and the rural world. They are not in any sense regional spokesmen, and their narrative concern is not only with local events, but also with their own explorations of the region. A special artistic sensibility results, involving subtle tensions between inner and outer, observer and observed.[18]

These passages particularly invite juxtaposition with ethnographic theory. It seems that Kemp is casting about looking for a term that would bring together several aspects of Frost's writing; ethnography is just such a term. For *chauvinism*, read *ethnocentrism*. For *artistic depth and complexity* in this case, read *thick description*. Jeffrey N. Wasserstrom sums up Geertz's famous term as follows: "Borrowing an illustration first used by Ryle, Geertz demonstrates what he means via reference to the many things that a person rapidly opening and closing an eye can signify. It can be an involuntary twitch, a conspiratorial wink, or even a parody of such a conspiratorial wink. A 'thin description' that just says that an eye opened and closed is not enough; assuming that every twitch is just a twitch will lead us astray in cultural analysis; what we need is a 'thick description' that separates twitches from winks and one sort of wink from another."[19] Keeping such terms in mind makes it clear that Frost's (or his narrative persona's) experience in his earlier poetry is fundamentally that of the ethnographic participant-observer. Positioning Frost's narrators as intermediary figures between the subject culture and the reading audience heightens the potential usefulness of ethnographic theoretical models in this situation, as does the attention to the nonnative narrators' strong interest in reflecting on the processes of their own explorations.

Besides analyzing Frost's narrative stances in order to see behind the poet's largely self-created personae (both the narrative persona and the public persona Frost invented and amplified in his numerous public appearances), Kemp persuasively explains that Frost's rural image made very good sense in terms of the market considerations of the earlier years of his literary career:

Frost's return to New Hampshire [from England] in 1915 and his assumption of the Yankee farmer's role could hardly have been better timed. Benjamin T. Spencer has identified a resurgence in American regionalism from about 1912 into the 1920s, noting that regionalism was especially dominant in American poetry from 1915 to 1925. At this time, American literature seemed to focus on regional environments: Ellen Glasgow's Dinwiddie, Virginia; Robinson's Tilbury Town; Carl Sandberg's Chicago; Willa Cather's Black Hawk, Nebraska; Edgar Lee Masters's Spoon River; Sherwood Anderson's Winesburg, Ohio; and Sinclair Lewis's Gopher Prairie, Minnesota. Thus it is highly understandable that Frost's residence on a White Mountain farm—together with his pose as the Yankee farmer poet and his promulgation of the Derry myth [the misconception that the time on the farm in Derry, New Hampshire was a time when Frost single-handedly eked out a living by the narrowest of margins by relying only on the income from his farm—this version overlooks significant details such as the presence of two knowledgeable hired men and the financial support Frost received from his grandfather]—had a profound effect on the literary community. *North of Boston*, released in New York just prior to his return from England in February 1915, went on the best-seller list and into its fourth printing during the summer before the poet was completely settled on his new farm. So adept was Frost at performing his rustic role, however, that during the spring of 1915, well before moving to the farm, he had beguiled interviewers, critics, and urban acquaintances into thinking that he was already engaged in agricultural work.[20]

The example above clearly shows Frost manufacturing ethnographic authority, fabricating something like rural New England authenticity in order to lend more weight (what Frost elsewhere called "the virtue of fact") to his work. Frost manufactured his special brand of ethnographic authority so successfully that he effectively convinced innumerable critics and readers that he was no mere observer and commentator on rural culture north of Boston; he became, for all literary intents and purposes, a representative voice (really *the* representative voice) of the culture region.

Lowell emphasized "that his photographic 'pictures' and 'characters' were 'produced directly from life,' " and declared, "He is not writing of people whom he has met in summer vacations, who strike him as interesting, and whose life he thinks worthy of perpetuation . . . He is as racial as his own puppets."[21] R. Clifton Spargo points out that in comparing "Frost to a local-color short-story writer such as Amy Brown, Lowell praised him for his unrelenting mimetic eye and for telling the reader 'what he has seen exactly as he has seen it.' "[22] In fact, in his notebooks Frost described his work and himself in very similar terms: "Im [sic] not a realist but an actualist. A realist is satisfied if what he writes seems as if it must have happened. I set nothing down that hasn't [here the word "actually" is crossed out] to my knowledge actually happened in words and tones I have actually heard. No book words."[23]

It is worth mentioning that at least once, in her 1922 long poem *A Critical Fable*, Lowell describes Frost's work in lines that simultaneously poke fun and recall the prevalence of the social-science discourse about the perceived ills of rural New England:

> There's Frost with his blueberry pastures and hills
> All peopled by folk who have so many ills
> 'Tis a business to count 'em, their subtle insanities.
> One half are sheer mad, and the others inanities.
> He'll paint you a phobia quick as a wink
> Stuffed into a hay-mow or tied to a sink.
> And then he'll deny, with a certain rich rapture,
> The very perversion he's set out to capture.[24]

Given the description of his varied background that Frost provides Lowell in a 1917 letter, it is all the more remarkable that Lowell generally persisted in thinking of Frost as some kind of pure figure of rural New England life:

> Doesn't the wonder grow that I have never published anything except about New England farms when you consider the jumble I am? Mother, Scotch immigrant. Father oldest New England stock unmixed. Ten years in West. Thirty years in East. Three years in England. Not less than six months in any of these: San Francisco, New York, Boston, Cambridge, Lawrence, London. Lived in Maine, N.H., Vt., Mass. Twenty five years in cities, nine in villages, nine on farms. Saw the South on foot. Dartmouth, Harvard two years. Shoe-worker, mill-hand, farm-hand, editor, reporter, insurance agent, agent for Shakespearean reader, reader myself, teacher in every kind of school public and private including psychological normal school and college. Prize for running at Caledonia Club picnic; prizes for assumed parts at masquerade balls; medal for goodness in high school; detur for scholarship at Harvard; money for verse . . . Presbyterian, Unitarian, Swedenborgian, Nothing. All the vices but disloyalty and chewing gum or tobacco.[25]

The list sounds a bit like the résumé of a young man on the make, though by this time Frost had already achieved a good deal of literary success and had joined the faculty at Amherst College. (He wrote the letter on the letterhead of the Amherst College English Department.)

Although Frost alerted Lowell to the numerous aspects of his identity that had little to do with the growing image of Frost as some ur-Yankee, at other times he was not above willfully misrepresenting his background, downplaying or omitting (and sometimes purposely distorting) significant details in order to strengthen his homespun Yankee persona, and sometimes even tailoring his image to different parts of rural New England in order to reinforce his own ethnographic authority. In this, Frost seems an excellent example of a species of nonnative resident that sociologists Wendy Griswold and Nathan Wright call "cowbirds, people who come in [move to a new region] and absorb the cultural characteristics of their new homes, just as cowbirds infiltrate and thrive in the nests made by other birds."[26] In a 1938 letter to the editor of *New Hampshire: A Guide*, Frost bends the truth considerably, emphasizing entirely different aspects of his life, residence, and identity than he does in the aforementioned letter to Lowell and creating the impression that he has thoroughly absorbed the cultural characteristics of his adopted home region:

> I lived, somewhat brokenly to be sure, in Salem, Derry, Plymouth, and Franconia, New Hampshire, from my tenth [eleventh] to forty-fifth [forty-sixth] year. Most of my time out of it I lived in Lawrence, Massachusetts, on the edge of New Hampshire, where my walks and vacations could be in New Hampshire. My first teaching was in a district school in the southern part of Salem, New Hampshire. My father was born in Kingston, New Hampshire. My wife's mother was born in New Hampshire. So you see it has been New Hampshire, New Hampshire with me all the way. You will find my poems show it, I think.[27]

Lawrance Thompson corrects some numerical inaccuracies, indicated in brackets above, and also points out that Frost's first teaching job was actually in Methuen, Massachusetts, rather than New Hampshire. It is worth noting the significant difference between the busy mill city of Lawrence, Massachusetts, and the state of New Hampshire at the end of the nineteenth century. Frost's long poem "New Hampshire" celebrates this difference, praising at length the state's complete lack of anything like the industrialization that characterized the Lawrence area.

To see Frost trying out or trying on the rural Yankee identity he would eventually personify in the minds of innumerable readers and critics, one need only look to the early prose pieces Frost published in two poultry-farming trade journals, *The Eastern Poultryman* and *Farm-Poultry*, from 1903 to 1905 (collected and edited as *Robert Frost: Farm-Poultryman* by Edward Connery Lathem and Lawrance Thompson). In these prose writings, Frost attempts to speak as an insider, a bit of imposture twice over, in that at the time he was a newcomer to rural New England and a newcomer to poultry farming. It should come as no surprise to learn that Frost was not especially successful in this early attempt to pass himself off as a Yankee farmer. In fact, he exposed himself inadvertently with embarrassing results. Lathem and Thompson describe the circumstances:

> The mistake of consequence, made by Frost in his reporting the activities of John Hall [the poultry farmer whose domestic arrangements were the basis for Frost's poem "The Housekeeper"], had nothing to do of course with the domestic arrangements of the Hall household. It was, rather, a purely technical blunder—that of letting his imagination supplement his knowledge by claiming that Hall's geese roosted in trees, something that geese in fact do not do; this mistake

prompted a letter to the editor from a Massachusetts poultry farmer gently making fun of Frost's imaginative elaboration. In a published reply, Frost unwittingly emphasized his ignorance of the subject matter by remarking that Hall's geese did not need coops. The editor, recognizing that Frost was making things worse for himself, printed a commentary along with Frost's letter. The editor's commentary, although worded mildly, could not disguise the fact that Frost had exposed himself as doubly uninformed about his subject matter, a fact that the editor makes clear in his first sentence: "Mr. Frost seems not to be aware of the fact that geese generally remain out of doors by choice practically all the time."[28]

Lathem and Thompson also describe the lengths Frost went to in order to attempt to reestablish his authority once he had blown his cover and exposed himself as anything but an expert: "Unfortunately, however, before his own letter (with this unexpected editorial comment and correction) appeared, Frost had decided it might be well to protect himself further by having John Hall write a letter in his defense. But, as all his friends and enemies knew, John Hall had little schooling, and his talents did not include epistolary abilities. The best he could do was to enter into collusion with his friend by giving approval to a letter actually composed by Frost." That letter attempted to reestablish Frost's claim to the status of a knowledgeable insider versed in country things; in it, "Hall" claimed, "I don't know how Mr. Frost made that mistake [about geese roosting in trees], for of course he knows better."[29] Frost later admitted that he had written the letter, and that the ideas therein were his own rather than Hall's, thereby making it clear that the latter was a fiction intended to recuperate his ethnographic authority; that this ethnographic authority was itself inherently fictitious (given Frost's newcomer status in the area and his lack of familiarity with poultry farming) emphasizes the lengths Frost went to in order to misrepresent the disparity between his background and the background of the narrative persona he was in the process of constructing. In a 1913 letter to John Bartlett (who had gotten himself in trouble by embellishing and sometimes fabricating facts and details in his work as a journalist), Frost makes it clear that he understands the power inherent in this kind of ethnographic narrative persona by referring to another published account in which Frost had purposely misrepresented the truth:

> You mustn't fake articles any more. Not even in details. Them's orders. I'll tell you why. It's taking an unfair advantage. Of whom? Of the public? Little I care for them. They would deceive themselves were there no one else to deceive them. Of your fellow journalists then? I suspect that they can hold up their end. No it is taking an unfair advantage of the gentlemen who profess fiction. I used to think of it when I faked in a small way for another paper named the Sun which was published in Lawrence Mass. All I had to do was to claim for my yarns the virtue of fact and I had story writers of twice my art and invention skun a mile . . . It had occurred to me previously that some

fiction not purporting to be true otherwise than as fiction is true, true to the life of the farm and especially the poultry farm, wouldn't derogate from the serious not to say solemn interest of a poultry journal.[30]

This recognition of the rhetorical power of the ethnographic insider persona (as opposed to a narrative participant-observer who remains cognizant of an original outsider status that is fundamentally unchangeable) makes it clear that Frost was well aware of the added weight such a persona (whether as a narrative persona or as what we might call, somewhat awkwardly, a personal persona— the face Frost prepared to meet the faces he would meet for most of his highly public literary career) could lend to his writing.

That Frost remained cognizant of the distance between this sort of persona and his actual experience is evident in a 1920 letter to Louis Untermeyer. The letter gives an idea of Frost's less-than-masterful farming, as well as his self-consciousness about not being what his rural neighbors would regard as a real farmer: "[I] took up my new life as a farmer today by absently boring a hole clear through a two foot maple tree and out onto the other side. 'Amatoor!' all the leaves began to murmur. 'Book-farmer!' "[31] Kemp refers to Lawrance Thompson's account of Frost's status among his neighbors, an account that suggests the words Frost imagined hearing in the murmuring leaves were quite similar to the sentiments of Frost's neighbors: "Thompson, noting Frost's financial reliance on the annuities of his grandfather's will during the Derry period, points out that by the time he took up teaching, 'Everyone in the region knew he did very little farming, and not much with hens.' "[32]

Frost's creative representations of his own subject position with regard to his ability to speak of (and eventually for) rural New England with some degree of cultural authority go beyond what most professional ethnographers would consider ethical, but they are not without similarities to some contemporary ethnographic theory. Clifford's inclusive models of ethnography recognize that ethnographic accounts are always already partial and creative. Whereas traditional models of ethnographic theory might prohibit or deny a hybrid narrative position such as Frost's, Clifford's understanding of the inherent elements of creativity and fictionality in all ethnographic narratives accommodates Frost's complex subjectivity. "Ethnographic texts are orchestrations of multivocal exchanges. The subjectivities produced in these often unequal exchanges—whether of 'natives' or of visiting participant-observers—are constructed domains of truth, serious fictions,"[33] Clifford writes. This acknowledgment of the artifice involved in the composition and presentation of any ethnographic text closes the gap between ethnographic production and literary production, and this identification of the complications inherent in literary presentations of multivocal exchanges is especially helpful for readers of Frost's narrative poems, in which multiple characters often offer contending interpretations of facts in attempts to establish or discover some truth.

Frost's early sonnet "Mowing" provides a useful poetic complement to Clifford's theory of literary ethnography. The most famous line in "Mowing"— "The fact is the sweetest dream that labor knows"—suggests an understanding of the creative energies underlying the production of what, in ethnographic contexts or in more general contexts, people accept as facts. (Frost would have been aware that the Latin roots of "fact" and "fiction" suggest similarities between the two words; there is an element of constructedness inherent in the word roots that might suggest a deep kinship or a Latinate pun.) Kemp describes "Mowing" as a landmark poem because of its use of the cultural-insider voice with which Frost's rural New England verse would eventually become identified: "His greatest achievement in 'Mowing' was the virtual elimination of distance between his speaker and the regional world of the poem. Instead of parading the 'poetical' voice he had cultivated during his years of apprenticeship, he struck boldly at the unadorned poetic power of human speech, aiming not to describe or comment, but to dramatize the personal engagement of a regional character in a specific, rustic activity."[34] In short, "Mowing" shows us Frost going native, or pretending to, for the first time. Siobhan Phillips points out that "[Frank] Lentricchia describes how Frost 'define[d] and proudly advertise[d] himself as ordinary' in pointed contrast to high modernist company."[35] "Poetry and Poverty," Frost's 1937 Haverford College Address, is another excellent example of Frost's self-fashioning and also indicates his complex subject position: "When I speak of my people, I sort of mean a class, the ordinary folks I belong to," Frost said. Later in the same talk, Frost described his earlier years in rural New England in terms reminiscent of extended ethnographic fieldwork: "I spent all that part of my life, over twenty years of it, with just country neighbors around me . . . I was brought up in a family who had just come to the industrial city of Lawrence, Massachusetts."[36] Characteristically, Frost seems to be trying to have it both ways.

Frost's remarks purposefully align him with "a class, the ordinary folks," thus obliterating distinctions between rural and urban people; they also demonstrate his awareness of himself as different and separate from the rural Yankees he came to regard as subjects for literature. The extent of this perceived difference (which Frost tended to downplay while fashioning and presenting his popular farmer-poet persona) is perhaps debatable; however, it should be noted that Frost distinguishes not so much between New Englanders and other Americans (a distinction that might resonate personally for him because of his childhood years in California), but between urban and rural New Englanders. Kemp's accounts of the Frost family's relationship to the developing urban-rural divide in New England make it clear that Frost's identity was based more in the bustling life of the region's mill cities than in the bucolic settings with which most readers and critics tend to associate him:

> It is significant that in creating his mythical background Frost always glossed over the distance between country life and the social position his family had attained by the end of the nineteenth century. The Frosts were well-established townsfolk by then, and their cultivation was *not* of the soil. The family home, to which Frost's mother returned after his father's death in 1885, was in Lawrence, Massachusetts, a highly industrialized city for its day and one of the world's leading textile centers. The paternal grandfather, William Prescott Frost, an important figure in Frost's early life, was a bespectacled, stylishly bearded patriarch who had worked his way up to an overseer's position at the Pacific Mill.[37]

Kemp also points out that Frost's first in-depth encounter with rural New England life resulted in no sense that the writer and his primary subject matter had finally met. His description also makes it clear that the young Frost did not even have a great deal of interest in well-known literary treatments of the region:

> Ironically, when Frost, who was to become New Hampshire's twentieth-century "Rustic Bard," took a summer job as a farmhand in 1891, he happened to work on the very farm where New Hampshire's nineteenth-century "Rustic Bard," Robert Dinsmore (the original farmer poet extolled by Whittier), had cultivated his potatoes and poems more than sixty years before. It is indicative of Frost's early indifference to New England's rural literature that he never realized the significance of the Dinsmore farm. Furthermore, his distant relationship to the farm country is suggested by his inability to get along with the other hired hands or with Dinsmore's descendants. After only three weeks, he ran away—too discomfited to ask for his pay—and returned home with complaints about "the coarseness, the profanity" of rural folk.

With this incident in mind, and with Frost's generally urban and sophisticated background taken into account, we should be able to appreciate—as many commentators have *not*—that the move to Derry was a departure into an alien world.[38]

Frost describes the rural space north of Boston as removed from industrial capitalism, in some sense insulated from the realities of the encroaching American economy by a sort of moral or intellectual economy that supersedes market considerations, "For no matter how educated or poor a man is, a certain level up there in Vermont and New Hampshire stays about the same."[39] This confusion of education and financial status ("educated or poor" rather than "educated or uneducated" or "rich or poor") typifies Frost's desire for rural New England to stand for a world not governed by the forces of industrialism and market pressures. Education, it would seem, is a sort of wealth in Frost's imagined rural spaces. It is, nevertheless, an alternative form of wealth that allows Frost to disguise it at his convenience in order to perpetuate an image of himself as a poor (and therefore typical) New England farmer. A comment Frost made in a 1941 interview in the *New York World-Telegram* shows him promoting the perception that (despite being highly educated by any standard) he was at bottom no different from the rural people who often inspired his verse: "A woman said to me once, 'You've written so nicely about the poor.' And I said, 'If I did that, it was when I was so poor myself that I was looking up to them.' It's neither the rich nor the poor that I was writing about. Just about people like us."[40]

To attend to the ways remarks such as this one and turns of a phrase such as "educated or poor" de-emphasize or gloss over financial issues is not to say that Frost's depictions of rural New England refuse to register the pressure of market capitalism. Far from it. Economic realities frequently obtrude in Frost's poetry. He writes more often and more eloquently about work than any of the major modern poets with whom he is usually compared, and his poems of work are often marked by the presence of industrial capitalism. Poems such as "The Self-Seeker," "New Hampshire," "The Egg and the Machine," " 'Out, Out—,' " and "A Lone Striker" deal directly with the consequences of industrialism and market pressure. Collectively, these poems function as a series of ethnographic accounts of the pressures of capitalism on the society Frost examines. These poems embody the kind of ethnography by synecdoche Clifford describes, finding the widely applicable in the local, the whole in the parts.

Frost's narrative techniques frequently resemble ethnographic narrative accounts in their presentation of events with minimal apparent narrative intrusion, as if the function of the author or narrator were the direct presentation of simple truths. Such a narrative approach (in Frost's poetry and in other ethnographic accounts) of course creates an added appearance of veracity and thus heightens the impact of the accounts on readers. Striking anecdotes make readers willing to go along with the ethnographic project, willing to take the selected parts as representative of the whole. "The Self-Seeker" presents just such a striking narrative with little obvious intrusion by the narrator. The gruesome subject matter of "The Self-Seeker" makes evident the cost/benefit relationship of industrial capitalism to the anonymous maimed worker identified by the narrator as "The Broken One."[41] The maimed man explicitly describes his mangled feet and legs in the only terms industrial capitalism recognizes: "The lawyer's coming for the company. / I'm going to sell my soul, or, rather, feet. / Five hundred dollars for the pair, you know."[42] When the lawyer arrives he appears solicitous and begins to address the maimed man, but he cannot remember the man's name and so refers to him only as "Mister——."[43]

The maimed man, the company, and the lawyer all remain nameless, as if to emphasize the point that their individual identities are less important than their value as exemplars, their ability to evoke broader truths about their respective cultures. The distinction between cultural groups or cultural identities is crucial to Clifford, and, I believe, is a prerequisite to identifying and understanding the ethnographic elements of Frost's work. Clifford writes, "A 'culture' is, concretely, an open-ended, creative dialogue of subcultures, of insiders and outsiders, of diverse factions."[44]

Although in some sense ethnographic accounts always attempt to speak about sizeable cultural groups, they inevitably reveal the existence of smaller groups and divisions within the culture. Frost's poems demonstrate an awareness of such cultural divisions, and "The Self-Seeker" in fact identifies multiple divisions. The maimed man and the lawyer in "The Self-Seeker" clearly belong to different subcultures or cultural groups. The lawyer is the socially acceptable face of industrial market capitalism as embodied by the company, and the maimed man is obviously not part of the same cultural group. The man is different in part because of his injury and his social class and in part because of his temperament. His passion, it seems, is wildflowers. The man's friend Willis implores him, "But your flowers, man, you're selling out your flowers."[45] As if readers could ignore the symbolic associations of wildflowers in a narrative of the body's (and, by the injured man's admission, the soul's or the self's) destruction by the forces of industrial capitalism, Frost introduces Anne, a young girl who shares the injured man's love of wildflowers and so emphasizes his separation from the culture of industrial capitalism. Willis, aware that the meeting is in part a meeting of representatives of distinct cultural groups, replies to the lawyer's empty assertion ("'We're very sorry for you.'") with a disdainful rhetorical question that emphasizes the cultural differences: "Willis sneered: / 'Who's *we*?—Some stockholders in Boston?'" The injured man explains Willis's hostility to the lawyer after Willis leaves and does so in terms that again emphasize the poem's symbolic opposition of rural life to industrial urban market forces: "'He [Willis] thinks you ought to pay me for my flowers. / You don't know what I mean about the flowers. / Don't stop to try now. You'll miss your train.'"[46]

The train reappears as a symbol of industrialism in "The Egg and the Machine," in which an unnamed man seethes with Luddite anger and fantasizes about destroying the railroad and the train: "He gave the solid rail a hateful kick" and later "He wished when he had had the track alone / He had attacked it with a club or stone / And bent some rail wide open like a switch / So as to wreck the engine in the ditch."[47] The man eventually finds a turtle's egg buried in the sandbank of the train track and threatens to throw it against the windshield of the next train that passes. That the gesture would be ineffectual is part of the point of the poem, in that the poem opposes a fragile organic projectile against an immense symbol of expansionist industrial power.

Clifford describes ethnographic narrative techniques as falling into two major classes. One style seeks to conceal the presence of the narrator, rendering the ethnographer as a disembodied narrative voice. The other style includes the ethnographic narrator as a character present in the narrative.[48] "The Self-Seeker" approximates the first approach, as the felt presence of a narrator is minimal. Other Frost poems of work fall somewhere between the two stylistic poles, incorporating elements of narrative presence and authorial self-consciousness but often leaving readers with questions about the identity of the narrator. "'Out, Out—,'" for instance, resembles "The Self-Seeker" in its concern with the terrible impact of industrial capitalism on human life, but its narrative technique depends far more on the presence of a narrator. An awareness of the economic consciousness underlying the poem is crucial to any understanding of what happens and why. The boy in the poem has apparently been working all day cutting wood on a buzz saw in the yard of his family's home, "big boy / Doing a man's work, though a child at heart,"[49] presumably because his family needs the money his labor will help generate. Again, industrial capitalism encroaches on childhood and home life, again with disastrous results for the human body. The boy loses his concentration, then his hand, then his life.

Unlike "The Self-Seeker," which proceeds almost entirely by way of quotations from the various characters in the poem, "'Out, Out—'" manifests a strong, although indeterminate, narrative presence throughout. The only lines of dialogue come when the wounded boy begs his sister not to let the doctor amputate his hand. The rest of the poem depends entirely on the narrator. Frost foregrounds his narrative presence by using a first-person pronoun early in the poem: "Call it a day, I wish they might have said."[50] By including "I" and referring to the narrator's retrospective wish, Frost forces readers to account for the fact that they know nothing about the controlling consciousness that is generating the narrative. Clifford identifies this type of unavoidable yet unknowable narrative presence as a common element in ethnographic accounts. Such a destabilizing "invasion by an ambiguous person of questionable origin" undermines claims to monologic authority from within the narrative.[51] Readers who remain conscious of the unknown (and therefore inherently unreliable) narrator will attend to the multiple layers of subjective interpretation present in the poem's final lines: "No more to build on there. And they, since they / Were not the one dead, turned to their affairs."[52]

Because the lines deliver the narrator's interpretation of what the narrator must infer from the family's reaction, readers should regard them as less than absolutely stable or reliable. The language of the lines, in fact, registers the pressure of industrial capitalism even after the boy's death. Finally, describing the situation in terms of utility value ("No more to build on there.") reminds readers that the market does not care about the death of the nameless boy any more than it cares about the mangled feet of the unnamed man in "The Self-Seeker." Kemp's interpretation of the startling, blunt final lines meshes nicely with an attempt to understand the poem's ethnographic elements: "In the closing lines, after the boy's death, Frost gives the regional apothegm, 'No more to build on there.' Yet he neither elaborates it nor lets it stand as a lesson to the reader. Instead, he turns attention to the regional people, and in so doing, reaffirms his speaker's separation from them: 'And they, since they / Were not the one dead, turned to their affairs.' "[53] This separation emphasizes the ethnographic element of the poem, which turns on the fact that the boy's family literally cannot afford to turn for long from their affairs: The family (like the rural culture in general) is not wealthy, and financial pressures remain noticeable regardless of the emotional consequences of certain events. In fact, since the boy had already been pressed into service doing adult labor, it is logical to conclude that his death would be a serious financial setback to his family as well as an awful emotional blow. Identifying the poem's most jarring line as a regional apothegm makes clear another ethnographic element of the poem (albeit one that disciplinary ethnographic theory has not addressed). Building a poem around a local maxim such as "No more to build on there" (or, elsewhere and more famously, "Good fences make good neighbors") is in a strange sense ethnographically descriptive: The poem is largely a work of fiction, of course, but in incorporating local sayings (perhaps as the verbal and ideological equivalents of material cultural artifacts), the poem strengthens its claims to the kind of truth Frost describes in his aforementioned discussion of fabricating accounts and misrepresenting them as accurate descriptions of the truth; the poem becomes more like, in Frost's terms, a kind of truthful fiction, faithful to the life of the rural culture it represents.[54]

Clifford describes the effect of "the perceptual frame," a narrative reminder to readers that the narrative is in part the product of a consciousness separate from the action it describes. This reminder "redirects our attention to the observational standpoint we share, as readers, with the ethnographer."[55] Clifford explains the way such reminders simultaneously distinguish narrators from narratives and implicate readers in narratives: "Every use of *I* presupposes a *you*, and every instance of discourse is immediately linked to a specific, shared situation."[56] That is, the simple act of reading a first-person narrative constitutes a sort of shared situation that involves readers in the narrative. Given this, what are readers to make of "The Vanishing Red," a poem with which most readers would scarcely want to identify themselves? The narrative technique of the poem's first lines is indirect and reports the popular account of the story to come: "He is said to have been the last Red Man / In Acton. And the Miller is said to have laughed—." But the narrative then turns to the reader ("If you like to call such a sound a laugh.") and suddenly involves the reader in the kind of identification Clifford describes, "implicat[ing] readers in the complex subjectivity of participant observation . . . the second person construction brings together reader and native in a textual participation."[57]

A narrative such as "The Vanishing Red" also brings together reader and narrator, although in the end the reader may wish that it had not. Frost reminds readers of the difference between narrative and reality by alluding to the ways narrative cannot represent events in their entirety and so always holds something back: "You can't get back and see it as he saw it. / It's too long a story to go into now. / You'd have to have been there and lived it."[58] This sounds much like Clifford's claim that "to understand discourse 'you had to have been there,' in the presence of a discoursing subject . . . The ethnographer always departs, taking away texts for later interpretation."[59] Frost's narrative evinces awareness of this inherent element of fictionality within all narrative accounts (including its own), but this does not release readers from the grasp of the direct second-person address.

The uneasy relationship between the reader and the narrator proves extremely disturbing as the narrator's final lines reveal that the Miller kills the "Red Man" John by shutting him in the wheel pit of the mill and then intensifies as the narrator savors the irony of the phrasing and the means of John's murder: "Oh, yes, he showed John the wheel-pit all right."[60] Readers cannot help but wonder if the narrator expects laughter in exchange for his gruesome joke, and they must recognize the poem's title as a pun on the Miller's murder of John. As with "The Self-Seeker," the poem's allegorical elements are immediately evident and are fraught with such symbolic value that readers can scarcely overlook them, especially when considering the ethnographic aspects of Frost's work: The Miller (Frost capitalizes the M, as if to identify the Miller as a type) functions as a figure of industrial capitalism not unlike the company lawyer in "The Self-Seeker," and both poems identify mills as destroyers of human bodies and lives; John represents noncapitalist, unindustrialized consciousness; when John meets the Miller and the mill, the Miller has the last laugh, emphasizing industrial capitalism's disregard for the people it destroys.

Clifford suggests a corrective measure against the kind of monologic authority evident in "The Vanishing Red": "One may also read against the grain of the text's dominant voice, seeking out other half-hidden authorities, reinterpreting the descriptions, texts, and quotations gathered together by the writer. With the recent questioning of colonial styles of representation, with the expansion of literacy and ethnographic consciousness, new possibilities for reading (and thus for writing) cultural descriptions are emerging."[61] Attempting to read against the dominant voice of "The Vanishing Red" produces a realization of the extent to which Frost encourages or even forces this. Frost undermines the dominant voice of "The Vanishing Red" by calling attention to the narrator's apparent approval of the murder. The poem's narrator is the antithesis of the detached, scientific recorder of data, and his involvement on all levels of the poem is itself a way of compelling readers to recognize him as a sort of unreliable narrator and read against or behind the narrative. (I use masculine pronouns above because when in doubt readers and critics typically assume that Frost's narrators are male, a tendency Frost encouraged in his talks and via his general interest in rural masculinity.)

Frost's long poem "New Hampshire" seemingly offers fewer opportunities for readers to read against the dominant narrative voice. The poem is a first-person explanation of the reasons the narrative voice (I will call it Frost) thinks New Hampshire is wonderful. As is often the case, however, Frost destabilizes his own narrative, both by way of the nature of his claims about New Hampshire and by way of his self-conscious commentary at the end of the poem. From the first lines, the poem fits into the larger pattern of Frost's ethnographic consciousness and examination of market capitalism: "The having anything to sell is what / Is the disgrace in man or state or nation."[62] Frost describes New Hampshire as a sort of anticapitalist economic paradise where people are not "soiled with trade,"[63] where even a gold mine yields "not gold in commercial quantities, / Just enough gold to make the engagement rings / And marriage rings of those who owned the farm. / What gold more innocent could one have asked for?"[64]

New Hampshire is the site and inspiration of the poem, but, Frost drolly mentions, "Anything I can say about New Hampshire / Will serve almost as well about Vermont."[65] This assertion includes Vermont in Frost's nonindustrial and anticapitalist moral economy, and it also undermines the uniqueness of New Hampshire, which is purportedly what occasioned the poem in the first place. Frost complicates readers' understandings of his own narrative position by saying, "Because I wrote my novels in New Hampshire / Is no proof that I aimed them at New Hampshire."[66] The Frost readers know is not a novelist, but a poet, and this strange stray detail keeps readers slightly unsure of what Frost is up to as he constructs his narrative persona within this poem. At the end of "New Hampshire," Frost offers readers a version of himself more in line with the public Frost persona readers would come to expect, but this version too reveals itself as constructed and fundamentally unstable:

> I choose to be a plain New Hampshire farmer
> With an income in cash of say a thousand
> (From say a publisher in New York City).
> It's restful to arrive at a decision,
> And restful just to think about New Hampshire.
> At present I am living in Vermont.[67]

By explicitly mentioning his conscious choice of persona and repeating "say" to emphasize the fact that this narrative is an imaginative product, Frost prompts readers to recognize the multiple layers of fictionality surrounding the narrative. Locating himself in Vermont in the present of the poem emphasizes this sense of narrative instability. It also enables Frost to tweak the noses of readers who have taken him at face value throughout a poem about New Hampshire that repeatedly reminds readers that it is perhaps really not about New Hampshire at all.

Clifford offers a description of anthropologist Bronislaw Malinowski that works equally well with regard to Frost's self-conscious self-presentation in "New Hampshire" and throughout his career: "His revelations about himself and his work were exaggerated and ambiguously parodic. He would strike poses . . . challenging the literal-minded to see that these personal truths were in some degree fictions. His character was staged but also truthful, a pose but nonetheless authentic. One of the ways Malinowski pulled himself together was by writing ethnography. Here the fashioned wholes of a self and of a culture seem to be mutually reinforcing allegories of identity."[68] Frost, of course, entertained himself throughout his career as a public figure by toying with his audiences and with literary critics. He purposely blurred the distinctions between Robert Frost the living person and the narrative "I" of his poems and also purposely confused the issue of which Robert Frost was the real person—Frost the classicist scholar and former student at Harvard and Dartmouth, Frost the former mill worker and native Californian, or Frost the self-described "plain New Hampshire farmer."

Frost's narrative position often seems most complicated in poems where the speaking character is clearly not Frost but is a man. Frost is able to explore local rural notions of masculinity, but the invented characters distance Frost the author from the words of the poems in ways the first-person narrative voice alone cannot. Because these poems address the roles of men in a particular culture, they invite consideration as examples of literary ethnography. In the poems, Frost's characters often refer to male characters and their conduct in terms of certain cultural notions of manliness, and these accounts of masculine identity construction and evaluation comprise a series of literary-ethnographic narratives of maleness.

"The Code" is the most salient example of a Frost poem that explicitly deals with the social expectations surrounding maleness. A farmer and two hired men are piling hay in a meadow when one hired man suddenly and wordlessly puts down his pitchfork and walks off toward his home. The other hired man explains that, half an hour before, the farmer had tried to tell the first hired man how to do his job, a big mistake because, "The hand that knows his business won't be told / To do work better or faster."[69] The hired man then tells the farmer a cautionary tale that explains his point and also illustrates how much worse things could have turned out for the farmer. The hired man tells of a similar situation in which another farmer offended the hired man by telling him how to do his job, which, the hired man makes clear, threatens a man's basic masculine identity: "Never you say a thing like that to a man, / Not if he values what he is. God, I'd as soon / Murdered him as left out his middle name."[70] In fact, the hired man reacted by trying to kill his employer by burying him alive under a load of hay. After explaining that the farmer survived this attack, the hired man delivers the moral of the story: The farmer did not even fire the hired man because "He knew I did just right."[71] The attempted murder in effect agrees with the prevailing cultural notions of masculinity.

It is important to note that Frost distinguishes between the rural cultural group in which such an assault is acceptable masculine behavior and the cultural group that would consider such an attack an unacceptable and criminal act. As is often the case in Frost's work, the rural landscape is a cultural site with expectations distinct from those common to urban areas. The poem explicitly separates rural masculinity from urban masculinity: "The town-bred farmer failed to understand" why the first hired man found the farmer's remarks offensive. The second hired man explains, "He thought you meant to find fault with his work. / That's what the average farmer would have meant."[72] Rural masculinity is distinctly different from "town-bred" masculinity, then, not only in its expectations about respect and autonomy but also in its acceptance of murderous rage as a culturally appropriate response to a perceived insult. The distinction between town masculine culture and rural masculine culture calls attention to the constructed aspects of culture, but the potentially deadly aspect of rural masculinity is no less real for being constructed. Clifford touches on this simultaneous fictionality and reality of culture and succinctly explains the importance of cultural expectations to individuals: "Culture, a collective fiction, is the ground for individual identity."[73] The hired man's cultural concept of masculine identity is such that any work-related slight seemingly threatens the core of his being.

The cultural value of self-directed male behavior becomes increasingly evident in "Snow." Meserve, the distant neighbor who has stopped at Fred and Helen Cole's house because he was caught in a snowstorm, is determined to go back out into the snow and make his way home against the advice of the Coles and his wife. Fred Cole says of Meserve, "'That sort of man talks straight on all his life / From the last thing he said himself, stone deaf / To anything anyone else may say.'"[74] Although this sounds like a complaint, Fred's subsequent reactions to Meserve's masculine stubbornness reveal Fred's identification with and admiration of Meserve's conduct. When Helen says of Meserve, "'I don't like what he's doing, which is what / You like, and like him for,'" Fred's response evinces the importance of self-directed behavior (especially in defiance of female advice) to the cultural notion of masculinity:

> Oh, yes you do.
> You like your fun as well as anyone;
> Only you women have to put these airs on
> To impress men. You've got us so ashamed
> Of being men we can't look at a good fight
> Between two boys and not feel bound to stop it.
> Let the man freeze an ear or two, I say.—[75]

Better, it seems, to risk frostbite (and, by implication, to risk death) than to risk the dissolution of one's masculine identity by acting insufficiently manly. Fred again reveals his admiration for Meserve's single-mindedness by saying, " 'If you were the kind of man / Paid heed to women, you'd take my advice.' "[76] Fred admires Meserve precisely because Meserve refuses to listen to women. This relates to the overall difference between the Cole household and the Meserve household as sites of masculine behavior. Helen Cole is an outspoken woman who does not defer to Fred; Meserve's wife, on the other hand, is named Lett Meserve. The symbolic value of her name indicates her submissive role and her likely deferral to Meserve's self-directed masculine behavior. Meserve's reaction to Helen's attempts to make him stay (" 'Save us from being cornered by a woman,' " he says) emphasizes the diminishment of perceived masculinity that would result if he took Helen's advice. He explicitly identifies his decision as a masculine necessity, and so overrides Helen's objections by referring to a code of rural masculinity to which she has no access: " 'Well, there's—the storm. That says I must go on. / That wants me as a war might if it came. / Ask any man.' "[77] Of course, the storm is nothing like a war, and there is no need for Meserve to risk his life, but Helen's inadvertent threat to his masculine identity inspires him to create this simile that appears to justify his decision, even though it lacks any basis in fact.

Frost presents contending versions of masculinity again in "A Hundred Collars," and again the difference between urban masculine identity and rural masculine identity is at the heart of the poem. When Dr. Magoon (an urban professor) finds himself sharing a hotel room with a large and drunken specimen of rural masculinity, he reacts with distaste and, primarily, fear: "The Doctor looked at Lafe and looked away. / A man? A brute."[78] The professor is visibly shaken by Lafe's imposing physical presence, and Lafe clearly recognizes the professor's fear. When the terrified academic climbs into bed without taking off his shoes, Lafe offers to pull his shoes off for him, and this reduces the professor to pleading, "Don't touch me, please—I say, don't touch me, please. / I'll not be put to bed by you, my man."[79] Lafe exacerbates the professor's concern by remarking on the professor's fear of him and exclaiming, "Who wants to cut your number fourteen throat!" The number 14 refers to the professor's collar size and establishes the considerable difference in stature between Magoon and Lafe, who wears a size 18. Lafe further frightens the professor by offering to send him all his old size 14 collars and thus attempting to learn the professor's address. The doctor functions as an effete figure of cultivated urban masculinity (Frost capitalizes the D in "doctor," thus suggesting that the Doctor is a type via the same technique applied to the Miller in "The Vanishing Red") and emphasizes the danger and potential brutality of rural masculinity.

Frost's portrayals of cultural conflict between men with differing notions of masculinity succeed in part because they are unflinchingly realistic fictions. Clifford identifies this element of realism as a necessary element of any ethnographic text: "In both novels and ethnographies, the self as author stages the diverse discourses and scenes of a believable world."[80] Although Clifford specifically refers to novels, the larger context of his critical approach indicates that Frost's narrative poems would satisfy the same criteria. Frost's poems stage discourse and create realistic scenes as skillfully as any novel, and Frost may in fact have abstracted several poems (particularly "The Death of the Hired Man") from his early uncompleted novel that dealt with conflict between rural and urban ideas of masculinity via the character of a college student and his experiences as a hired hand on a New England farm where he works with rural men up close.

"The Death of the Hired Man" presents another look at rural masculinity and is perhaps the most poignant of Frost's ethnographic poems examining masculinity because of its focus on rural masculinity in decline. Silas, the hired man of the poem's title, never actually appears or speaks in the poem. Mary and Warren, the couple Silas formerly worked for, try to figure out what to do with the old and infirm man, who has returned to live with them and still pretends to intend to do some work in order to preserve his pride. Mary, mindful of the rural masculine self-concept, says to Warren, "Surely you wouldn't grudge the poor old man / Some humble way to save his self-respect."[81] "Silas' one accomplishment"[82] is that he can build a skillfully arranged load of hay, and now that his physical strength is gone he is struggling to maintain his rural masculine identity. Silas' absence from the poem and his death emphasize the sense in which without his masculine identity Silas becomes nothing.

The centrality of work to the cultural concept of rural masculinity becomes increasingly evident in "The Housekeeper." The poem resembles "The Death of the Hired Man" in several respects: John, the man at the center of the poem's commentary, appears to be losing his grasp on socially approved masculinity, he is absent from the scene for the majority of the narrative, and other characters discuss his failing masculinity with some concern. John's long-time domestic partner has left him because he has consistently refused to marry her. This refusal seems a violation of standard masculine behavior, and the poem describes John's conduct in terms of insufficient masculinity. The woman's mother (the housekeeper of the poem's title) lived with the couple and still lives there after her daughter leaves John. When an unidentified male neighbor arrives, the housekeeper complains about John's failure to be sufficiently masculine in the wake of her daughter's departure:

> He's awful!
> I never saw a man let family troubles
> Make so much difference in his man's affairs.
> He's just dropped everything. He's like a child.
> I blame his being brought up by his mother.[83]

John's failure to live up to the cultural model of masculinity scandalizes the housekeeper, who identifies John's behavior as a source of shame. This fundamental departure from masculinity has implications for John's overall worth and identity as perceived by his culture. In violating the cultural code of masculinity—apparently the same one discussed in "The Code," in which the rural culture is the same—John unwittingly threatens his own identity, undermining his own masculinity in a way the rural hired men of "The Code" would recognize as unacceptable. As "The Code" makes clear, the proper response to such a threat to the core of one's masculine identity is anger and possibly violence. Such responses are means of reasserting masculine identity if that identity is threatened, but because John has diminished his own masculine identity, no such compensatory responses are available to him.

In his 1935 introduction to Edwin Arlington Robinson's *King Jasper*, Frost remarks on the tenuous connection between individual men and the collective social fiction of masculinity. Frost refers to a man's awareness that he may fail to measure up to social ideals of masculinity as, "the fear of Man—the fear that men won't understand us and we shall be cut off from them."[84] This statement demonstrates an ethnographic consciousness of compulsory masculinity, which was a significant influence on Frost's writing and his creation of a persona. In "On Extravagance: A Talk," Frost's 1962 Dartmouth College Address, Frost once again refers to the widespread American cultural notion that poetry itself is somehow not masculine: "When I catch a man reading my book, red-handed, you know, he usually looks up cheerfully and says, 'My wife is a great fan of yours.' Puts it off on the women."[85] This statement manifests Frost's awareness that American culture harbors doubts about whether poetry is a sufficiently masculine pursuit for men and also suggests the extent to which

Frost consciously compensated for this cultural doubt in constructing his public persona. By emphasizing the aspects of his life that most closely agreed with cultural notions of masculinity (farming, chopping wood, mending walls, and rejecting outwardly refined speech, for instance), Frost effectively established his masculine credentials in cultural terms. Demonstrating his masculinity in such conventional ways made it possible for Frost to pursue poetry—an interest that is culturally positioned outside the realm of standard masculine behavior—without inviting a perceived diminishment of masculine identity akin to that identified in "The Code," "The Housekeeper," and "The Death of the Hired Man."

Although the connections may not be as obvious, Frost's ethnographic examinations of industrial market capitalism involve the same kinds of connections between cultural models of masculinity and Frost's creation of a culturally acceptable masculine poetic persona. By demonstrating the destructive effects of industry and arguing against the logic of capitalism, poems such as "The Self-Seeker," "The Vanishing Red," and "New Hampshire" lay the groundwork for later poems such as "The Egg and the Machine" and "A Lone Striker." These two later poems unite Frost's ethnographic concerns, bringing masculinity and industrial capitalism into direct conflict. "The Egg and the Machine," the last poem in *West-Running Brook* (1928), introduces the theme of defying (and perhaps destroying) the emblematic engine of industrial capitalism. "A Lone Striker," the first poem in *A Further Range* (1936), extends this theme by implicitly advocating a man's refusal to continue to work in a mill. These poems unite the logic of Frost's poems about masculinity with the logic of Frost's poems about industrial capitalism. (I use the reductive "about" to streamline this argument. The aforementioned poems that deal with aspects of masculinity are of course about more than masculinity, just as the poems that deal with aspects of industrial capitalism also deal with other issues.)

In his earlier poems, Frost establishes a version of masculinity that privileges self-directed behavior. "The Egg and the Machine" begins the association of masculinity with a rejection of the profoundly other-directed behaviors of industrial capitalism. "A Lone Striker" completes the figure: Truly masculine men do not let individuals tell them what to do (as in "The Code" and "Snow"), therefore neither should they let industrial market capitalism tell them what to do. This logic frees Frost's unnamed male character in "The Lone Striker" from any requirement to prove his masculinity by working in a mill. Rejecting mill work and going out into the woods suddenly appears to be not only an acceptably masculine course of action but in fact the only inherently masculine course of action.

The resonance of this logic in Frost's own life can scarcely be overstated. Several biographers have noted Frost's own uneasiness about relying on money from his grandfather to keep him afloat during his early years as a writer. (Jay Parini describes a humiliating incident when the local bank teller mocked Frost as Frost deposited a check from his grandfather, for example.) The poetic logic that culminates in "A Lone Striker" effectively redeems Frost's masculinity by constructing an elaborate argument that insists that true masculinity demands a rejection of industrial market capitalism and thus authorizes Frost's repudiation (as expressed in "Two Tramps in Mud Time," the poem that appears immediately after "A Lone Striker" in *A Further Range*) of the sort of other-directed wage labor that characterizes industrial market capitalism: "My object in living is to unite / My avocation and my vocation / As my two eyes make one in sight."[86] Frost's poetic logic enables him to unite cultural notions of masculinity with a repudiation of standard wage labor and thus allows him to frame his own nonconformist literary lifestyle as authentically and supremely masculine, thereby resolving his own anxieties (at least on paper) and presenting a poetic persona more accessible to the public (particularly to American males) because of its apparent mastery of the cultural tropes of masculinity.

Recognizing Frost's personal and professional involvement in the cultural issues his poems examine should not ultimately diminish the ethnographic elements of the poems. Clifford frequently reminds readers that ethnographic narratives, like any narratives, are inherently partial and creative. The ethnographer is always to some extent involved in the narrative of culture, and this involvement does not invalidate ethnographic narratives but requires readers to account for the influence of the ethnographer, the fact of the author's presence in the text. Readers must also account for Frost's complex narrative presence throughout his poems and must balance the implicit truth claims of the narratives with their existence as fictions and their origins in the mind of Robert Frost, a man enmeshed in the culture his poems explore. Clifford's words provide useful final advice for readers regarding Frost's ethnographic narratives: "The best ethnographic fictions are . . . intricately truthful; but their facts, like all facts in the human sciences, are classified, narrated, and intensified."[87]

CHAPTER 3

"I Knew That World"
Warren's Southern Ethnography

Now, I don't mean to say that that is the only kind of valuable criticism. Any kind is good that gives a deeper insight into the nature of the thing—a Marxist analysis, a Freudian study, the relation to a literary or social tradition, the history of a theme. But we have to remember that there is no *one, single, correct* kind of criticism—no *complete* criticism. You may have different kinds of perspectives, giving, when successful, different kinds of insights. And at one historical moment one kind of insight may be more needed than another.

—Robert Penn Warren

I just want to ask one question before anything starts. I just want to ask where you're from.

—Southern law student to Warren in the early 1950s
at a group discussion of segregation

Since the revised version of Robert Penn Warren's 1953 book-length poem *Brother to Dragons* appeared in 1979,[1] numerous scholarly responses have concentrated on the political implications of the poem's central event, the 1811 murder of a slave by two nephews of Thomas Jefferson in rural Kentucky. Such critiques have too often taken for granted that Warren's magnum opus should be considered exclusively as a poem, a generically stable and exclusively literary construct that should be evaluated according to certain inviolable criteria. As Michael Kreyling notes while examining *Brother to Dragons*, " 'Poetry' is the name we customarily give to cultural products that are privileged, by canons of reading and interpretation, to boast the closure, meaning, finishedness that lived history negates."[2] Such a concept of poetry (which one could extend to literature in general) serves poorly in an examination of *Brother to Dragons*, because Warren's poem continually destabilizes its own meanings, refuses authoritative closure and finishedness, and presents itself not as a pure poem but as a complex literary hybrid.

The conceptual models developed in works of contemporary or postmodern ethnographic theory—most notably Clifford's *The Predicament of Culture*—provide particularly well suited critical apparatus with which to examine *Brother to Dragons* as a work of creative ethnography. Although Clifford's work will serve as the theoretical starting point of this chapter, I will refer to a number of contemporary ethnographic theorists in order to address other possibilities for ethnographic literary criticism that such theorists explore. Clifford's status as the preeminent theorist of the interdisciplinary connections between ethnography and literature is as yet unchallenged. No other ethnographic theorist has paid a comparable amount of attention to the interdisciplinary possibilities of ethnographic theory and its potential applicability to literary criticism, and Clifford's prominence in recent ethnographic critical discourse is confirmed by the amount of time other critics in the field spend responding directly to his work.

This chapter will move back and forth between Warren's *Brother to Dragons*, *Segregation: The Inner Conflict in the South* (1956), *Who Speaks for the Negro?* (1965), and a number of ethnographic theoretical texts, reading Warren's works by the lights of the various theorists' comments on the interrelationships between ethnography and literature, and recognizing the similarities between various paradigms of ethnography and Warren's approach to American cultural issues. This will call attention to the extent to which the works analyze and construct versions of America and national forms of injustice and complicity, particularly those traditionally identified with the South. Ultimately, however, this juxtaposition of ethnographic theory and Warren's works may prove most useful because of discrepancies between Warren's texts and the ethnographic theoretical models. Noticing the ways the theoretical models fail to accommodate Warren's narrative strategies will provoke readers to consider the ways Warren's works deconstruct themselves and continually complicate the very questions readers might expect them to resolve.

During Warren's lengthy literary career, he published some fifteen books of poetry, ten novels, one book of short stories, six books of nonfiction prose (not counting his literary criticism), one play, textbooks (including the remarkably influential *Understanding Poetry* with Cleanth Brooks) in multiple editions, and a great deal of critical writing covering everything from literature to broad social issues. He also amassed numerous awards and honors, including three Pulitzer Prizes (two for poetry, one in 1958 and one in 1979, and one for fiction, in 1947), and in 1986 became the first designated U.S. Poet Laureate Consultant in poetry (a new title for a post he first held from 1944 to 1945). As Stuart

Wright puts it, "Warren was almost certainly, by the time of his death in 1989, America's most highly decorated man of letters ever."[3]

Walter Sullivan expresses a conviction—common among Warren scholars— that "the autobiographical element is stronger in Warren's poetry than in his fiction."[4] It is stronger still in Warren's nonfiction prose writings on race. Because Warren is best known—at least outside academic circles—for his novel *All the King's Men*, a decision to turn critical attention away from his prose fiction may seem perplexing. Although one could extend an ethnographic reading of Warren's work into his novels, the element of disguise surrounding the novels' narrators would ultimately make such a critical pursuit less fruitful than an ethnographic consideration of *Brother to Dragons, Segregation*, and *Who Speaks for the Negro?* Whatever autobiographical elements biography-minded critics may discern in Jack Burden of *All the King's Men* or Jed Tewksbury in *A Place to Come To*, for instance, Burden and Tewksbury do not appear to represent Warren directly in the ways that the narrative voices of *Brother to Dragons, Segregation*, and *Who Speaks for the Negro?* do.

Warren's ethnographic consciousness in *Brother to Dragons* is evident even before the body of the poem begins. The epigraphs to the poem include an extract from the 1893 Annual Report of the Bureau of Ethnology and a passage from W. H. Perrin's 1884 *History of Christian County* in which unnamed native informants relate their worldviews to white auditors. In his foreword, Warren uses the vocabulary of ethnographic research to explain the origins of his project: "The poem . . . had its earliest suggestion in bits of folk tale, garbled accounts heard in my boyhood." Warren then presents the adult poet-ethnographer rummaging through factual accounts of the events surrounding the murder using language that hints at the complexities of voice and viewpoint in the poem to come: "As the poem began to take shape in my head, I went to Smithland and sought out in the dim and dusty hugger-mugger of a sort of half-basement room (as I remember it) the little bundles of court records, suffering from damp and neglect, but sometimes tied up in faded red tape or string."[5]

The poem is on one level—the literal level—a creative work, something generated by Warren's imagination, but there are numerous moments when Warren makes assertions such as "this really happened," moments that claim for the poem a measure of authenticity. Despite the apparent differences between the poem and standard ethnographic texts, such claims are not necessarily at odds with recent ethnographic theory. In his essay "Textual Play, Power, and Cultural Critique: An Orientation to Modernist Anthropology," Marc Manganaro explains Clifford Geertz's account of the inherently creative textuality of ethnographic accounts: "Geertz's recent book, *Works and Lives: The Anthropologist as Author*, affirms an essentially textual approach to ethnography, claiming that the anthropologist's ability to convince is based primarily not upon the suitability or solidity of fieldwork, but upon the very writerly task of convincing us "that what they say is a result of having actu-ally penetrated . . . another form of life, of having, one way or another, truly 'been there.'" "[6] Warren's parenthetical "as I remember it" shades into Warren's awareness of the fundamental unreliability and inherent creativity of narrative, and suggests a gruesome submerged pun on Warren's attempt to put everything, including the dismembered body of the murdered slave, back together again. The pun serves as a way of distinguishing *Brother to Dragons* from even the sort of self-consciously tex-tual ethnography Geertz describes, in that the wordplay indicates another height-ened form of attention to textuality at the level of the individual word.

Clifford's introduction to *The Predicament of Culture* begins with a brief examination of the ethnographic aspects of William Carlos Williams's "To Elsie," which begins with the oft-quoted declaration "The pure products of America / go crazy."[7] This, quite simply, is the subject matter of *Brother to Dragons*. Thomas Jefferson himself appears in the poem as the thinker behind the idea of Ameri-can democracy and tries throughout the poem to reconcile his deist humanism and democratic ideals with the murder committed by his relatives. Jefferson also wrestles with the idea of his complicity in the killing via his role in perpetuating slavery and tries to put to rest his guilt over the disgrace and death (apparently by suicide) of his kinsman and surrogate son Meriwether Lewis.

Instead of setting the poem in 1811 and thus producing a fairly conven-tional historical narrative, Warren takes a radically different approach:

> The main body of the action lies in the remote past—in the earthly past of char-acters long dead—and now they meet at an unspecified place and unspecified time and try to make sense of the action in which they were involved. We may take them to appear and disappear as their urgencies of argument swell and sub-side. The place of the meeting is, we may say, 'no place,' and the time is 'any time.' This is but a way of saying that the issues that the characters here discuss are, in my view at least, a human constant.[8]

Focusing on Warren's word choices in the passage above may yield a sort of reductive preliminary understanding of Warren's narrative techniques in *Brother to Dragons*. In this context the word *body* seems another grisly pun on the dis-membered body of the murdered slave. The repeated use of *we* suggests a certain commonality between author and audience, and so begins the poem's extended process of implicating readers to varying degrees in the systems and actions ren-dered by the poem. The use of *my* also prepares readers for the periodic intru-sion of Warren's first-person voice as the character R.P.W. throughout *Brother to Dragons*. Warren's claim of universality must strike contemporary readers as inherently suspect. Clifford takes issue with a similar claim implicit in Wil-liams's "To Elsie," and in doing so summarizes the conventional ethnographic-literary project: "The ethnographic modernist searches for the universal in the local, the whole in the part."[9] Clifford explains that "Elsie disrupts the project, for her very existence raises historical uncertainties undermining the modernist doctor-poet's secure position."[10] Elsie's presence as another potential speaking subject undermines Williams' implicit claim to authority in the same way the other speaking subjects in *Brother to Dragons* undercut—or at least appear to undercut—R.P.W.'s periodic attempts to control their narratives.

Warren complicates his own universalizing claim on a number of levels, and Clifford's analysis of authorial position and power provides suitable material for comparison: "A useful—if extreme—standpoint is provided by Bakhtin's analysis of the 'polyphonic' novel. A fundamental condition of the genre, he argues, is that it represents speaking subjects in a field of multiple discourses. The novel grapples with, and enacts, heteroglossia."[11] Clifford then poses a fundamental question for contemporary ethnographic literature: "Does the ethnographic writer portray what natives think by means of Flaubertian 'free indirect style,' a style that suppresses direct quotation in favor of a controlling discourse always more or less that of the author? . . . Or does the portrayal of other subjectivities require a version that is stylistically less homogeneous, filled with Dickens' 'different voices'?"[12] *Brother to Dragons* answers a single, indeterminate yes to the questions Clifford poses above. That is, Warren creates a sort of synthesis, a literary vehicle that moves—or at least seems to move—back and forth between univocal and polyphonic styles.

Warren destabilizes his own narrative by writing it as a series of vocal exchanges between up to a dozen people, all of whom, with one important exception, are long dead. Warren himself is the exception. He appears in a list of the poem's characters as "R.P.W.: *The writer of this poem,*"[13] narrates certain sections of the poem, and more or less mediates the free-form discussion between the poem's characters, moving in and out of the discussion as a participant-observer. This element of self-reflexivity throughout *Brother to Dragons* indicates Warren's consciousness of the inherent problems of claims to monologic textual authority. R.P.W. explains the poem's apparently polyvocal form as an attempt to correct for the inherent problems and distortions involved in constructing a narrative out of actual events and records, saying that he had originally intended to cast the narrative in ballad form, "but the form was not adequate to the material." R.P.W. decides he must tell the story by a more complex form, but Jefferson replies, "There is no form to hold / Reality and its insufferable intransigence"[14] and so reminds readers of the disparity between even the dramatic vocal poetic form and reality itself.

Questions regarding the adequacy of particular forms of representation persist in contemporary ethnographic theory, which has increasingly viewed the so-called realism of the classic ethnographic monograph with suspicion. In an interesting coincidence of phrasing and imagery, Manganaro mentions the growing belief among ethnographic theorists that "the vessel of representation is inadequate to hold the cultural truth; rather, Clifford and others echo Nietzsche in questioning the existence of a cultural truth removed from discursive processes."[15] One should not make too much of this resemblance, but the similarities do direct attention to the concerns with representation, authenticity, and the inherently discursive nature of any written account that occupy so much space in both contemporary ethnographic theory and contemporary literary criticism and so suggest the great potential for interdisciplinary exchange.

By immediately calling attention to his multilayered presence in the poem, Warren effectively signals readers that *Brother to Dragons* is a self-deconstructing text. The poem knows and demonstrates how it cannot in fact do what it claims or appears to do, cannot mean what it claims or appears to mean, because it is a work of literature rather than a historical document. Moreover, as Clifford indicates and R.P.W. strongly suggests, ethnographic and historical accounts are always already partial and creative. Because of the multilayered presence of the persona of R.P.W. moving within the poem as a participant-observer and the existence of the actual Robert Penn Warren standing outside the poem as the controlling consciousness behind the words, *Brother to Dragons* self-consciously enacts the problems of perspective, voice, and interpretation that surround ethnographic texts.

Clifford refers to ethnography as "a state of being in culture while looking at culture, a form of personal and collective self-fashioning."[16] This project requires a degree of language fluency such that the ethnographer "could 'use' the vernacular to ask questions, maintain rapport, and generally get along in the culture while obtaining good research results in particular areas of concentration."[17] One of the more disturbing aspects of *Brother to Dragons* is R.P.W.'s repeated use of the word *nigger* in his remarks about African Americans throughout the poem. Clifford's account of the necessary use of the vernacular by the ethnographer provides a sort of explanation for R.P.W.'s persistent racist speech, but such an explanation rings somewhat hollow.

Early in the poem, R.P.W. describes Smithland, Kentucky—the town nearest the home of Jefferson's kinsmen, the Lewises, the home where the murder took place—as an idyllic small Southern town, but his language draws attention to race and racism: "It looked the sort of town Sam Clemens might / Grow up in then and not be much worse off. / River and catfish, nigger in the shade."[18] Later, when R.P.W. climbs a hill to visit the site of the Lewis home, he comments on the stifling summer heat and remarks, "But niggers don't mind heat. At least, not much," then uses the racist epithet as an adjective and refers to the ruins of the house as "Poor nigger stonework."[19] R.P.W. also refers to the murdered slave as "the nigger boy named John,"[20] describes the charred flesh of John's mutilated body as "Fire-black and nigger-black,"[21] and speaks of the other slaves who saw Jefferson's nephew Lilburne Lewis kill John as "the niggers hunkering by the wall."[22] These instances are remarkable not so much as simple evidence of racist discourse as for the fact that they represent the words of the author. By stating that R.P.W. is the writer of the poem, Warren clearly intends for readers to interpret R.P.W.'s words and actions as directly related to Warren himself.

Here the usefulness of Clifford's explanations of ethnographers' necessary use of the vernacular drops off sharply. This is an instance where ethnographic theories fail to explain *Brother to Dragons*. In fact, this self-conscious use of racist epithets is one of the ways *Brother to Dragons* refuses to explain itself. R.P.W. not only records the vernacular of racism but also uses it himself both early and often. The racist remarks of R.P.W. are all the more troubling given that many of the remarks are phrased in the present tense. This suggests that R.P.W. utters them not in 1811 but in the continuing *now* of the poem, presumably no earlier than 1979 in the 1979 version of the poem.

At the end of the 1970s, creating racist characters (particularly racist villains) in literature was one thing; writing *oneself* into literature as a racist character was another thing altogether. What does it mean to do this in 1979 as opposed to 1953? Any answer must take into account the amount of time lapse and the significance of the social changes separating the two editions of *Brother to Dragons—Brown v. Board of Education* (1954), desegregation, civil rights legislation, Black Power and Black Pride, the American Indian Movement, and the feminist movement, to name just a few. Simply by keeping R.P.W. a racist presence, Warren defies polite social, intellectual, and literary expectations and so strengthens his position in a sense even as he apparently contradicts his own public disavowal of racist views. This is particularly remarkable in that, as Kreyling points out, Warren's repudiation of racism had and has a sort of symbolic cultural significance in addition to its significance for Warren more directly: "For a significant band of twentieth-century Southerners (most of them male), *being Southern* means *having been racist* . . . Warren's conversion is crucial to the narrative of southern cultural 'awakening' and progressive growth; he is the biographical 'fact' that grounds so much faith in a fictional-cultural character like Harper Lee's Atticus Finch: the white southern male who is deeply identified in his people and his place, but also able to rise above and move forward from 'the sins of the fathers.'"[23] By implicating himself via his use of racist language long after his public rejection of racism, Warren establishes a counterintuitive sort of moral authority that enables him to implicate the readers, who are thereby encouraged to engage uneasily in the sort of identification with the primary narrative voice that monologic first person narrative literature practically demands.

Part of the difference between creating a racist character and portraying oneself as a racist character lies in the disparity between the role or position of the ethnographer and the position created and occupied by R.P.W. in *Brother to*

Dragons. Clifford explains "the persona of the fieldworker" as a researcher and a literary presence: "The professional ethnographer was trained in the latest analytic techniques and modes of scientific explanation."[24] Substituting *poetic* for *scientific* creates a fair description of Warren as a scholar, critic, and poet circa 1979. Despite ethnographers "mastering the vernacular and undergoing a personal learning experience comparable to an initiation," Clifford says that ethnographers traditionally "did not speak as cultural insiders but retained the natural scientist's documentary observational stance." In fact, absorption into the subject culture was actively discouraged and considered professionally counterproductive because "intuitive, excessively personal understanding . . . could not confer scientific authority."[25]

R.P.W. speaks from a position that is inherently more complex than Clifford's ethnographic participant-observer model. R.P.W., in fact, acts in the poem as both participant-observer and native informant, effectively feeding his own opinions and interpretations into the ongoing polyphonic discourse of the other characters. Instead of keeping a traditional aesthetic or ethnographic distance, R.P.W. injects himself into the action of the poem and speaks with the very sort of intuitive, personal, native understanding that traditional ethnography supposedly disallowed. Manganaro calls attention to the actual historical association between ethnography and literary art: "In the years after 1922 anthropologists often performed dual roles as students of culture and artists . . . others, such as Malinowski, worked as anthropologists but conceived of themselves as author figures; both Clifford and Stocking refer to Malinowski's claim that '[W.H.R.] Rivers is the Rider Haggard of anthropology; I shall be the Conrad.' "[26] Malinowski, long regarded as an exemplar of ethnographic practice and monograph production, stands in as a representative figure of the discipline. By insisting on Malinowski's self-conscious author function, Manganaro implicitly insists that such a complicated issue inheres in every act of ethnographic writing.

R.P.W. calls attention to his own complex position and his Kentucky roots with a reference to "my own Todd County"[27] early in the poem and later emphasizes his position as a Southerner: "Now, anybody raised down home—down South— / Will know in his bones what the situation was."[28] This seems another gruesome submerged pun on the charred bones of the murdered slave and also adopts what Kreyling refers to as the Quentin Compson model of Southern ethnography as a closed system[29] (that is, the idea that only Southerners can understand the South). R.P.W. later expands this idea of pan-Southern understanding in a passage that indicates both a white subject position and a white resentment of African Americans: "Who doesn't know down home / The intolerable eye of the sly one, and the sibilant / Confabulation below / The threshold of comprehension."[30] This particular passage is doubly disturbing because the word choice connotes simmering hatred and a degree of identification with Lilburne Lewis, Thomas Jefferson's slave-murdering nephew. R.P.W.'s position as a cultural insider forecloses any possibility of maintaining traditional ethnographic distance and allows him to implicate all Southerners, including himself. In this, *Brother to Dragons* functions as a work of internal ethnography. The temptation, especially for non-Southern readers, is to take the poem as an ethnographic fiction about America as a whole, but it is certainly possible to read the poem as an extension of the Quentin Compson thesis. All the characters, including R.P.W., are Southerners, and although readers may immediately identify Thomas Jefferson with America in its entirety, it is also possible to read Jefferson as a symbolic figure of distinctly Southern identity.

In "Forecasting Theory: Problems and Exemplars in the Twenty-First Century," Stanley R. Barrett draws important distinctions between the classic outsider anthropologist who appears in a non-Western environment and "insider anthropology, the term applied to anthropologists from dominant groups who do research at home."[31] Barrett further distinguishes between basic insider anthropology and what Lila Abu-Lughod calls "halfie anthropology": "[According to Abu-Lughod,] Halfies are 'people whose national or cultural identity is mixed by virtue of migration, overseas education, or parentage.' "[32] Readers familiar with Warren's biography will recognize migration (Warren's moves between Guthrie, Kentucky; Nashville, Tennessee; Berkeley, California; Oxford, England; Memphis, Tennessee; Baton Rouge, Louisiana; Minneapolis, Minnesota; New Haven, Connecticut; and West Wardsboro, Vermont) and overseas education (Warren's Rhodes Scholar years at Oxford). Barrett's elaboration of halfie anthropology pertains, it would seem, not only to Warren but to numerous Southern writers who approach Southern cultures with more or less ethnographic intentions: "In halfie anthropology things are more complicated. When halfies do research within their own community, the self and other are synonymous. But as in the case of feminist anthropology, a different kind of other, negative in connotation, always lurks in the shadows: mainstream, dominant society. In this context, the self and other are not only separate, but antagonistically opposed."[33]

Manganaro's appraisal of internal ethnography complements Barrett's by emphasizing the possible advantages of such a complex authorial position: "The recent upsurge in doing ethnography 'at home' has brought to many a greater awareness of the issues of alterity and power . . . the reflexive tendency to construct an allegory that shuttles [the anthropological subject] to the exotic margin becomes confounded. And the fact that the ethnographer is of the same culture as the subject may make the ethnographer more aware of the interpersonal liberties that the ethnographer, as a member of a sanctioned discipline, takes for granted when conducting interviews and 'writing up' the results."[34]

Manganaro's comments should provoke readers to reconsider what has already been identified as a complex authorial position in *Brother to Dragons*. In this light, R.P.W.'s aforementioned comments that "anybody raised down home—down South— / Will know in his bones what the situation was"[35] and "Who doesn't know down home / The intolerable eye of the sly one, and the sibilant / Confabulation below / The threshold of comprehension"[36] seem more than disturbing: They seem duplicitous.

By 1979, Warren had written *Segregation: The Inner Conflict in the South* (1956) and *Who Speaks for the Negro?* (1965), two nonfiction prose works with very strong ethnographic elements. It is highly unlikely that by 1979 Warren would have been so careless as to conflate *anybody* with *any white person* accidentally. This seems a purposeful play on the too-long-persistent ideas that so-called *real* or *true* Southerners were *white*, that the authentic Southern experience was the experience of Southern whites, that African Americans were somehow excluded even at a conceptual level, and that African American experience ultimately did not count.[37]

A return to Barrett's discussion of Abu-Lughod will provide further interpretive strategies for an analysis of Warren's tactics: "Abu-Lughod . . . has declared that the time has come for anthropologists to write against culture. Her argument is that the concept has begun to resemble race. It promotes a viewpoint in which people around the globe are separated into distinctive blocks, homogenized and stereotyped, and arranged in an implicit hierarchy of superiority and inferiority."[38] One could—and, I believe, should—apply this logic to R.P.W. and white Southerners as well as to black Southerners. It is clear that R.P.W. is making essentialist statements about both groups; it is not so clear whether, when, or to what extent his tongue is planted in his cheek. As a narrative technique, this no doubt makes careful readers uneasy. It also implicates them to varying degrees in R.P.W.'s racist discourse and the social system that produced it. This is especially true for Southerners—"anyone raised down home, down South"—but it also holds true for Americans in broader senses. Hierarchies are tricky here because, as *Brother to Dragons* repeatedly insists, socioeconomic superiority and moral superiority are two very different things.

Jefferson—as a Southerner, as a slave owner, and as a governing figure of American discourse—calls attention to R.P.W.'s complex role in the poem by way of an ongoing struggle between the two over narrative control. Over the course of the poem, Jefferson and R.P.W. debate the relative merits of Jefferson's American project and interrupt each other frequently, attempting to control the narrative or steer the discourse in a particular direction. This jockeying for narrative position marks a significant difference between *Brother to Dragons* and the ethnographic model Clifford presents, which responds rather differently to multiple speaking subjects. "If ethnography produces cultural interpretations through intense research experiences, how is unruly experience transformed into an authoritative written account?" Clifford asks. His answer: "The process is complicated by the action of multiple subjectivities and political constraints beyond the control of the writer. In response to these forces ethnographic writing enacts a specific strategy of authority. This strategy has classically involved an unquestioned claim to appear as the purveyor of truth in the text. A complex cultural experience is enumerated by an individual."[39]

Brother to Dragons refuses to remain within the limits of Clifford's model and simultaneously refuses to move completely outside those limits. R.P.W. is "the writer of this poem,"[40] a persona, a participant-observer, a native informant, and a constant reminder that although *Brother to Dragons* presents ongoing polyphonic exchange, the governing intellect behind it all is that of Robert Penn Warren. The moments when other characters interrupt R.P.W. are moments of virtual heteroglossia. Although at times the poem appears to be the literary equivalent of an online chat room, Warren produces and sustains this appearance by way of monologic authorial control.

It is worth noting that the poem is primarily a series of speech acts by dead white males. Not only does Warren control the apparently polyphonic narrative by virtue of his position as author, but all the most prominent speakers share a number of characteristics with Warren himself: They are all white male Southerners.[41] Furthermore, all the main characters except Warren either are blood kin to one another or are slaves held by family members. The women in the poem play minor roles, and the only slave woman to speak is Aunt Cat, a character Warren admittedly invented "from whole cloth."[42] In the 1953 edition of *Brother to Dragons*, Aunt Cat has dozens of spoken lines and a certain amount of agency, which she demonstrates by consciously torturing Lilburne with near-references to the murder when his wife Letitia's brother visits.[43] The 1979 edition leaves Aunt Cat with no such agency. She seems no more than a type of the slave mammy, diminished as a character and nearly devoid of the intelligence and understanding of speech acts evident in the original version. The murdered slave John (named George in reality and in the 1953 version), whose grisly murder is at the conceptual center of the narrative, is silent for the first 117 pages of the poem, then speaks barely at all (only six lines). Manganaro's explanation of ethnographic polyvocality is helpful here: "Some texts . . . use openness itself as a ploy, employing multiple voices in order to bolster the semblance of equality that in turn lends more authority to the author. In other words, polyvocality has to be read in a fuller context of power relations."[44] Thus the appearance of heteroglossia in *Brother to Dragons* obscures what is in most important ways a monologic text that resembles what Clifford calls "new paradigms of authority"[45] only on the surface. In this, *Brother to Dragons* appears unmarked by Clifford's "insistent, heteroglot voices, by the scratching of other pens."[46]

Warren persistently complicates this—and indeed any—understanding of the poem, simultaneously reminding the reader that *Brother to Dragons* is a work of imagination by way of his presence as R.P.W. throughout the narrative and claiming a measure of authenticity for the poem, by turns suggesting and insisting that things really happened and that he is not always in control of the narrative movement. When other characters interrupt R.P.W. at various points in the poem, these interruptions undercut the idea of a unitary narrative and give the sense that no one mind is governing expression and interpretation. R.P.W. makes multiple references to his archival research and actual historical records[47] and even includes several pages of notes appended to the poem.[48] The notes are largely composed of excerpts from historical documents, complete with variant spellings or misspellings to underscore their authenticity. These excerpts function as artifacts, tangible objects that lend a veneer of authenticity to *Brother to Dragons*. Similarly, R.P.W. seems surprised when Meriwether Lewis appears without his hat, thus exposing his fatal head wound. R.P.W. exclaims, "My God!—it's Meriwether!"[49] Such a shocked response gives the impression that R.P.W. does not imaginatively create or control Meriwether Lewis's image, that he is somehow taken by surprise.

At a previous point in the poem, however, R.P.W. moves from an authorizing reference to a preexisting narrative to an expression of his own narrative control over the poem. He recounts the folk version of the Lewis brothers' reaction to the enormous New Madrid earthquake that actually occurred shortly after Lilburne had killed, burned, and buried the young slave. Then, after Isham Lewis tells him that the folk version is not accurate, R.P.W. replies, "I never thought so. You see, that version / Would violate Lilburne's deepest character, / We know that Lilburne's not the Devil's son."[50] In the space of a few lines, R.P.W. gestures toward the preexisting folk account, then overrides it with his own account, analyzing Lilburne's character at a distance of a century and a half. The seemingly innocuous pronoun *we* connotes a number of possible levels of identification with Lilburne and once again includes and implicates readers of the poem.

This awareness of R.P.W.'s narrative influence manifests itself in the poem's repeated interruptions and rephrasings, the moments when R.P.W. overrides another character's speech or reinterprets it in his own words. Phrases such as "As I was saying"[51] and "In other words"[52] signal R.P.W.'s narrative control and remind readers of the multileveled presences and functions of R.P.W. both within and outside the text. The most blatant instance of R.P.W. seizing control of the narrative involves his momentary adoption of slave vernacular. Clifford identifies this tactic as inherently problematic for ethnography, but not for works of fiction, which—as mentioned above—may employ "Flaubertian 'free indirect style,' a style that suppresses direct quotation in favor of a controlling discourse always more or less that of the author . . . Some use of indirect style is inevitable, unless the novel or ethnography is composed entirely of quotations, something that is theoretically possible but seldom attempted. In practice, however, the ethnography and the novel have recourse to indirect style at different levels of abstraction. We need not ask how Flaubert knows what Emma Bovary is thinking, but the ability of the fieldworker to inhabit indigenous minds in always in doubt."[53] Even if readers choose to ignore the possibilities of insider ethnography or halfie ethnography (in which the binary opposition of fieldworker and indigenous mind breaks down), accepting Clifford's comments as true for works of fiction does little to resolve the complex issues of voice and representation in *Brother to Dragons*.

Warren is clearly aware of ethnographic issues, and he presents numerous implicit comparisons between the poem and ethnography. The action of the poem is in fact entirely composed of quotations, although they are quotations created by Warren and sometimes filtered through the persona of R.P.W. In this, *Brother to Dragons* exists both inside and beyond the boundaries of ethnographic paradigms as what Clifford refers to as a "para-ethnographic"[54] work, "a living impure product"[55] of America gone crazy. When R.P.W. describes the slaves' relationships with their mistress, he appropriates slave speech, "mastering the vernacular"[56] in a way Clifford never intended the phrase. R.P.W. says, "In other words, they liked her 'tol-bul well.' / Might say: 'Ole Miss, she know a nigger feel.' / And if that's not love, then it's something that will do"[57] and "They'd say: 'Ole Miss—you know she jes lak dat.' "[58] In such acts of narrative control, Warren effectively answers his own question of who speaks for the Negro.

Clifford's comments about presenting quotations may help elucidate Warren's strategies of representation: "The staging of indigenous speech in an ethnography, the degree of translation and familiarization necessary, are complicated practical and rhetorical problems. But [ethnographer Victor] Turner's works, by giving visible place to indigenous interpretations of custom, expose concretely these issues of textual dialogism and polyphony."[59] Warren presents readers with a phony polyphony, an ongoing series of apparent exchanges that is subjective rather than intersubjective and so does not give any visible place to authentic indigenous interpretations other than his own. R.P.W. does not imagine or perform all the slave speech in *Brother to Dragons*—Aunt Cat, John, and an unidentified male slave do speak for themselves in the poem— but even the moments of supposedly unmediated slave speech are of course the imaginative products of Warren the author. By foregrounding his authorial presence, however, Warren exposes issues of textual dialogism and polyphony. The method of exposure differs from that of conventional ethnographic works but achieves a similar effect. By relentlessly reminding readers of his multiple roles in the poem, Warren draws attention to the poem's illusory dialogism and simulated polyphony.

Given Warren's amply demonstrated consciousness of his own authorial control and his repeated gestures toward ethnographic paradigms, what are readers to make of the appearance of intersubjectivity throughout *Brother to Dragons*? Clifford downplays the significance of frequently quoting, as R.P.W. appears to do, from native informants:

> Such a tactic only begins to break up monophonic authority. Quotations are always staged by the quoter and tend to serve merely as examples or confirming testimonies. Looking beyond quotation, one might imagine a more radical polyphony that would 'do the natives and the ethnographer in different voices'; but this too would only displace ethnographic authority, still confirming the final virtuoso orchestration by a single author of all the discourses in his or her text. In this sense Bakhtin's polyphony, too narrowly identified with the novel, is a domesticated heteroglossia. Ethnographic discourses are not, in any event, the speeches of invented characters.[60]

Clifford's distrust of monologic authority in works of fiction seems derived from Foucauldian concerns about the author function, and imagining literary polyphony free of monologic authority would appear to lead toward an aesthetic of the online chat room. In *Brother to Dragons*, Warren creates a poem that attempts to render polyvocal discourse while working primarily from within traditional paradigms of authorship. Warren's displayed self-consciousness about the problems of representation and interpretation inherent in *Brother to Dragons* simultaneously comprehends and refuses to abide by the real distinctions between fiction and ethnography. Warren moves toward collapsing such distinctions in his foreword, stating, "Historical sense and poetic sense should not, in the end, be contradictory, for if poetry is the little myth we make, history is the big myth we live, and in our living, constantly remake."[61] Ethnographic theorist Paul Bohannon claims, "We all know that history has to be re-written every generation. Even if the historical 'facts' do not change, the context in which they are to be read and interpreted does change."[62] Again, the similarity between the wording of *Brother to Dragons* and the wording of the ethnographic theory calls attention to a recognition on both sides of the ethnography-literature divide of the interdisciplinary possibilities implied by common techniques and similar theoretical assumptions.

Warren's statement manifests an awareness of the inherent elements of fictionality and authorial control in any written account. Clifford, despite his understandable emphasis on the actual existence of native informants, is also aware that written accounts are inseparable from elements of authorial control. He argues that converting polyphonic discourse into narrative fundamentally changes the discourse and renders it effectively monologic: "Experiences become narratives, meaningful occurrences, or examples . . . The data thus reformulated need no longer be understood as the communication of specific persons."[63] In light of such statements, the fundamental difference between fictional characters and native informants in an ethnographer's narrative seems far less significant. Clifford explains that "to understand discourse, 'you had to have been there,' in the presence of the discoursing subject."[64] This sounds like a version of the Quentin Compson thesis, much like R.P.W.'s aforementioned remarks about growing up down home, down South, being the key to understanding the racially charged discourse of *Brother to Dragons*, but Clifford also suggests a corrective measure against monologic authority: "One may also read against the grain of the text's dominant voice, seeking out other half-hidden authorities, reinterpreting the descriptions, texts, and quotations gathered together by the writer. With the recent questioning of colonial styles of representation, with the expansion of literacy and ethnographic consciousness, new possibilities for reading (and thus for writing) cultural descriptions are emerging."[65] Attempting to read against the dominant voice of *Brother to Dragons* produces a realization of the extent to which Warren encourages or even forces this by way of his exhibited authorial self-consciousness. Warren visibly deconstructs the dominant voice of *Brother to Dragons* by calling attention to R.P.W.'s complicated status as participant-observer, native informant, and "writer of this poem."[66] R.P.W. is the antithesis of the detached, scientific recorder of data, and his involvement on all levels of the poem is itself a way of compelling readers to recognize him as a sort of unreliable narrator and read against or behind his narrative. Clifford's description of the ways ethnographic accounts attempt to represent entire cultures is particularly relevant to a consideration of *Brother to Dragons*:

> Since culture, seen as a complex whole, was always too much to master in a short research span, the new ethnographer intended to focus thematically on particular institutions. The aim was not to contribute to a complete inventory or description of custom but rather to get at the whole through one of its parts. I have noted the privilege given for a time to social structure. An individual life cycle, a ritual complex . . . could also serve, as could categories of behavior like economics, politics, and so on. In the predominantly synechdochic rhetorical stance of the new ethnography, parts were assumed to be microcosms or analogies of wholes. This setting of institutional foregrounds against cultural backgrounds in the portrayal of a coherent world lent itself to realist literary conventions.[67]

Brother to Dragons, like *Segregation* and *Who Speaks for the Negro?*, does ethnographic work on a number of the levels mentioned above. Warren deals with social structure—the slaveholding practices of 1811 Virginia and Kentucky—and takes the complex of events around the murder of the slave John as having wider implications for America, particularly for the South. Warren also focuses

on the economic underpinnings of slaveholding society and highlights the economic issues surrounding the murder.

In fact, Warren represents the poem's entire landscape as suffused with economic concerns. Jefferson speaks of the West, the land he acquired via the 1803
Louisiana Purchase, as property belonging in some sense to him in particular:
"I never saw it. Never crossed / The mountains to Kentucky and my West"[68]
and later "My West—the land I bought and gave and never / Saw."[69] With this
paradigm of economics and property in mind, readers will notice that such concerns permeate *Brother to Dragons* and define interactions between the poem's
characters. Women function as property in the poem, as the male characters
continually worry about protecting the honor of the white womenfolk. This
preoccupation reflects not only a legitimate concern for the well-being of the
individual women, but also a concern for the figurative commodity value of
the honorable woman, the credit she brings to the males of her family.

Lilburne's dog is obviously an item of property, and its privileged traditional
position as both commodity and friend or companion loads the dog with symbolic value in the poem. In fact, Lilburne's first act of violence against the dog
adumbrates his first act of violence against his slaves. Immediately following the
description of Lilburne kicking the dog, Warren writes, "That night he strikes a
slave."[70] The parallelism between dog and slave is unmistakable. Both are regarded
as forms of property and are more or less defenseless against Lilburne. John, the
slave Lilburne eventually murders, is Lilburne's body servant, the slave whose dual
relationship as commodity and companion most closely resembles that of the dog.

Warren underscores the slaves' commodity status by describing them in terms
of their exchange value. When the sheriff comes to investigate reports of trouble
at the Lewis house after Lilburne has killed John, Lilburne tells him that John
ran away. The sheriff is impressed by the way Lilburne shrugs off the loss of such
a valuable commodity: "That shrug's impressive to the frontier Sheriff. / Five
hundred dollars gone, and a Lewis shrugs."[71] The notes appended to *Brother to
Dragons* illustrate this economic sensibility by including a historical document,
a court-ordered appraisal of the cash value of every slave belonging to the Lewis
estate.[72] The poem's concern with economic matters extends even to the axe
with which Lilburne kills John: "*Lilburne Lewis, he with an axe / Of the value
of two dollars ($2.00) / Held in his hands, did willfully and maliciously/ And with
hate, cut a death wound—.*"[73] The inclusion of this inessential detail emphasizes
the poem's pervasive concern with economic elements.

In order to justify and perpetuate the commodity culture of slavery, white
characters in *Brother to Dragons* continually refuse to consider slaves in any terms
other than economic ones. Jefferson's rhetorical question sums up the position
of slaves in the social order: "Oh, what's one nigger more / In the economy of
pain."[74] Clearly, white discourse restricts the slave's position to that of an

economic marker. Warren makes it clear that this economic consciousness under-
lies Lilburne's murder of John, both in the larger sense of identifying slaves as
chattel and in the more direct sense of providing a motive for the crime. The
aforementioned passage in which Lilburne kicks his dog tells only part of the
story of how and why he turns on his own property and begins to act out against
things he owns. Lilburne strikes the slave for accidentally breaking a cup that
Lilburne's recently deceased mother had habitually used for her morning tea.
The destruction of an item associated with his mother is what sets Lilburne off
initially. He soon becomes obsessed with protecting such items, and the slaves
steal or break his mother's spoons and cups surreptitiously in order to torment
him. Warren describes how "the first cup in innocence broken / Is succeeded by a
dozen broken by design. / But who has broken them? Nobody knows. / They just
aren't there any more, on hook or shelf. / Spoons disappear. Where do they go?"[75]

Lilburne murders John immediately after John has broken the late Mrs.
Lewis's favorite pitcher. (The 1953 edition makes it clear that Lilburne at least
sets John up and perhaps even breaks the pitcher himself.)[76] The association of
the deceased Lucy Lewis with her cups and spoons extends the poem's theme of
women as commodities and makes the protection of such items a point of honor.
Lilburne and—to a less maniacal extent—Isham regard the assault on their dead
mother's tableware as an assault on her person and her honor. Thus the protection
of cups and spoons takes on the familiar rhetoric of defending the white Southern
woman against contact with or assault by black hands. Lilburne and Isham explicitly discuss this after both have been arrested for John's murder. Isham recounts
the discussion: "[Lilburne said] 'Well, Ishey-boy, we sort of killed the nigger!' /
And me: 'But just a nigger'—and my breath got choked— / 'Just a nigger you said
had done our mother wrong.' "[77]

Clifford declares that "the time is past when privileged authorities could
routinely 'give voice' (or history) to others without fear of contradiction."[78]
This archaic ethnographic paradigm seems to be behind what is perhaps the
most bizarre and inexplicable part of *Brother to Dragons*, the passage in which
R.P.W. advances an interpretation of John's murder that blames the victim for
the crime:

> R.P.W.: If you would speak of responsibility,
> There's the not unfashionable notion to consider
> That John himself was in a strange way responsible.
> . . .
> R.P.W.: Only because he wanted, in the end,
> To curl on the meat-block, draw his knees up little,
> And squinch his eyes and know the expectant deliciousness
> Before the axe fell—[79]

This line of reasoning becomes too much to bear even for Jefferson, who desperately wants to shift the blame for the murder away from his kin and himself. When Jefferson rebukes R.P.W. for this, R.P.W. responds with what seems to be both a disavowal and an identification with the principle of blaming the victim:

> *R.P.W.:* No, don't blame me, I just report a notion.
> The victim
> Becomes the essential accomplice, *provocateur*—
> No, more, is the principal. And the real victim
> Is he whose hand was fatally elected to give the stroke,
> But is innocent.[80]

R.P.W.'s theorizing here presents an extreme example of the perversion of reality that is possible under the archaic model of ethnography Clifford discredits. From a position as a uniquely privileged authority, R.P.W. gives voice to John's unspoken desire, regardless of the fact that the scenario he describes lies far beyond the limits of plausibility. The explanation appears to be a notion concocted by a member of a ruling class in order to explain away responsibility for the crime, and in this sense it resembles the very cultural logic that perpetuated slavery.

Brother to Dragons repeatedly returns to such depictions of speech versus voicelessness. Speech acts are primarily the domain of white characters, while the slaves normally remain voiceless. Aunt Cat is the only slave to make any kind of attempt at achieving a measure of narrative control within the poem. Because she wet-nursed Lilburne in his infancy, she insists on her relationship with Lilburne as a form of motherhood. She refers to Lilburne as "my Chile and Honey"[81] and cites nursing him as a form of proof in her attempts to authorize her claim, saying "I'm yore Mammy, too. I give you tiddy."[82] Lilburne finally turns on Aunt Cat and repudiates her claim of connection in language that bluntly denies her right to such a speech act because of her inferior social position. Lilburne says, "Ain't no nigger gonna call me Honey."[83] R.P.W. clearly recognizes what is at stake in such a struggle over privileged speech and oppressed voicelessness. He explains Aunt Cat's attempts to create a special form of identity for herself as a "struggle / for Lilburne's love, for possession of her Chile."[84] Questions of possession and racial influence are especially tangled because of the apparent racial coding of Lilburne throughout *Brother to Dragons*. Lilburne's face is repeatedly described as beautiful and dark,[85] his eyes shine darkly,[86] and he is equated with a variety of animals, including a cat,[87] a bobcat, and a painter or cougar.[88]

In a progression of silencing that indicates the differences between Clifford's ethnographic model of polyvocality and Warren's ersatz polyvocality, Aunt Cat's culturally imposed figurative voicelessness gives way in *Brother to Dragons* to symbolically loaded images of literally voiceless slaves. When John is tied up immediately before Lilburne kills him, the adjective "nigger-mum"[89] describes his silence. Lilburne's brother Isham describes John as without voice even during the murder:

> *Isham:* Yeah, that fool nigger spread his mouth to yell.
> You got to yell if ever they start chopping.
> But me, I ne'er heard—
> Like all that nigger could yell was just a hunk
> Of silence—you don't even hear it when the meat-axe
> Gets in, gets through, goes *chunk*, chunks on the wood.
> It's funny how that *chunk* just won't come clear.
> Yeah, the axe comes down,
> But not a sound, and that nigger spreads his mouth,
> And I strain and strive
> To hear—oh, Lord, if only—
> Then maybe something gets finished.[90]

Isham's account indicates the figurative speechlessness of slaves and in his desire to hear John also comprehends the degree to which the culturally enforced voicelessness of slaves was essential to maintaining the cultural logic of slavery. Lilburne uses the murder as a brutal demonstration of this cultural logic of enforced voicelessness and commodity consciousness by turning to the rest of his slaves after murdering John directly in front of them and saying, "You better pray / God'll help you keep count on my mother's spoons. / You've seen that nigger John. Well, now you know."[91] Lilburne frames the killing as an object lesson in applied commodity culture. Praying that God will help them be efficient slaves is the only speech act suggested or permitted for the slaves, and this suggestion ultimately reinforces the awareness of their voicelessness. John literally and figuratively gains the power to speak only after death: His first spoken lines come long after his death in the poem, and it is the discovery of John's charred jawbone that leads to Lilburne's eventual arrest for the murder. In this, John gains the power to speak once he has become a sort of archaeological object and thereby achieves a symbolic voice that he never would have been permitted while he was living in a slaveholding culture.

Beyond the boundaries of Anglo-American culture, race relations in the poem take on decidedly different values. Meriwether Lewis describes punishing his slave York in terms that indicate a certain amount of awareness of the value of slave speech: "I flogged him. / He screamed at the dawn-stripes. / The Indians, watching, wept. / And I would have wept in my heart, for I knew him, / And knew him to be only another of us, / In long travel."[92] Significantly, Lewis is able to hear his slave's voice when they have figuratively and literally moved beyond America and its cultural practices on Lewis and Clark's expedition. Other marginalized people can also hear the screams of the slaves York and John. Aunt Cat hears John's scream and later likens it to the screech of an owl.[93] Letitia not only hears John scream, she also tries to scream but cannot.[94]

According to Clifford, "[images of] inarticulateness stand for groups marginalized in the bourgeois West: 'natives,' women, the poor."[95] This statement not only relates to the previously discussed cultural positions of women and slaves in *Brother to Dragons* but also draws attention to the cultural group that haunts the poem from the margins. The spectral presence of Native Americans appears throughout the poem, and Warren's epigraphs indicate his awareness of America's systematic mistreatment of various Native American tribes. The epigraphs drawn from a Bureau of Ethnology report and an American history book stand as reminders that Native Americans were, and continue to be, studied and summarily explained by numerous ethnographers. The epigraph extracted from the letter of Wovoka—the messianic figure who began the nineteenth-century Native American religious revitalization movement known as the Ghost Dance—is both an ironic reference to the earthquake that follows Lilburne's murder of John and a reminder of the abysmal living conditions that made so many Native American tribes receptive to Wovoka's message.

Native Americans first appear in *Brother to Dragons* as literally haunting presences. Aunt Cat recalls when she would nurse the infant Lilburne and "Sing fer the moon to skeer the Bugaboo, / Sing fer the Cher-kee never come not nigh / To skeer my punkin Little Baby-Bear, / And no Raw-Head-and-Bloody-Bones to come."[96] A related image of Native American menace also is visible in a sort of fantasized Indian captivity narrative that Jefferson delivers: "Listen, when some poor frontier mother, captive, lags / By the trail to feed her brat, the Indian, / He'll snatch its heels and snap / The head on a tree trunk, like a whip, / And the head pops like an egg."[97]

The imagined presence of hostile Native Americans in the woods also appears in R.P.W.'s rhetorical question about John's effective captivity at the Lewis estate: "For where, in those days, could a nigger run? / Starvation or the scalping knife, that's all."[98] Later, Meriwether Lewis confronts Jefferson with a reminder of the price Manifest Destiny exacted from Native Americans: "Ask the Christian Cherokee / How the heart bled westward on the Trail of Tears."[99] This example of Native American disenfranchisement and marginalization is especially troublesome because it goes to the heart of American culture. Although many of the Cherokee had adopted Christianity, which they thought was a basic value of American culture, they found out the hard way that expansionist American economic imperatives took precedence over religious niceties. R.P.W. quickly picks up on Meriwether's cue and tells Jefferson how "In Eddyville, down in the tavern there, / Some heroes of our national destiny / Kicked an old Chickasaw to death, for sport."[100]

This attention to Native Americans as the victims of Manifest Destiny accounts for their haunting presence in *Brother to Dragons* in terms of national guilt on at least two levels. First, the cultural practice of racism enabled expansionist America to force tribes off the best land with no justification other than the cultural imaginary of Manifest Destiny. In addition to the multifaceted awareness of racism in *Brother to Dragons*, there is also a barely suppressed consciousness of America as stolen property.[101] The persistent emphasis on exchange value and Jefferson's reflections on having bought the West provide a context for understanding the relative silence and absence of Native Americans in the poem as representative of their systematic exclusion from and victimization by American exchange culture.

The poem's oblique references to the Ghost Dance emphasize this exclusion of Native Americans from commodity culture. One of the principal appeals of the Ghost Dance Movement to many tribes was its twofold promise that the whites would disappear from North America and Native Americans would be restored to relative wealth. Details apparently varied slightly from tribe to tribe, but all versions shared this vision of increased prosperity of some sort. The Plains tribes, for instance, reportedly believed that the Ghost Dance would bring back the buffalo herds that once supported their respective cultures. In a perfect example of mastering discourse, Warren (via Meriwether Lewis and the other characters) appropriates the name, the function, and the imagery of the Native American revitalization movement, applying it to white discourse and using it to resolve the poem's struggles with guilt and complicity:

Meriwether: Dance back the buffalo, the Shining Land!
        Our grander Ghost Dance dance now, and shake the feather.
        Dance back the whole wide gleaming West anew!

All (singing):   Dance back the morning and the eagle's cry.
        Dance back the Shining Mountains, let them shine!
        Dance into morning and the lifted eye.
        Dance into morning past the morning star,
        And dance the heart by which we must live and die.

Jefferson: My Louisiana, I would dance you, though afar!

Meriwether: For nothing we had,
        Nothing we were,
        Is lost. All is redeemed,
        In knowledge.

Again, Warren's word choices ("Our grander Ghost Dance," for example) indi-cate an awareness of his appropriation of Native American themes and imagery, his mastering of Native American discourse. To Warren's credit, he eschews the closure and certainty of a pat happy ending. By having R.P.W. contest Meri-wether Lewis's claim of redemptive closure and insist on remembering the poem's marginalized characters, "those who could not end in joy,"[102] Warren pre-vents readers from walking away from *Brother to Dragons* with a neatly wrapped bundle of narrative satisfaction and so refuses to claim the closure his poem would traditionally be granted.

It is important to note that Warren's references to Native American practices such as the Ghost Dance presuppose that a reader has some knowledge of such matters. Of course, the only way for most readers to acquire or describe such knowledge is via the very ethnographic practices that Warren foregrounds and Clifford interrogates. Thus serious attempts to understand *Brother to Dragons*, its references, and its ethnographic literary influences implicate readers by involv-ing them inextricably in the ethnographic practices in question. To understand *Brother to Dragons*, readers and critics must receive and perform ethnography themselves.

Unlike *Brother to Dragons*, Warren's *Segregation: The Inner Conflict in the South* (1956) seems wary of associating itself on the surface with ethnography as defined and practiced by academic specialists. Instead of the suggestive epigraph from the U.S. Bureau of Ethnology Report that prefaces *Brother to Dragons*, *Segregation* presents readers with an author's note that is as much a disclaimer as an assertion of authority: "This report comes out of travel in Kentucky, Tennessee, Arkansas, Mississippi, and Louisiana, the parts of the South that I have known best. It does not pretend to represent a poll-taking or a mathematical cross-section of opinion. It is a report of conversations, some of which had been sought out and some of which came as the result of chance encounters." This modest disavowal of scien-tific or statistical authority in fact does little to diminish the importance of the book's extensive ethnographic elements. A lay audience would likely be untrou-bled by the fact that Warren makes no claim to present hard scientific results or polls with minimized margins of error. Readers more familiar with the practices of ethnography would realize immediately that professional ethnography in fact makes no pretenses about generating the kind of verifiable, statistically representa-tive data that Warren carefully does not claim to offer. Further, such readers would know that the intermingling of planned interviews with chance encounters is per-fectly acceptable in—indeed is integral to—conventional ethnography. Geertz's famous account of a Balinese cockfight exemplifies the importance of chance encounters: Geertz and his wife did not plan on having to run from the authori-ties who conducted a surprise raid on the cockfight. This chance encounter was (in Geertz's opinion) the key to a deeper, almost-insider understanding of Balinese culture; indeed Geertz describes it as a sort of initiation ritual by which he and his wife gained a much greater measure of acceptance than they had achieved prior to the incident.

The source of Warren's credibility in *Segregation* is twofold: first, and perhaps most important to the editors of *Life* magazine (which published sections of the book), Warren's academic credentials were impeccable; second, and perhaps most important to a general readership, Warren self-identified as a Southerner. In this, he had advantages unavailable to Geertz and other traditional academic ethnographers, who typically studied societies geographically distant from and significantly different from their own cultures of origin. Warren could claim a large measure of native knowledge even as he represented native knowledge in his text, and thus could to a great extent act as his own native informant.

Modern ethnographic theory has recognized that even a privileged position such as Warren's involves a number of factors that might prevent an ethnographer from presenting an accurate representative account of a culture he or she claims as native. Muriel Dimen-Schein points out that "very often, people's views of their lives differ drastically from the observer's view" regardless of whether the observer originates within or beyond the culture in question. Dimen-Schein cites "the American theorist, Marvin Harris, [who] has drawn a fundamental distinction between these two views. He calls the viewpoints of those who are observed the *emic* view, and that of the observer the *etic* view. Harris's distinction resembles the Marxist position that one should not necessarily trust people's views of themselves. In fact [major schools of ethnographic thought] also mistrust self-explanation by the observed, but they do not say this so clearly."[103] Dimen-Schein revisits this issue later in the same chapter: "My analysis of our own culture, for example, rests on a combination of (1) what I observe with my own outsider's training (i.e., etics), (1) [*sic*] what I experience as an insider (emics), and (3) what others have observed and think about it (etic and emic). In all this, I try to keep the ideal and the real separate. Our reports of other cultures try to do the same, and likewise depend on an interplay between etics and emics."[104] Dimen-Schein's observation about the frequency with which "people's views of their lives differ drastically from the observer's view" glosses over the problems this perceptual conflict may present for ethnographers in the field; the statement is self-evident and irrefutable, but it hardly hints at the real difficulties involved in trying to do ethnographic fieldwork among people who are distrustful of or hostile to the ethnographic enterprise in general or to the ethnographer in person.

Segregation clearly registers the varying degrees of hostility and distrust Warren encountered on his ethnographic forays. Warren recounts a tense exchange between himself and a local woman during one of his stays in Tennessee:

"Excuse me," she suddenly says, but addressing me, not the husband, "excuse me, but didn't you say you were born down here, used to live right near here?"

I say yes.

She takes a step forward, coming out of the shadow. "Yes," she says, "yes," leaning at me in vindictive triumph, "but you never said where you're living now!"

Warren follows this account with a brief description of sitting down with a group of Southern students; one (a law student) confronts him with a blunt question before discussion can get underway: "I just want to ask one question before anything starts. I just want to ask where you're from." When Warren identifies such questioning as evidence of a general Southern "Suspicion of the outlander or of the corrupted native,"[105] contemporary readers would likely agree, in part because such Southern provincialism is widely identified with the racist ideology of segregation. Readers would also likely agree because of Warren's privileged position in the text. He is in some sense both native informant and ethnographic participant-observer (though at the time he wrote *Segregation*, some Southerners might have regarded Warren as an outlander or a corrupted native, as he was then living in New Haven, Connecticut, and teaching at Yale); moreover, he is the readers' guide through the moral underworld of the segregated South, by turns Virgil and Dante, and always the narrative mind behind the text's multiple voices.

Although Warren generally downplays the idea of plural Souths in favor of a narrative of more-or-less unitary Southernness (as was common among scholars during that time period), *Segregation* also contains passages that undermine the simplistic notion of some Southern essence inherent in everything or everyone throughout the region. At times, Warren's text draws readers' attention to the complexity and diversity of the South by highlighting scenes of regionalism within regionalism rather than some mythical pan-Southern solidarity. In a Clarksdale, Mississippi motel lobby, for instance, a generalized "suspicion of the outlander or of the corrupted native" means some uncomfortable moments for Warren the observer: "I see the eyes of the man behind the desk stray to the license of our car parked just beyond the glass front. It has a Tennessee license, a U-Drive-It from Memphis."[106] Warren tries to engage the desk clerks and a male guest in a conversation about race relations, but once they identify him as an outsider, they become reticent and preoccupied. (This passage also presents an example of ethnographic effacement or editing—Warren refers to *our* car, but the text makes no further mention of anyone with him on that leg of the trip.) Warren follows this account of regionalism within regionalism with a related anecdote that underscores the same point:

My Tennessee license, and Tennessee accent [Warren actually grew up in Kentucky], hadn't been good enough credentials in Clarksdale, Mississippi. But on one occasion, the accent wasn't good enough even in Tennessee, and I remember sitting one evening in the tight, tiny living room (linoleum floor, gas heater, couch, one chair, small table with TV) of an organizer of a new, important segregation group (one-time official of the Klan, this by court record) while he harangues me . . . He is a hill-man, come to town from one of the counties where there aren't too many Negroes, but he's now out to preserve, he says, 'what you might name the old Southern way, what we was raised up to.'[107]

To this day, anyone who has spent much time in Tennessee will be aware that the state has three distinct regions—West Tennessee, Middle (*never* "Central") Tennessee, and East Tennessee—and that the residents of the regions do in fact distinguish between their respective regions and the other two. The three stars on the Tennessee state flag symbolize the three distinct regions, and remind people of the topographic, demographic, and cultural differences between the three areas. In short, Memphis and Knoxville are in the same state, but they are poles apart, and Nashville is somewhere in between them.

At some level, Warren's account recognizes this element of internal diversity and subregional differentiation. The "hill man" almost certainly comes from East Tennessee, where the population of African Americans has historically been far smaller than in Middle Tennessee or West Tennessee. It would be an exaggeration to say that slavery and segregation had no effects on East Tennessee; however, East Tennessee's combination of topography and economy (much like that of the rest of the Appalachian South) did not encourage large-scale slave-labor plantation agriculture; moreover, the relative scarcity of African Americans in the region meant that many Appalachian Southern areas experienced questions of segregation and race relations as somewhat less pressing than lowland Southerners found them to be. (A simple reference to the cultural unconscious may reinforce this point, if not prove it outright: The images of the Civil Rights movement most Americans recall come almost exclusively from the lowland South rather than the Appalachian South.)

Warren's observation that the hill man comes from an area where there are few African Americans (although "too many Negroes" need not be read quite so innocently) simultaneously undercuts the hill man's comments about defending a common Southern heritage of racial intolerance ("what you might name the old Southern way, what we was raised up to") and suggests the submerged or ignored truth of Southern diversity—what I have called regionalism within regionalism—that makes possible this racist fiction of common heritage and common experience. The establishment and growth of Appalachian Studies programs indicates the extent to which scholarly communities are trying to account for the cultural diversity that has often been written out of the master narratives of Southern literature and Southern history. The simple fact that the

South is so vast—that the boundaries, broadly conceived, could encompass or have encompassed Maryland, Florida, Missouri, and Texas—and so varied both topographically and culturally should alert people to the problems inherent in sweeping rhetorical gestures or essentialist accounts of the region.

Throughout *Segregation*, Warren moves back and forth between a traditional concept of Southern culture as unitary and the verge of explicitly realizing a multifaceted concept of plural Southern cultures more like the ones that have gained widespread currency in Southern Studies quarters. Though clearly aware of Southern diversity or regionalism within regionalism in specific instances, Warren never makes the conceptual leap that would be necessary to incorporate this awareness fully into a thoroughgoing account of Southern social attitudes. In part, this conceptual limitation belongs to Warren's age rather than to Warren the man in particular. I will invoke W. J. Cash and C. Vann Woodward as exemplars of a tradition of generalizing about cultures in an attempt to reduce cultures to easily comprehensible patterns, relationships, attitudes, or formulas (as in Cash's 1941 *The Mind of the South* and Woodward's 1960 *The Burden of Southern History*, both of which influenced generations of Southern scholars and continue to provoke scholarly responses). According to Dimen-Schein, "This [type of] reasoning bares another assumption of the culture concept, that such societies are so homogenous and stable that a lone fieldworker can learn their culture by living in them for a year or so. Until the 1950s, most anthropologists rejected the study of complex cultures because their heterogeneity, size, and changeability proved too much for this underlying holistic orientation."[108]

Heterogeneity (however frequently overlooked) and size have characterized the South since the early antebellum period; most South-watchers would now add changeability to the list. These terms make clear the impediments to any essentializing account of Southern culture, but I want to focus more on Dimen-Schein's previous sentence. Although it might not seem to apply to Warren at all, the model of the nonnative academic fieldworker who purportedly knows a culture thoroughly after roughly a year's time in residence in fact relates to Warren's ethnographic project in provocative ways.

In the cowritten introduction to *Talking with Robert Penn Warren*, a collection of interviews spanning Warren's lengthy literary career, Floyd C. Watkins, John T. Hiers, and Mary Louise Weaks offer this assessment of Warren: "He remains a Southern personality though he is no longer a citizen of the South."[109] This description reminds readers that Warren spent the majority of his adult life living and writing outside the South (including periods of residence in California, England, Minnesota, Connecticut, and Vermont). It also, perhaps inadvertently, refers to the idea that the South is completely separate from the rest of America: *citizen* and *resident* are, after all, quite different things. Giving up residence is perhaps not momentous; it can presumably be reclaimed or reestablished. Giving up citizenship sounds far more serious and more permanent.

In light of this notion of renounced Southern citizenship (or at least lengthy residence outside the South) Warren's own remarks in interviews may lead readers back toward Dimen-Schein's troublesome model of an outsider "knowing" a culture. In a 1969 interview with Richard B. Sale at Yale University, Warren says that even before he wrote *Segregation* and long before *Who Speaks for the Negro?* he realized that the South he once knew had largely disappeared: "There was a time—twenty years ago—when I considered going back permanently to Tennessee to live. I even got far enough to try to locate a place [to live]. I discovered the world had changed; it would have been artificial. That is, the world I'd be going back to would not be the one I was remembering."[110] In this context Warren's realization is more than just the trite idea that one can never really go home again. It relates to Warren's earlier remarks connecting "the outlander" and "the corrupted native" in that it makes these identity categories suddenly seem less than distinct and less than stable. Later in the same interview, Warren says, "Only several years later [that is, several years after leaving Vanderbilt], after I'd been away from Tennessee for a little while, I began to discover Tennessee."[111]

Eight years later, the *New York Times Book Review* published an interview by Benjamin DeMott in which Warren remembers the same series of events: "I began to look for a place down there, but suddenly I saw it was a different world. The people aren't the same people. Oh more prosperous and all that, but not the kind I had known."[112] The tense change from "was" to "aren't" is likely unintentional, the sort of thing that can easily happen in conversation; nevertheless, it demonstrates the problem of time lapse that theories of halfie ethnography overlook. If one accepts Dimen-Schein's concept of cultural "changeability," then the duration and legitimacy of a returning native's claim on *citizenship* rather than simple residence—that is, a return to the cultural-insider status which the special legitimacy of such an ethnographer's accounts depends upon—is increasingly difficult to determine.

In Warren's case, problems of elapsed time arise on both ends of the ethnographic process, during the simultaneous acculturation and fieldwork (at that point not recognized as such) of Warren's youth and early adulthood in Kentucky and Tennessee[113] as well as during what ethnographers typically refer to as the "writing-up" process of converting field notes and recollections into a coherent narrative, which takes place after the ethnographer has returned from the field location and concluded the fieldwork. Warren's remarks in a 1969 interview with Marshall Walker manifest both forms of problems with elapsed time:

> As long as I was *living* in Tennessee and Kentucky and knew a great deal about various kinds of life there from the way Negro field hands talked or mountaineers

talked, what they did and what they ate, on up to the world of Nashville, Tennessee, I had no romantic notions about it. I was just naturally steeped in it and I knew that world . . . Then, as soon as I *left* that world of Tennessee and went to California, and then to Yale and Oxford, I began to rethink the meaning, as it were, of the world I had actually been living in without considering it.[114]

One aspect of the time-lapse problem involves the temporal and physical distances between Warren's experiences of Southern life (which he describes as various, thereby recognizing its diversity on one hand while obscuring it with the other) and his rethinking of it after he leaves; the other involves the time lag between these earlier procedures and the writing-up phase in which he converts his cultural knowledge into written accounts.

Such realizations do much to trouble any easy notions of *Segregation*'s Warren as a largely unproblematic cultural insider bringing to bear on the subject a keen eye, impeccable academic credentials, what he calls "my native ear,"[115] and a reliable Southern perspective that allows him to say both implicitly and explicitly that "I know what the Southerner feels." Any such notions appear increasingly untenable in light of Warren's comments in a 1982 interview with Thomas L. Connelly:

> *Connelly:* After graduating [from Vanderbilt] you went to California and then went to graduate school and became in a sense, a non-Southerner. How important do you think it is in your own writing that you had a quality of what you would call alienation, being out of the South?
>
> *Warren:* May I interrupt just a second? I think I became a Southerner by going to California and to Connecticut and New England. When I was at Vanderbilt, I couldn't have been paid to go to the Scopes trial. I was right there by it. I was not concerned with it, at all. My Civil War was primarily anecdotal from my acquaintance with old soldiers. They were my old soldiers all right. When I went west I began to read, much more than in some of the graduate courses I had, Southern history and American history. That continued. I really became a Southerner by not being there.[116]

This is not an uncommon sentiment, to be sure, but it is an important one with regard to constructing realistic narratives that purport to extend beyond literary realism and represent particular realities accurately. (Think again of Faulkner's Quentin Compson at Harvard—an easy comparison, but also an apt one. When Quentin complies with Shreve McCannon's request to tell about the South, he runs into trouble: The South is too big, too confusing, and he is no longer there.) Anyone who has stayed among nontourists in a foreign country for any length of time will have some idea what Warren means—what it is like to be held up as a *representative* American, for instance, all of a sudden (*"You're* a Yank. What do *you* think?"). The implications of Warren's remarks for his own ethnographic authority are profound, and they reach beyond the type of realization of partiality at which the native abroad must suddenly arrive when asked to play Quentin. Because of the era and the very nature of Warren's ethnographic enterprise, admissions of partiality were generally discouraged. Whereas in the decades to follow, ethnographers would to varying degrees accept and even celebrate their own inherent inability to become the cultural equivalent of an Emersonian transparent eyeball, the model of anthropological thought behind Warren's work did not encourage foregrounding the fact that an ethnography's narrator had at most a severely limited form of cultural omniscience. Ethnographies of this type did not always completely obscure the issue, but neither did they foreground it the way a number of postmodern ethnographers eventually would.

Warren deviates from the conventional ethnographic practices of the era by drawing attention to the instability or unreliability of his medium. *Segregation* deals directly with three distinct varieties or three different effects of the instability and partiality of language: (1) The inability of particular individuals to communicate with particular other individuals because of differences in sociocultural backgrounds or experiences. (2) The inability of a participant-observer-writer to understand correctly and represent accurately the thoughts, feelings, and actions of others in general. (3) The ability or inability of such an individual to understand himself or herself, including private thoughts, emotional responses, and public speech acts. An exchange between Warren and an unidentified African American man exemplifies the first effect of linguistic instability and partiality; the recollection it prompts manifests the second:

> There is another suspicion story. A Negro told me this. A man from New Haven called on him, and upon being asked politely to take a chair, said, "Now, please, won't you tell me about the race problem."
>
> To which the Negro replied: "Mister, I can't tell you a thing about that. There's nothing I could tell to you. If you want to find out, you better just move down here and live for a while."
>
> That is the something else—the instinctive fear, on the part of black or white, that the massiveness of experience, the concreteness of life, will be violated; the fear of abstraction. I suppose it is this fear that made one man, a subtle and learned man, say to me: "There is something you can't explain, what being Southern is."[117]

It is not entirely clear whether particular demographic factors, the general partiality and instability of language, or (most likely) a combination of the two prevents the man from saying anything at all about segregation and racial tension to his white Northern questioner, but words clearly will not convey anything like the reality the man perceives. Warren's recollection shifts the focus to the larger question of whether it is possible for him to carry out the fundamental goals of his intellectual project. Between the anxiety about violating the truths of life and experience and the learned man's declaration (the meaning of which hinges on whether a reader interprets the *you* as *one* or as Warren in particular— the declaration itself displays linguistic instability even as it apparently warns of the problem), the outlook is not especially promising.

Warren continues to question his ability to perform his multifaceted roles as participant-observer-writer by explicitly directing attention back to language in a figure of textual interpretation: Even when people appear willing to talk candidly with him about controversial issues, he wonders, "But how fully can I read the words offered in the fullest effort of candor?" Directly after this question, Warren remembers being driven through a town in Louisiana: "I am riding in an automobile driven by a Negro, a teacher, a slow, careful man, who puts his words out in that fashion, almost musingly, and drives his car that way, too." The man's remarks to Warren further undermine the idea of an "outlander," especially a white one, producing an accurate ethnographic account of African American Southerners: "Then, putting his words out that slow way, detachedly as though I weren't there, he says: 'You hear some white men say they know Negroes. Understand Negroes. But it's not true. No white man ever born ever understood what a Negro is thinking. What he's feeling.' The car moves on down the empty street, negotiates a left turn with majestic deliberation. 'And half that time that Negro,' he continues, 'he don't understand, either.'"[118] If readers assume that this man does not subscribe to racist notions that African Americans are less introspective than whites, this final sentence calls into question the ability of a participant-observer to know others and calls into question an individual's ability to understand himself or herself. This concern (the third item in the list above) also appears at the end of Warren's account of the "subtle and learned man":

> "There's something you can't explain, what being a Southerner is." And when he said that, I remembered a Yankee friend saying to me: "Southerners and Jews, you're exactly alike, you're so damned special."
> "Yes," I said, "we're both persecuted minorities."
> I had said it for a joke.
> But had I?[119]

At this point, the very ability of Warren the ethnographer to know his own mind and actions is in question. Such self-reflexivity, second-guessing, and self-doubt is far more characteristic of postmodern ethnography than the sort of midcentury positivist anthropological works Warren would have encountered prior to embarking on his own interdisciplinary fieldwork. Significantly, this moment of fundamental linguistic self-doubt appears early in *Segregation* and thus situates all subsequent accounts and analyses against a background of profound uncertainty.

As in *Brother to Dragons*, Warren keeps readers somewhat off balance throughout *Segregation*. Although the text makes it clear that Warren is generally opposed to racism and in favor of integration, his word choices and his sense of humor make it difficult for readers (contemporary readers, at least) to be completely comfortable or self-congratulatory about identifying with him. Racial category labels such as "mulatto" and "yellow" might seem at odds with the overarching concern of the book (though such labels were of course quite common in the South in the 1950s), but it is the matter-of-fact mention of a lynching joke that brings readers closest to the type of uneasy feeling of complicity Warren generates in *Brother to Dragons*: "There is, of course, the old joke that after the Saturday night lynching, the congregation generally turns up a bit late for church."[120] Again, it is the small words that bear the most weight: *of course*, *generally*, and *the* (rather than *a* in "the Saturday night lynching") together create the horrible sense that while strange fruit rots in Southern trees, church and life go on just as usual, perhaps with a nod and a wink from the pulpit.

One could read these elements as evidence of Warren's conflicted cultural position and the extent to which racial insensitivity was accepted in an era that predated political correctness; one could also read these elements as strategic devices deliberately employed by Warren in part to make readers somewhat uncomfortable, as *Brother to Dragons* does at points. By virtue of such knowledge, Warren and readers are implicated in the cultural systems that make such things possible. Readers do not necessarily share the same degree of complicity. Southern readers or readers who know the old joke differ significantly from other readers; even putatively innocent readers do not escape unsullied, though: There lingers a disquieting sense of being included in some disgusting secret, a feeling of unease because someone thought that one would nod knowingly and laugh at the joke.

The sketchily described man from New Haven mentioned above contributes to this growing sense that readers should perhaps not be completely comfortable with Warren as their native guide and interpreter. The potential destabilizing significance of this man becomes most clear when one compares him with another shadowy figure in *Segregation*. Several pages after mentioning the man from New Haven, Warren recalls an exchange with another man, "a college professor": "Yes, he was a segregationist. I didn't have to ask him. Or ask his reasons, for he was talking on in his rather nasal voice—leaning happily back in his chair at the handsome office, a spare, fiftyish man, dark suited, rather dressy, sharp-nosed, with some fringe remnants of sandy hair on an elongated, slightly-freckled skull."[121] Careful readers might suspect that these underidentified characters are versions of Warren himself, that Warren is perhaps at one level playing the same sort of game he plays in *Brother to Dragons* by insisting on his own multilayered presence in the text. The overt, realistic ethnographic project of *Segregation* insists on Warren's presence on a surface level, to be sure. The man from New Haven and the segregationist college professor should make readers wonder if there is not another, more literary level to the text as well. By the mid-1950s, it would have been perfectly accurate to describe Warren himself as a man from New Haven because of his employment at Yale. Moreover, the man from New Haven visits the African American man in order to ask the exact sort of question ("Now, please, won't you tell me about the race problem.") that Warren himself presumably asked time and time again during his fieldwork.

The case of the college professor is somewhat more complex and conjectural, in that Warren's description of the man involves a little linguistic sleight of hand, a manifestation of linguistic instability that might easily escape notice. Warren sets his description of the man in the past tense. This appears unremarkable unless one notes that the encounters and conversations with people throughout *Segregation* are set almost exclusively in what ethnographers refer to as the ethnographic present. This means describing events in the present tense even when writing about events that happened years before, much like the practice of referring to literary texts in the present tense throughout critical essays. I say *almost exclusively* in order to account for the events and conversations Warren clearly frames as flashbacks.

The main narrative action of *Segregation* takes place in the present tense. The anomalous past-tense description of the college professor suggests that perhaps Warren is once again exploiting the power of inherently unstable language to create multiple simultaneous levels of narrative meaning. The difference between writing "he was a segregationist" (as Warren does) and "he is a segregationist" (as he does not) is the difference between an accurate description of Warren himself circa 1956 (looking back on his defense of status-quo segregation in "The Briar Patch," his contribution to the 1930 Agrarian essay collection *I'll Take My Stand*) versus a description that could no longer apply to him. The man's physical characteristics (*spare, fiftyish, sharp-nosed*, and so on) sound more than a little like Warren's own. In this scenario, it makes sense that Warren could say of the man, "Yes, he was a segregationist. I didn't have to ask him. Or ask his reasons."

It is not quite possible to declare these individuals or characters completely fictional (merely aspects of Warren rather than representations of other real people) or completely real (accurate representations of other real people). The latter would suggest that Warren emphasized certain aspects of these real men because he recognized these aspects within himself and that he did so in order to destabilize his own position as ethnographer and narrator. It is finally impossible, however, to rule out either interpretation completely. Choosing between the two becomes increasingly problematic because of the final pages of *Segregation*. Warren presents a lengthy interview with another man who is very similar to the ones mentioned above. The man's answers to Warren's questions are often provocative and somewhat poetic, as is the case in this exchange:

> Q. Do you think it is chiefly the red-neck who causes violence?
> A. No. He is only the cutting edge. He, too is a victim. Responsibility is a seamless garment. And the northern boundary of that garment is not the Ohio River.[122]

The man's most provocative response is, except for Warren's surprising one-sentence conclusion to the book, the last thing readers encounter in *Segregation*:

> Q. Has the South any contribution to make to the national life?
> A. It has made its share. It may again.
> Q. How?
> A. If the South is really able to face up to itself and its situation, it may achieve identity, moral identity. Then in a country where moral identity is hard to come by, the South, because it has had to deal concretely with a moral problem, may offer some leadership. And we need any we can get. If we are to break out of the national rhythm between complacency and panic.

With a short declarative sentence, Warren ends *Segregation* and reminds readers once again of the interrelated elements of partiality and instability inherent in his accounts of things, in ethnographic accounts in general, and of the linguistic medium of these accounts: "This is, of course, an interview with myself."[123]

This issue—the complex issue of voice and authentic representation—is one of the relatively few points at which my project intersects with the works of other Warren critics. Although Warren critics have not explicitly made reference to ethnography in their work, a number of contemporary critics have done provocative work on Warren and issues of voice or representation. Karen Ramsay Johnson directs attention to Warren's structural choices in "The Briar Patch" in a way that suggests links between the narrative devices of the notorious early essay and Warren's techniques in *Segregation* and *Who Speaks for the Negro?*:

> "The Briar Patch" is a monologue; most of the few questions that arise are overtly rhetorical, and it seems clear that Warren has never asked a real person, black or white, any of them. The only persons quoted in the essay are Juvenal and

Booker T. Washington, who is literally quoted and is also presented as speaking words imagined for him by Warren. These two speakers echo and illustrate Warren's points; their voices thus merge with his own. For example, Warren imagines Booker T. Washington's response to a "radical": "'My friend,' Washington might well reply to such a critic, 'You may respect yourself as a man, but you do not properly respect yourself as a Negro." Shortly thereafter, Warren consciously paraphrases "Washington's" words: "What the white workman must learn, and his education may be as long and laborious as the Negro's, is that he may respect himself as a white man, but, if he fails to concede the Negro equal protection [from exploitation by employers], he does not properly respect himself as a man." Of course, Warren is actually paraphrasing himself, although the reader is likely, several pages after the fact, to remember the original quotation as Washington's own, and thus to perceive Warren's words as a gesture of respect rather than as a rhetorical strategy.[124]

Ramsay Johnson's explanation of the complexities of issues of voice and representation in "The Briar Patch" brings out the similarities between Warren's narrative strategies in the early work and his representations of speaking subjects in *Segregation, Who Speaks for the Negro?*, and *Brother to Dragons*. By paraphrasing and quoting actual people in his imagination—thus removing their words from their control—Warren presents narrative accounts that demand closer scrutiny. Taking them purely at face value is at times akin to blaming someone you know for their behavior in a dream you had: The actions the dream version of the person performs are no more connected to the actual person than, say, Thomas Jefferson's words in *Brother to Dragons* are connected to the actual Thomas Jefferson. Ramsay Johnson goes on to elaborate on Hugh Ruppersburg's reading of *Segregation*, concentrating particularly on a passage in which Warren figuratively locates the action within himself by saying,

> I was going back to look at the landscapes and streets I had known—Kentucky, Tennessee, Arkansas, Mississippi, Louisiana—to look at the faces, to hear the voices, to hear, in fact, the voices in my own blood. A girl from Mississippi had said to me: "I feel it's all happening inside of me every bit of it. It's all there."
> I know what she meant.[125]

Ramsey Johnson explains,

> Warren problematizes the idea of voice; as Ruppersburg suggests, the entire essay can be seen as occurring in Warren's mind, a sustained meditation as he gazes out of the airplane window. Both Warren's and the girl from Mississippi's formulations have the rather creepy quality of Faulkner's reference to Quentin Compson as a "barracks filled with stubborn back-looking ghosts," and *Segregation* shares *Absalom, Absalom!*'s narrative uncertainty, in which the narrator simultaneously provides knowledge and undermines it. Names are scarce in *Segregation*, and this

reinforces the extent to which these are "voices in . . . [Warren's] own blood." Yet they are clearly not figments of his imagination, and their voices are distinctly individual if anonymous.[126]

Ramsay Johnson's insistence on the reality or authenticity of the unidentified voices in *Segregation* is perplexing, especially in light of her earlier recognition of the complexities of Warren's treatment of Booker T. Washington in "The Briar Patch." Ruppersburg's point about the possibility of interpreting the entire book as a meditation rather than an actual report seems nearly as plausible as Ramsay Johnson's insistence that the narrative refers directly to the actual speech of actual people outside Warren's imagination.

Anthony Szczesiul's work on Warren's poetry reminds readers that even when Warren insists that his work accurately represents specific facts, readers should not necessarily take him at his word. Szczesiul explains the disparity between the historical record and what Warren repeatedly claimed actually happened in the event that precipitated his 1975 poem "Old Nigger on One-Mule Cart Encountered Late at Night When Driving Home from Party in the Back Country":

> In interviews Warren has emphasized the authenticity of the poem's recollection, claiming that the incident described in the poem "really happened." However, a closer look at the poem, along with evidence from the Robert Penn Warren Papers, shows that the poem is an exercise in self-invention; Warren privileges fiction over fact as he rewrites and reinterprets an event from his past in order to offer a retrospective narrative of his changing views on race—and poetry. While the narrated incident itself foregrounds the issue of race, the poem is also very much about the act of writing poetry—and the self.[127]

Kristina Baumli's archival research in the Warren collection at Yale's Beinecke Rare Book Library has extended this line of reasoning to Warren's nonfiction prose and has established a middle ground between Ruppersburg's idea of *Segregation* as an account of a meditation—an account, that is, that should not be taken at its word—and Ramsay Johnson's idea of *Segregation* as what amounts to a reliable record of Warren's Southern ethnography. Baumli reports of the files for *Segregation*,

> The entire set of notes consisted of a couple of small notepads with scrawled notes, and there was a typed transcript of one conversation. (Judging by other files, Warren was a man who kept every scrap of paper.) Most of the "conversations," I firmly believe, were made up—the notes that do exist show serious deviations in the text of *Segregation* from the recorded notes. I don't think Warren was lying; he was sticking to his ideas of the truth—and these remembered

'Everyman' conversations represented the 'truth' about the south . . . But there is no evidence that Warren actually performed the extensive research he claims.[128]

Who Speaks for the Negro? (1965) deals extensively with the issues Warren raises in the final lines of *Segregation*. Once again, Warren appears as an ethnographer moving among people who essentially function as native informants during the course of his fieldwork. *Who Speaks for the Negro?* departs somewhat from the impressionistic techniques of *Segregation* in that Warren generally identifies people by name and provides background information that effectively establishes their credentials as reliable or significant representatives of their culture. The text includes Warren's own voice, feelings, and reactions to situations, as well as a number of poetic descriptions and literary flourishes. It is important to note that such elements are not at all uncommon in traditional ethnographic narratives. Foregrounding the ethnographer's own subjectivity and partiality is a relatively recent practice within the discipline (although even this is a matter of degree and intensity—simply appearing in the narrative as a participant-observer does this to some extent), but literary flourishes designed in part to increase the readability and narrative appeal of ethnographies are nothing new. Once again, Warren presents readers with a disclaimer before the body of the narrative begins: "This book is not a history, a sociological analysis, an anthropological study, or a *Who's Who* of the Negro Revolution. It is a record of my attempt to find out what I could find out. It is primarily a transcript of conversations, with settings and commentaries. That is, I want to make my reader see, hear, and feel as immediately as possible what I saw, heard, and felt." Much like the author's note appended to the front of *Segregation*, this statement implies much about Warren's intentions and about the divisions in American academic intellectual culture Warren was trying to overcome in writing the two books. Insofar as the rest of *Who Speaks for the Negro?* clearly contradicts the disclaimer (much as the third sentence of the disclaimer contradicts the first), the disclaimer itself seems a product of a midcentury sense of academic disciplinary limitations. In an age much less interdisciplinary than our own, scholars were not encouraged to play fast and loose with disciplinary boundaries and practices. (Indeed, a critical approach such as my own would have been effectively prohibited by senior scholars and disciplinary protocols in English departments and anthropology departments.)

Despite Warren's protestations to the contrary, *Who Speaks for the Negro?* clearly has more to do with anthropological inquiry via an ethnographic approach than with anything else. It also has strong elements of sociological analysis and much in common with *Who's Who*; Warren explicitly mentions the listing of notable people twice, and he often relies upon the same sorts of lists of personal accomplishments that *Who's Who* exemplifies in order to demonstrate the social significance of his African American informants. Indeed, a partial list of the people Warren interviews reads much like a *Who's Who* of African Americans circa 1964: Martin Luther King, Malcolm X, Stokely Carmichael, James Baldwin, and Ralph Abernathy are just a few of the well known African American men who speak with and through Warren. I say *men* rather than *people* advisedly: Like *Segregation* (indeed, like many traditional midcentury ethnographic accounts) and *Brother to Dragons, Who Speaks for the Negro?* focuses almost entirely on men, thereby implying a potential answer about who is not authorized to speak.

The dedication ("*With thanks to all those who speak here*") indicates that the book is straightforward reportage, an accurate, true-to-life presentation of the words of the African Americans Warren interviewed; Warren's disclaimer insists on this element of accuracy in a detailed, defensive explanation of his technique: "The interviews were recorded on tape. In almost all instances the person interviewed checked the transcript for errors. Many of the interviews were long, sometimes several hours, and in a few cases there was more than one conversation. It would have been impossible, and undesirable, to publish all the transcripts. I have chosen the sections which seem to me most significant and exciting, and within these sections have sometimes omitted repetitions and irrelevancies. I have not indicated such omissions. But except for a rare conjunction, transition, or explanatory phrase, I have made no verbal changes." Although Warren surely intended this passage to establish the impartiality of his approach and the accuracy of the book's interviews, the wording of this explanation is rife with evidence of the ethnographer's narrative control. I do not mean to suggest that Warren intended this passage to be misleading or that his intentions were less than honest. Rather, I mean to draw attention to the types of ethnographic narrative control that this explanation perhaps unintentionally obscures. Although Warren points out that the people interviewed reviewed the transcripts of the interviews, this really does not relate to editorial decisions Warren made later, during the crucial writing-up process when notes, transcripts, and recollections gradually become a more or less unified narrative text. The transcripts people checked may well have been complete and accurate. As Warren makes clear, however, *Who Speaks for the Negro?* is a highly edited presentation of these transcripts, along with the circumstances surrounding the interviews and a number of Warren's own interpretive remarks about race relations in America. It is impossible for readers to determine what was omitted and what elements of context disappeared in the gaps between the transcripts and the published text.

Clifford's aforementioned warning about framing or staging conversations or quotations (cited in the discussion of *Brother to Dragons* above) deserves attention again here. By reminding readers that conversations or quotations, even if reported verbatim, are always staged or framed by the ethnographer who constructs the larger narrative, Clifford insists on the pervasive power inherent in the writing-up process, even with respect to linguistic events (such as direct quotations and conversations) that would appear to have their own inherent integrity. The potential for significant gaps in conversations is evident in Warren's remarks about choosing particular parts of interviews while leaving others out.

Who Speaks for the Negro? frequently presents the written equivalent of sound bites, short excerpts from conversations, framed to address complex problems in very brief statements. Warren's interview with Wyatt Tee Walker, a minister who was among the best-known associates of Martin Luther King in the Southern Christian Leadership Conference, provides representative examples of this ethnographic framing or staging technique: In the space of one page, Warren presents brief excerpts from his conversation with Walker. Presented out of context, the disparity between the complexity of the issues and the brevity of the answers is almost laughable, as is evident by simply listing the boldface labels that set off the quotations: "On Busing:, On 'Passing':, On the White Man and this Historical Moment:, On the South and Reconciliation:"[129] Again, all this, along with Walker's excerpted comments, appears on one page.

At times, Warren makes it clear that some gaps are unavoidable, whether because of technological constraints or because of the fundamental differences between piecemeal ethnographic inquiry and the production of unified ethnographic narratives. In a conversation with Martin Luther King, for example, simple recording technology leads to a significant gap in the transcript:

> *King:* I think there may be some truth in it [an assertion that there may be less communication between whites and African Americans in the large cities of the North than there is in the South]. In the South you have a sort of contact between Negroes and whites, an individual contact that you don't have in the North. Now that is mainly a paternalistic thing, a law of servantry—
>
> And here there was a change of tape. By the time the new tape was on I was asking how he interpreted the slogan "Freedom Now," in the light of historical process.[130]

I am of course aware that I am staging or framing this entire scene even as I explain Warren's power to stage or frame quotations and that my own bracketed explanation of the situation involves the same sort of editorial or narrative control I identify in Warren's texts. I am also aware that the special circumstances of King's tragic early death and his iconic status in contemporary America stack the deck against Warren in this case, that these things make the question of what was lost during the time between tapes in this particular conversation especially poignant. The same is true of Warren's conversations with Malcolm X, who was murdered before the book appeared in print; Warren includes a special note on Malcolm X's death. These facts simply underscore the importance of an ethnographer's power to frame and stage quotations and conversations. I have staged the incidents and framed the quotations in the service of my own narrative, just as an ethnographer would do.

Although less dramatic for the lack of the actual words of an iconic figure such as King or Malcolm X, Warren's brief descriptions of himself jotting recollections and impressions in notebooks after conversations are equally important to an understanding of ethnographic narrative power and the ways it circulates in *Who Speaks for the Negro?* A glimpse of this after the conversation with King provides an example: "*Something of a platform rhythm*, I wrote in my notebook when I stood again in the street. Then added: *Or is the platform rhythm itself out of a deep natural rhythm of feeling, of vision?* Then I wondered if that deep balance of rhythm had some relation to the attempt to deal with and include antitheses, to affirm and absorb the polarities of life."[131]

It is not just the poetical and speculative jottings (all conjecture based on King's speech pattern) that deserve attention; Warren's account of the sequence should also make readers pause. This passage demonstrates not only the extent to which an ethnographer may be drawn away from things that are in any sense subject to observation, and toward speculative interpretations that, although ultimately unverifiable, may well influence the tone or the framing of an ethnographic account; it also demonstrates multiple levels of removal from the actual observable event. Warren jots his notes down after he leaves King (converting experience into notes via short-term memory); much later, he returns to those jotted notes in order to reconstruct a coherent narrative of the events; later still, he presents those events and fills in gaps ("Then added," and "Then wondered") in the account of the note-taking activity by way of his overarching narrative voice.

All this attention to narrative practically demands some consideration of audience, the intended target of narrative technique. In a passage midway through *Who Speaks for the Negro?* Warren makes it clear that his intended audience is not as broad as contemporary readers might expect. Warren recounts a story about Malcolm X and a white student:

In a seminar . . . on race and religion there was a serious-minded and idealistic young girl, from, I think, Alabama. Among various guests who spoke to the seminar was Malcolm X, who pronounced his usual repudiation of the white devils. The girl asked him if there wasn't anything she could do—not anything—to be acceptable. "Not anything," he said. At that she burst into tears . . .

There is something of that little white girl in all of us. Everybody wants to be loved. The member of the White Citizens Council always gets around to telling you how Uncle Billy just loved the kids, would have cut off his right hand for 'em, and how Aunt Sukie or Sallie just loved the whole family and they all loved her right back and when she died they all cried and buried her in the family burying ground. But Malcolm X, even now, will have none of this.

Warren quickly shifts his attention to a different gendered response to Malcolm X's rhetoric: "But Malcolm X, in his symbolic function, does something else, quite paradoxical. Besides the little girl, there is in you too that hard, aggressive, assertive, uncompromising and masculine self that leaps out of its deep inwardness to confront Malcolm X with a repudiation as murderous as his own saying, 'OK, OK, so that's the way you want it, let her rip!' We must confront that wild elation in ourselves: 'Let her rip!' "[132] These give one a sense of Warren's presumptive readership or target audience. The prevailing sense is that the reader is white, and probably male, which reinforces interpretations of Warren as an ethnographic fieldworker intent on producing a narrative of the exotic for consumption elsewhere by an audience much like him.

The passages above also relate to a formula Warren presents near the end of *Who Speaks for the Negro?*:

As a basis for indicating this difference [between North and South in race relations], we may set up a little formula:

In the South, the Negro is recognized but his rights are not.
In the North, the rights of the Negro are recognized, but he is not.

But the formula needs a little footnote. If, in the South, as white Southerners like to claim, the Negro is recognized as a human, this occurs only when the Negro is in certain roles. If, in the North, the Negro's rights are recognized, they are recognized only in the legal sense; the shadow of a "human right" rarely clouds the picture.[133]

I juxtapose these passages because of what they do with pronouns, and what those pronouns do to readers, and I quote this passage in its entirety in order to avoid distorting Warren's argument, as omission of Warren's so-called footnote certainly would. In the first quotation, Warren speaks of *us* and to *you*; in the second, to *you* again, and of *we* and *ourselves*; in the third quotation, of *we* again. This sort of pronoun manipulation directly implicates readers in the action. Moreover, it demonstrates that the ethnographer's narrative power extends beyond the limits theorized by Clifford and Dimen-Schein. This power is not necessarily limited to native informants and the other people an ethnographer portrays within a given text. In implicating readers, ethnographers such as Warren may effectively extend their influence beyond the text itself. By drawing readers in, such narratives involve readers in the ethnographic practices being described—and in the second example above, in the explosive racial tension of Warren's intellectual project. As is the case with *Brother to Dragons* and *Segregation*, *Who Speaks for the Negro?* forces readers to receive and perform ethnography themselves, this time with the troubling realization that perhaps they are expected to be white males in order to do so fully.

CHAPTER 4

Making Strange

Heaney and Literary Ethnography

> Post-this, post-that, post-the-other, yet in the end
> Not past a thing. Not understanding or telling
> Or forgiveness.

Those are the first lines of a poem called "On His Work in the English Tongue" from Seamus Heaney's 2001 collection *Electric Light*. Over the past few decades a great deal of the criticism of Heaney's work has concentrated on postcolonial aspects of his poetry. There have been notable exceptions, of course (Helen Vendler's apparently apolitical attention to Heaney's work, for example), but the word *postcolonial* has attached itself firmly to Heaney's poetry, at least as it is commonly presented in colleges and universities, at conferences, and in scholarly books and journals. My purpose in this chapter is not so much to quarrel with critics who take postcolonial approaches to Heaney's works as it is to suggest an alternative methodology that complements the insights of the existing body of Heaney scholarship.

The opening quotation from Heaney serves notice that despite his long-standing association with writers (such as Seamus Deane, Tom Paulin, and the Field Day group) who are frequently identified with postcolonial thought, Heaney has some fundamental reservations about the applicability of the term *postcolonial* to the predicament of Northern Ireland. The simple truth, as Heaney implies, is that in 2001 the *post* in *postcolonial* did not apply to Northern Ireland in any tangible way. There were still colonial posts there; colonial power was by no means part of a gone world, and the extent to which it is remains debatable.[1]

This chapter will move back and forth between Heaney's poetry and works of contemporary ethnographic theory, juxtaposing Heaney's poetry with a number of theorists' comments on the interrelationships between ethnography and literature and recognizing the similarities between various paradigms of ethnography and Heaney's narrative strategies. This approach calls attention to the extent to which Heaney's poetry continually presents itself not simply as lyric or narrative verse but also as an ongoing project of creative ethnography. Ultimately, however, this juxtaposition of poetry and ethnography may prove most useful because of what the ethnographic-literary theories suggest about the potential value of this approach to a broader range of literary texts.

The differences between Heaney's works and the theoretical models highlight specific Northern Irish aspects of experience and discourse, both public (in Heaney's role as a sort of cultural ambassador) and private (as Heaney writes at times of family members and acquaintances killed in or scarred by Northern Ireland's sectarian conflict).[2] He also often writes of his own experiences of the remnants of the British imperium and the ways his distinctly Irish first name marked him as a Catholic Other and a presumptive nationalist in predominantly Protestant, British-controlled Northern Ireland). Noticing the ways ethnographic theoretical models fail to accommodate some of Heaney's narrative techniques will provoke readers to consider the limits of ethnographic approaches to literary production, as well as ethnographic criticism's potential to provide new perspectives on literary texts.

Since Heaney's first volume, *Death of a Naturalist*, appeared in 1966, critics have noted his attention to science in his observations of the natural word. Oddly enough, little has been said about the extent to which the logic of the social sciences—particularly ethnography—informs Heaney's work. The critics who have addressed the social science elements of Heaney's work have generally focused on archaeology rather than ethnography: Jon Stallworthy explains the archaeological elements in Heaney's *Death of a Naturalist* (primarily in "Digging") in his groundbreaking early essay "The Poet as Archaeologist: W. B. Yeats and Seamus Heaney." Brian McHale's "Archaeologies of Knowledge: Hill's Middens, Heaney's Bogs, Schwerner's Tablets," Christine Finn's *Past Poetic: Archaeology and the Poetry of W. B. Yeats and Seamus Heaney*, and Richard Rankin Russell's "Seamus Heaney's Regionalism" are also praiseworthy critical works that identify archaeological aspects, but not ethnographic aspects, of Heaney's work.

Heaney's first well-known poem, "Digging," which Heaney described in a 2008 interview as "truer to my phonetic grunting from south Derry than to any kind of iambic correctness from the books," shows the beginning of the ethnographic aspect of Heaney's literary project.[3] Heaney's narrators typically invite readers to identify the narrative voice with Heaney himself, as is the case in "Digging." By opening with the oft-quoted declaration "Between my finger and my thumb / The squat pen rests; snug as a gun," the poem locates Heaney with regard to the growing social tension of Northern Ireland in the 1960s. Despite his involvement in the daily life of Ulster, Heaney's stance is one of participant observation. He literally looks down on the scene he studies from the window of the upstairs room where he writes. The poem is in part a meditation on the traditional daily work of rural Northern Ireland and on the question of how a poet or a poet's work might relate to such matters. Heaney describes other men of his family engaged in the kind of activities that are self-evidently labor of the sort that a rural community openly admires and tacitly expects: Heaney's father digs up potatoes; his grandfather (apparently remembered from the poet's boyhood, though Heaney has said publicly that his great-uncle Hugh was the real-life model for the grandfather in the poem) digs and cuts turf into useable sods. When Heaney concludes, "I've no spade to follow men like them. / Between my finger and my thumb / The squat pen rests. / I'll dig with it,"[4] the figure of writing as work is unmistakable and the resulting poems are clearly akin to potatoes and turf, things with use value. Here, in the first poem of Heaney's first book, readers see him as poet, but also as a participant-observer studying culture and writing out the essential details for readers to consume. There is more at stake than production and consumption, of course, and more under way than ethnography. It would be a mistake to overlook these things, though, because one leads us to the other.

In 1964, after a few of his poems had been published to good critical notice, the publishing house Faber & Faber invited Heaney to submit a poetry book manuscript, which eventually became *Death of a Naturalist*. In signing with Faber & Faber—the same firm that published the poetry of T. S. Eliot, W. H. Auden, and Ted Hughes—Heaney became part of the English literary world in a very real way. His poetry and prose collections published by Faber and Faber led to wider critical acclaim. He resigned his secondary school teaching post, began writing full time, became a professor of poetry at Oxford and at Harvard, and eventually left Northern Ireland to settle in Dublin. This is a highly compressed account of things, but it highlights the fact that Heaney moved physically and socially away from his home turf in the years between his start with Faber & Faber and his selection for the Nobel Prize in 1995. This movement away from the land and the life of rural Northern Ireland—the land and the life that predominates in Heaney's poetry in the same way similar aspects of rural New England permeate Robert Frost's verse—is especially significant to the ethnographic elements of Heaney's ongoing literary project.

Heaney has been attacked by partisan critics on both sides of the Northern Irish Troubles for refusing to stake out a clear position, although many British critics have unsurprisingly lauded him for refraining from polemics. He has repeatedly praised the power of poetry and the role of the poet in essays such as "The Redress of Poetry" and the Nobel Lecture "Crediting Poetry." Although he has remained somewhat vague (perhaps strategically so) about exactly what he thinks the role of the poet is with regard to social conflict, he clearly does not think that it is to analyze the political situation, propose solutions, and sort the whole thing out. Instead, Heaney's take on Northern Ireland and its sectarian social conflict is largely ethnographic. In his Nobel Lecture, Heaney says that what he values in poetry is "its truth to life, in every sense of that phrase. To begin with, I wanted that truth to life to possess a concrete reality, and rejoiced most when the poem seemed most direct, an upfront representation of the world it stood in for or stood up for or stood its ground against."[5]

At times, however, Heaney's comments have not lent themselves so readily to an ethnographic-literary interpretation. As mentioned in previous chapters, this type of inconsistency does not invalidate the comments that manifest a poet's ethnographic tendencies; it merely reminds readers that poets are for the most part not systematic philosophers. Nevertheless, it would be a mistake for a study such as this one to pretend that such inconsistencies simply do not exist. In his 1988 essay "The Place of Writing," Heaney says, "Poetry is truly a vision of reality, and the creative imagination a truth-seeking and truth-augmenting faculty."[6] A *vision* is of course significantly different from a *representation* and, one suspects, might be quite different from reality as well. Heaney is writing of Yeats in this essay, so Yeats's *A Vision* is presumably not far from his mind when he describes poetry as a vision of reality.

As if to remind readers of this association, in his next lecture (Heaney originally delivered these essays as lectures to honor Richard Ellmann at Emory University) Heaney quotes Yeats's declaration that "art / Is but a vision of reality."[7] Although this declaration might seem to conflict with Heaney's remarks about his poetry being an upfront representation of the world, Heaney's explanation of the inherent doubleness of Northern Irish communication apparently accounts indirectly for both this contradiction and broader contradictions in Heaney's critical prose: Writing of a poem by Derek Mahon, Heaney explains that some linguistic details and some cleverly concealed meanings "may not be immediately evident to those unaccustomed to the minute inspections and pressures habitual to Ulster readers."[8] Though the idea of an entire society of readers attuned to Heaney's trademark etymological consciousness along with his verbal doublings and triplings and simultaneous insistence on multiple levels of meaning, an entire nation of readers at home with a sort of verbal cubism, is perhaps largely a Northern Ireland of the mind, even skeptics must concede that the social pressures of Ulster life would tend to focus the mind on the potential meanings concealed beneath even what Yeats (in "Easter 1916") called "polite meaningless words."

Accounting for this element of linguistic complexity at the level of the word is a challenge for even Irish and Northern Irish readers and critics of Heaney's work, to say nothing of critics from other countries. This is not as simple as merely dealing with place names, personal names, dates, and references to historical events—things that we might realize we do not know. It also has to do with the connotations of words that we might think we know. A brief example demonstrates Heaney's particular Northern Irish Catholic consciousness of the multiple levels of meaning of seemingly innocuous words. In 1989 the Dublin *Sunday Independent* presented Heaney with a special award in conjunction with the Irish Life Arts Awards. In his brief acceptance speech, Heaney talked about his discomfort with the word *special*, a word that has some unpleasant resonances among Northern Irish Catholics because of its association with the notoriously brutal Protestant special police squads known as the B-Specials (disbanded in 1970), which Heaney remembers quite well.

In their essay "Culture, Power, Place: Ethnography at the End of an Era," ethnographic theorists Akhil Gupta and James Ferguson describe ethnography in terms that relate closely to Heaney's occasional use of words and meanings that only fellow Northern Irish Catholics would be likely to understand completely:

> [The] often implicit conceptualization of the world as a mosaic of separate cultures is what made it possible to bound the ethnographic object and to seek generalizations from a multiplicity of separate cases.
>
> The later development of the idea of "a culture" as forming a system of meaning only reinforced this vision of the world. A culture, whether pictured as a semiotic system (Marshall Sahlins) or as a text to be read (Clifford Geertz), required description and analysis as an integrated totality. As a universe of shared meaning, each culture was radically set apart from other cultures, which had, of course, "their own" meanings, their own holistic logic.
>
> Today, it would be widely agreed that it has become increasingly difficult to conduct anthropological research in these terms. In ethnographic practice, as in theoretical debate, the dominant "peoples and cultures" ideal carries ever less conviction.[9]

Despite the trend Gupta and Ferguson describe, the idea of cultures as at least in part semiotic systems and/or texts to be read persists beyond the disciplinary boundaries of ethnography and anthropology. Heaney's misgivings about the word *special* draw readers' attention to part of the reason for this persistence. Moreover, when juxtaposed with the quotation from Gupta and Ferguson, they pose a significant para-ethnographic question that relates to the larger goals of this project: The question is how critics of culture, broadly construed (whether ethnographers or literary critics) should account for discrepancies between their theoretical models and the conceptual models widely employed by those they study. In this case, such critics must try to reconcile the fact that members of a particular social group still believe deeply in the notion of a social text with the fact that many contemporary theoretical models would disallow this understanding of culture.

Heaney's understanding of the ethnographic elements of literary production has much in common with Barrett's insider ethnography and Abu-Lughod's halfie model (both of which are discussed in the Warren chapter), insofar as Heaney and his work could fit into either conceptual category; neither category, however, would completely encompass the poet or his work. Another quotation from Gupta and Ferguson—this one from their essay "Beyond 'Culture': Space, Identity, and the Politics of Difference"—does more than the ideas of Barrett or Abu-Lughod to explain the extent to which Heaney considers Northern Irish culture to be both locally grounded and portable:

> The fiction of cultures as discrete, objectlike phenomena occupying discrete spaces becomes implausible for those who inhabit the borderlands. Related to border inhabitants are those who live a life of border crossing—migrant workers, nomads, and members of the transnational business and professional elite. What is "the culture" of farm workers who spend half a year in Mexico and half a year in the United States? Finally, there are those who cross borders more or less permanently—immigrants, refugees, exiles, and expatriates. In their case, the disjuncture of place and culture is especially clear: Khmer refugees in the United States take "Khmer culture" with them in the same complicated way that Indian immigrants to England transport "Indian culture" to their new homeland.[10]

Abdul JanMohamed's notion of the specular border intellectual, which Jan-Mohamed developed in a 1992 article on Edward Said and extended to Richard Wright in his 2005 book *The Death-Bound-Subject: Richard Wright's Archaeology of Death*, applies quite well to Heaney, complements Gupta and Ferguson's ideas about cultural portability, and suggests a reason Heaney might want to maintain the status JanMohamed describes. JanMohamed says of Said, "His entire oeuvre is centered around a tension produced by his location between cultures—a tension that manifests itself as the complex equilibrium of his intellectual stance, between 'worldliness-without-world' on the one hand and 'homelessness-without-home' on the other hand . . . Neither simply undivided nor simply divided, neither One nor Other (the one in *differance* from the Other, to borrow from Derrida)."[11] Despite the fact that Bellaghy (the village nearest to Heaney's childhood family farms), Derry or Londonderry (where he went to boarding school), and Belfast (where he worked and lived and enjoyed his first notoriety as a poet) are not all located on the border between Northern Ireland and Ireland (Derry is), Northern Ireland is small enough that one is never very far from the border. Moreover, one could argue that Northern Ireland, historically contested from without and from within, torn between Ireland and Britain, is a special case: The country itself is something of a cultural borderland. Gupta and Ferguson's comments about people who live a life of border crossing ("members of the transnational business and professional elite") also clearly apply to Heaney, who since the 1970s has lived and worked at times in Northern Ireland, Ireland, England, and America (though since 1972 his primary residence has been in Ireland).

Gupta and Ferguson's recognition of "the disjuncture of place and culture" perhaps resolves the problem of Heaney's move from his native Northern Ireland south to Ireland and also his periods of residence in England and America. Heaney addresses the issues of cultural portability and self-imposed exile or expatriation in "The Place of Writing," the title essay of his 1989 collection of lectures, saying of Louis MacNeice, "MacNeice provides an example of how distance, either of the actual, exilic, cross-channel variety or the imaginary, self-renewing, trans-historical and trans-cultural sort, can be used as an enabling factor in the work of art in Ulster." Here again, Heaney insists on multiple meanings of words that seem simple enough. In this case, removing the quotation from its context obscures the fact that *work* refers as much to social function (via a metaphorical treatment of levers and physics) as to any individual piece of art. Shortly thereafter, Heaney explains, "What is intractable when wrestled with at close distance becomes tractable when addressed from a distance."[12] Northern by birth, Southern by parentage (MacNeice was born in 1907, before Northern Ireland was separated from Ireland), educated in England, and largely absorbed into British cultural life (MacNeice studied at Oxford, taught at Birmingham University, and worked for the BBC from 1941 until his death in 1963), MacNeice faced many of the same cultural conflicts Heaney has faced, and Heaney is clearly aware of the similarities.

Heaney's enthusiastic responses to Ireland's most famous literary expatriate relate even more directly to the issues of cultural portability and accurate cultural description. In the September 13, 1984, issue of *The Irish Times*, Heaney describes James Joyce's literary project in terms that lend themselves to such a discussion: "There is an image I have often used of Joyce. He is like an immense factory ship that hoovers up all the experience from the bed of the Irish psyche. If you open *Ulysses* or *A Portrait*, or *Dubliners*, you are reading yourself."[13] An ethnographic-literary critical approach must recognize the limits of Heaney's Joyce, and by extension the limits of the mode of literary production and cultural reproduction he stands for in Heaney's mind. Despite the tremendous cultural content of *Ulysses* and the other works Heaney mentions, they all predate the modern Irish crises of civil war and partition, to say nothing of the Northern Irish Troubles. (Chapters of *Ulysses*, the most recent of the three works, appeared in *The Little Review* beginning in April 1918, and the events of the novel take place on June 16, 1904.) In this chronological sense there is much of the contemporary Irish self that cannot possibly be read in Joyce's works. Nevertheless, Heaney clearly considers Joyce to be an exemplar of the Irish artist as a cultural critic whose observations are in no way inferior to the kinds of observations a nonexpatriate or a social scientist might record.

In his essay "The Impact of Translation," Heaney indicates this belief in the accuracy of Joyce's expatriate works by approvingly citing and interpreting a comment made by the artist/Joyce character in Joyce's *A Portrait of the Artist as a Young Man*: "I am reminded of Stephen Dedalus's enigmatic declaration that the shortest way to Tara was via Holyhead, implying that departure from Ireland and inspection of the country from the outside was the surest way of getting to the core of Irish experience."[14] At first, this would seem to be an instance of accepting Joyce completely on his own terms (as expressed via Stephen Dedalus). Although Dedalus leaves Ireland for Paris to encounter "the reality of experience," a goal that would seem to have much in common with standard notions of ethnography, Dedalus does not have only French reality in mind. He leaves Ireland in part "to forge in the smithy of my soul the uncreated conscience of my race." Because both Heaney and Joyce are famously fond of employing multiple levels of meaning in individual words, readers should attend to the possibilities of *forge* (both in terms of metallurgy and in terms of misrepresentation or inauthenticity) and *uncreated* (in terms of an authentic organic thing found in some state of nature and perhaps in terms of something as yet uncreated, something the artist must therefore create) as well as the extent to which a vague, Joycean *conscience* might inform Heaney's sense of what it mean to "[get] to the core of Irish experience."

In "The Government of the Tongue," the title essay of his 1988 volume of critical prose, Heaney assesses the work of Elizabeth Bishop in terms that sound more scientific, less vague, and better suited to an ethnographic literary project. Heaney praises Bishop for "the discipline of observation"[15] she practiced in her work: "Typically, detail by detail, by the layering of one observation upon another, by readings taken at different levels and from different angles, a world is brought into being. There is a feeling of ordered scrutiny, of a securely positioned observer turning a gaze now to the sea, now to the fish barrels, now to the old man. And the voice that tells us about it all is self-possessed but not self-centered, full of discreet and intelligent instruction, of the desire to witness exactly."[16] It would be a mistake to suggest that everything an author writes in critical prose about other authors applies directly to his or her own work as well. The tradition of reading such prose for insights into the writer's own works, however, is well established. Because of the nature of Heaney's subject matter in his poetry, his stated interest in accurate representation, and his obvious affection for the techniques he describes in his comments on Bishop's work, it would be difficult not to read this passage as a metacritical treatment not only of Bishop's poetry but of Heaney's own work as well. Heaney describes Bishop's poetry in terms that apply directly to his own work, terms that could also serve to describe the Geertzian ethnographic practice of thick description by which an ethnographer produces a realistic narrative for readers.

Heaney's apparent sense that poetic truth and scientific truth are perhaps not so far apart is not entirely at odds with much contemporary thought on the matter. That is, readers need not take this as simply an isolated instance of a poet thinking that poetry is as good a form of knowledge as any. Arnold Krupat describes a larger contemporary interdisciplinary theoretical trend toward the kind of critical approach Heaney exemplifies: "The postmodern perception of a world organized in terms of signal/noise or figure/ground relations that are constantly shifting doesn't only blur genres, as Geertz might have it; rather . . . it blurs epistemological distinctions, asserting a kind of cognitive egalitarianism on the part of literature, ethnography, and even—at least at the highest theoretical level—the physical sciences."[17] Krupat explains the trend toward this kind of thought in ethnography as an outgrowth of literary criticism, although not, as readers might expect, originally from the later-twentieth-century French postmodernisms of Derrida and his ilk:

> In 1987, we have the publication of *Anthropology as Cultural Critique* by [George] Marcus . . . and Michael Fischer, which . . . turns to the Russian Formalist critics of literature of the early part of this [the twentieth] century, and takes their central concept, ostranenie, translated usually as *defamiliarization* or, simply, *making strange*, as authorizing experimentation and innovation in the writing of ethnography—a practice that might or might not . . . turn ethnographic writing from its traditional status as a "document of the occult" to an "occult document." I have referred once again, here, to the title of Stephen Tyler's essay in *Writing Culture*, one that defines the postmodern project of ethnography as indeed a shift from the production of documents of the occult to the production of occult documents. Such documents . . . would subsume all claims to "scientific" realism or "truth" to an essentially "literary" evocativeness. In Tyler's words, a postmodernist ethnography "*describes* no knowledge and *produces* no action," instead transcending these "by *evoking* what cannot be known discursively or performed perfectly." This "Evocation," for Tyler, "is neither presentation nor representation;" it is "beyond truth and immune to the judgment of performance." Occult document to be sure; for if one is to take Tyler seriously, ethnography's postmodern move beyond science . . . here passes beyond all literature except that which specifically attempts to give voice to the mystico-religious "silent realm" of the inexpressible, and inchoate—which, indeed . . . the postmodern scientist also values.[18]

Krupat misses the mark with his last literary comparison. In fact, Tyler's descriptions come as close to the theoretical underpinnings of some Language Poetry as to anything else. Krupat's insightful analysis of the radically destabilizing effects of modernist and postmodern thought, however, helps contextualize Heaney's understanding of the relationships between literary representation and scientific presentation or representation.

David Lloyd, a critic who is unabashedly hostile toward Heaney, finds fault with Heaney's work (specifically the poem "Punishment") because of some of the postmodern ethnographic qualities that Krupat describes, and generally derides what Lloyd apparently considers insufficient engagement with the events of Northern Irish society: "The cautious limits which Heaney's poetry sets round any potential for disruptive immanent questioning may be the reason for the extraordinary inflation of his current reputation. If Heaney is held to be 'the most trusted critic of our [sic] islands,' by the same token he is the most institutionalized of recent poets."[19] (The "[sic]" is Lloyd's own notation.) The apples-and-oranges comparison aside, Lloyd's complaint exemplifies the strain of literary criticism that might benefit most from the adoption of an ethnographic perspective.

A familiarity with ethnographic thought would have furnished Lloyd with critical tools that would have helped him make sense of the parts of Heaney's work he finds so frustrating, and also would have prevented this inexplicable criticism of Heaney's local subject matter: "[T]he celebration of regionalism dulls perception of the institutional and homogenizing culture which has sustained its apparent efflorescence at the very moment when the concept of locality, enclosed and self-nurturing, has become effectively archaic, and, indeed, functions as such."[20]

Many people in Northern Ireland still identify strongly with their counties of origin. It is not especially uncommon, for instance, for people from County Armagh to poke good-natured fun at people from County Derry (a number of other county combinations would suffice as well). Although a shop on Bellaghy's Castle Street rents out DVDs of recent Hollywood blockbusters, the lamppost outside the shop periodically bears a poster-sized photograph of hunger striker Bobby Sands, who was MP for Fermanagh and South Tyrone for a few weeks before he starved to death in 1981. To risk a sweeping generalization, Northern Irish culture seems to most observers to be neither homogenized nor institutional in the senses that Lloyd has in mind. When Lloyd's essay first appeared in print in 1993, the Northern Irish Troubles were still in full swing. As recently as August 2010, a large car bomb exploded outside a police station in Derry, police investigating bombings in the town of Lurgan were attacked with Molotov cocktails, and in the town of Bangor a booby-trap bomb fell from the bottom of a British army officer's car without detonating. Many of the road signs in the area read *Londonderry*—literal signs of colonial presence—but people routinely paint over parts of the signs, crossing out *London* or obscuring it entirely. This environment hardly seems an exemplar of some theoretical global or institutional homogeneity. (I realize that at this point I am engaging or inserting myself in the sort of ethnographic discourse I describe.)

I am not the first to observe that members of some communities resent the fact that they have just recently achieved independent subjectivity (so to speak) only to find that some theorists (mostly upper-class white males) have decided that the notion of stable subjectivity, even perhaps the notion of simple selfhood, is passé. (Numerous feminist critics and critics of race relations in literature and beyond have made this point.) Claiming that the notion of locality is passé is similarly offensive in the face of the historical facts of the Troubles, which insist rather firmly that locality matters—that it is, in fact, potentially still a matter of life and death.

Despite this, Lloyd makes valuable observations about Heaney's work and the questions it raises with regard to attempts at ethnographic literary criticism. Lloyd cites a remark of Heaney's that makes a distinction between the two aspects of ethnographic thought that prove most troublesome to this sort of enterprise, namely the distinction between the faithful reproduction or representation of observations and the creative generation of fictional representations of things (representations that might be realistic in the sense of literary realism but are not necessarily representations of specific observed facts, events, or statements): "So much in Ireland still needs to be done . . . the definition of culture, and the redefinition of it."[21] This remark (from an interview with John Haffenden) effectively makes it clear that Heaney is aware of the extent to which literature contributes to a culture's sense of itself, the issue mentioned above in association with Stephen Dedalus.

Jonathan Allison's essay "Magical Nationalism, Lyric Poetry, and the Marvellous: W. B. Yeats and Seamus Heaney" examines the complexities of realism and cultural representation in Heaney's poem "Lightenings" (from Heaney's 1991 volume *Seeing Things*), a poem "based upon an anonymous, early modern Irish legend, translated by Kenneth Hurlstone Jackson" in which a ship appears and sails in the air over an Irish monastery: "In an adjacent poem in the volume, the speaker admits it took him fifty years before he could learn to 'credit marvels,' and this poem among others is an admission, aesthetically and ethically, of the marvelous or supernatural . . . The poem appropriates fabulous matter from a traditional narrative, and the sense of national history is preserved with the phrase, 'the annals say' . . . The poem establishes a link between the magical thinking underpinning the nationalism of Yeats's revolutionary generation, paying tribute to that tradition, and hinting at its noble but altered continuance."[22] John Carey provides a detailed description of the original sources of this "air ship" narrative—a description that balances a scholarly skepticism with a scholarly acknowledgement of the surprising elements of the historical record:

Toward the middle of the eighth century—different sources propose the dates 743, 744, and 748/9—ships, with men aboard, were seen in the air over Ireland. Entries to this effect are included in the Annals of Ulster, of Tigernach, of Clonmacnoise, and of the Four Masters, as well as in annalistic material preserved in some manuscripts of *Lebar Gabála*. The date, the range of attestation, and the fact that the item was first recorded in Latin all suggest that we have here to do with a contemporary notice of an anomalous occurrence. We will of course never know what it really was which some person or persons saw overhead in the 740s, or how many retellings and mutations separated the first testimony from its distillation in the annals.[23]

Carey's analysis adds further weight to Allison's observation that "in his lyric adaptation of legendary narrative, Heaney questions the conventional relationship between the 'fantastic' and the 'real', in the context of the re-writing of a national story, as recorded in 'the annals.'"[24] This aspect of Heaney's work adumbrates his more recent poems based on quotations and found prose and also resembles the ethnographic elements of Yeats's work, particularly Yeats's treatment of supernatural issues such as belief in Irish fairies. Both poets appear to use supernatural elements as parts of their compensatory cultural strategies, ways to present, affirm, and dignify Irish folk beliefs, things beyond the ken of and utterly foreign to the foreign power that has exerted such cultural influence on and political control over Ireland. By foregrounding Irish supernatural elements, both Yeats and Heaney insist that such elements figure into readers' understandings of their poetic works and readers' understandings of Ireland itself.

It is this simultaneous definition and redefinition of culture that Lloyd apparently considers to be the most objectionable element of Heaney's work. In short, Lloyd argues that Heaney's poetry flattens history and makes it seem inevitable. According to Lloyd, Heaney's bog poems (the poems inspired by P. V. Glob's *The Bog People*) "reduce history to myth, furnishing an aesthetic resolution to conflicts constituted in quite specific historical junctures by rendering disparate events as symbolic moments expressive of an underlying continuity of identity."[25] Lloyd particularly objects to what he identifies as Heaney's "aestheticization of violence": "Heaney renders it symbolic of a fundamental identity of the Irish race, as 'authentic.' Interrogation of the nature and function of acts of violence in the specific context of the current Troubles is thus foreclosed, and history foreshortened into the eternal resurgence of the same Celtic genius . . . The unpleasantness of such poetry lies in the manner in which the contradictions between the ethical and aesthetic elements in the writing are easily resolved by the subjugation of the former to the latter in order to produce the 'well-made poem.'"[26] To charge a poet—or any artist, for that matter—with aestheticizing violence seems almost tautological. It accomplishes little, except perhaps to provoke readers to wonder what else art could do when describing or depicting violence. The war poems of World War I, Picasso's *Guernica*, and films such as *Apocalypse Now* and *Saving Private Ryan* all aestheticize violence in that they represent violent acts in works of art. Heaney's representations of social violence are aestheticized, but not at all in amoral, celebratory, or insensitive ways. Heaney's work refers to violence carefully and evocatively in ways that are generally quite disturbing to readers. These moments typically serve as points of departure for Heaney's considerations of what a relatively sensitive and sane person is to do or think or feel when his society—which is both his subject culture and his home culture—repeatedly lapses into cycles of violent retribution.

In his essay "Place and Displacement: Recent Poetry of Northern Ireland" Heaney says that the concepts and terms associated with anthropology and ethnography—"different history, heritages, cultural identity, traditions, call it what you will"—at least temporarily helped those in the region understand the Troubles from another, more analytical perspective, albeit without providing a clear solution to the real problems of violent social conflict:

> For a moment, the discovery and deployment of this language allowed us to talk of Planters and Gaels, rather than Protestants and Catholics, to speak of different heritages rather than launch accusations and suspicions at one another, to speak of history rather than the skullduggery of the local government. It was a palliative, true in its way, salutary in that it shifted the discourse into a more self-diagnosing frame of reference; but, as everyone including the poets knew, not true enough, another place where the mind could take shelter from the actual conditions. To locate the roots of one's identity in the ethnic and liturgical habits of one's group might be all very well, but for the group to confine the range of one's growth, to have one's sympathies determined and one's responses programmed by it was patently another form of entrapment. The only reliable release for the poet was the appeasement of the achieved poem.[27]

As mentioned above, other critics have also taken issue with Heaney's engagement (or lack thereof) with Northern Irish social violence. In fact, Heaney has taken issue with it himself rather extensively in his poetry, often by emphasizing his personal culpability, which functions to undercut the notion of inevitability and to implicate the poet in the matrix of social conflict, violence, and injustice. Vendler, whose work is quite dissimilar from the kind of politically oriented criticism that Lloyd's work exemplifies, at times directs her attention to Heaney's treatment of sectarian violence in her 1998 study *Seamus Heaney*. The differences between Vendler's comments and Lloyd's comments are instructive, both in a general sense and as examples of the ways very different literary critical approaches could benefit from the insights of ethnographic theory.

Vendler generally dislikes the kind of criticism that Lloyd's work exemplifies (political criticism rather than the apparently apolitical aesthetic criticism Vendler practices) and she regards politically based critical attacks on Heaney as entirely wrongheaded: "Heaney's adversary critics read the poems as statements of a political position, with which they quarrel. To read lyric poems as if they were expository essays is a fundamental philosophical mistake; and part of the purpose of this book is to read the poems as the provisional symbolic structures that they are."[28] This seems very much at odds with remarks Vendler makes just a few pages before about Heaney's intellectual and poetic progress and his willingness to reexamine or revise his previous political positions:

> As each decade of poetry unfolds, it illuminates and corrects the previous ones. With its autobiographical circuit, it is also an oeuvre of strong social engagement, looking steadily and with stunning poetic force at what it means to be a citizen of contemporary Northern Ireland—at the intolerable stresses put on the population by conflict, fear, betrayals, murders. Heaney has made one imaginative cast after another in an attempt to represent the almost unrepresentable collective suffering of the North, yet he has tried, equally consistently, to bring intellectual reflection to the emotional attitudes that too often yield the binary position-taking of propaganda.[29]

Besides overriding Vendler's aforementioned remarks about de-emphasizing or disregarding the expository elements of the poetry, this sort of language would seem to point the way to ethnographic considerations of Heaney's work. Indeed, Vendler includes a chapter entitled "Anthropologies: *Field Work*" that focuses on Heaney's acclaimed 1979 volume *Field Work*. That a critic as accomplished and insightful as Vendler decided to examine this aspect of Heaney's verse is unsurprising. What is surprising is the fact that, despite the chapter title, Vendler skims over the surfaces of the anthropological or ethnographic elements without producing the kinds of penetrating close readings (with regard to these elements) for which she is justly renowned.

Vendler asserts that "in *Field Work* Heaney is an anthropologist not only of the dead, but also of the living,"[30] then goes on to discuss a number of poems in terms that make no reference to the anthropological enterprise. When she picks up the idea again, it is to comment on a section of Heaney's "Glanmore Sonnets" (a poetic sequence which, in its preoccupation with Wordsworth and with a married couple removed from society in rural quietude, seems not to be ethnographic or anthropological at all) that makes mention of "Our first night years ago in that hotel," which Vendler surprisingly reads as an anthropological moment: "Idyllic though this is, and means to be, it introduces its down-to-earth anthropological note in mentioning the hotel."[31] Taking Vendler's remark this far out of context obscures the fact that the poem is indeed idyllic. Its anthropological note, however, is indistinguishable to my ear; even Vendler would have to concede that a brief mention of an undescribed hotel hardly rises near the level of what she (using Heaney's words as a title for one of her critical books) has identified as "the music of what happens."

Vendler's few explicit dealings with anthropology and ethnography at times produce provocative analogies and creatively turned phrases—"to the anthropologist every detail is a trading counter, useful insofar as it illuminates,"[32] for example. Overall, however, her concept of anthropology is extraordinarily loose and apparently includes just about any reference to any aspect of civilization, even one as brief and unremarkable as Heaney's mention of the hotel. Like Lloyd's criticism, Vendler's presents clear examples of situations in which the criticism would benefit greatly from a framework of or familiarity with disciplinary anthropology. Such a familiarity would give a critic such as Vendler the vocabulary to talk in greater detail and with greater accuracy about the ethnographic or anthropological elements in Heaney's poetry instead of being limited to a superficial treatment of a subject she obviously finds potentially engaging. Lacking this framework, Vendler's treatment of the anthropological elements of Heaney's work falls well short of her usual level. As is the case with Lloyd, she overlooks an element that the poetry itself fairly insists is both important and complex.

In "Punishment," the poem Lloyd discusses most extensively, Heaney identifies himself as clearly complicit in the Catholic community's retribution against local women who fraternized with British soldiers: "I who have stood dumb / when your betraying sisters, / cauled in tar, / wept by the railings."[33] Earlier in the same poem Heaney declares "I am the artful voyeur," an indictment of aestheticizing violence that should make it clear that the poem contains its own criticism of Heaney's participant-observer stance. In "Summer 1969," a section of the long poetic sequence "Singing School," Heaney brings up the issue of his absence at important moments of Northern Irish social violence, in this case represented by the fact that he was on a trip to Spain during an outbreak of anti-Catholic violence directed at Belfast's Catholic Falls Road area and overseen by Northern Ireland's police force, the Royal Ulster Constabulary, which at that time employed only Protestants: "While the Constabulary covered the mob / Firing into the Falls, I was suffering / Only the bullying sun of Madrid."[34] The line break after *suffering* sharpens the poem's note of self-accusation by momentarily causing the reader to expect some sort of equivalent suffering on the part of the poet, only to lead to the realization that Heaney is pointing out the disparity between the two situations (and, later in the poem, emphasizing it by revealing that he was reading a biography of Joyce while in Madrid, providing a self-parodying image of a not-yet-expatriate author reading about

Ireland's most famous literary expatriate instead of engaging directly with the social violence at home).

In the long poem "Station Island," Heaney moves from expressions of guilt and self-implications to a more complex and subtle treatment of his participant-observer status. "Station Island" includes encounters with the spirits of people Heaney knew, people who were killed in the North's sectarian violence, and Heaney appears in the poem itself as a speaking participant-observer whose recollection or report is, we are to assume, the poem itself. In conversations with the ghosts, Heaney is forced to deal with the distance that separates participant observation as an author from full-fledged participation as an actor or an activist. When confronted by the shade of one former acquaintance, Heaney responds, " 'Forgive the way I have lived indifferent— / Forgive my timid circumspect involvement,' / I surprised myself by saying."[35] Although this plea contains elements of the guilt and self-accusation cited in the poems above, it ultimately exceeds those poems in its subtle rendering of the poet as conflicted ethnographic participant-observer.

Heaney's indictment of his participant-observer stance is ultimately less surprising and less significant than the representation of his own surprise within the text of the poem. The element of surprise creates the sense that Heaney is not completely in control even as it creates a sense of truth to life. By introducing this aspect into the text of the poem's larger narrative of spiritual pilgrimage,[36] Heaney creates a rhetorical structure that buttresses his own constructed sense of ethnographic authority. Later in the poem, Heaney's encounter with the ghost of his murdered second cousin serves as a reminder not to lose sight of the facts of an event when aestheticizing it. Once again, the poet's physical removal from a scene of sectarian violence implies levels of cognitive removal. The ghost reminds him that he was at a gathering of writers in Jerpoint (about forty miles southwest of Dublin) at the time of his cousin's murder:

> "The red-hot pokers blazed a lovely red
> in Jerpoint the Sunday I was murdered,"
> he said quietly. "Now do you remember?
> You were there with poets when you got the word
> And stayed there with them, while your own flesh and blood
> Was carted to Bellaghy from the Fews.
> They showed more agitation at the news
> Than you did."
> "But they were getting crisis
> first-hand, Colum, they had happened in on
> live sectarian assassination.
> I was dumb, encountering what was destined."
> And so I pleaded with my second cousin.

"I kept seeing a grey stretch of Lough Beg
and the strand empty at daybreak.
I felt like the bottom of a dried-up lake."
"You saw that, and you wrote that—not the fact.
You confused evasion and artistic tact.
The Protestant who shot me through the head
I accuse directly, but indirectly, you . . ."[37]

Once again, an evocative line break (after *word*) intensifies Heaney's self-critique, this time contrasting the gathering of poets in celebration of words with receiving word of the sectarian murder at home. The description of Heaney's reaction to the news (visualizing the grey lake and an empty shoreline at dawn) also lends itself to a bitterly parodic portrayal of a poet aestheticizing an event to the point where it becomes literally and emotionally unrecognizable to others. As is the case earlier in the poem, Heaney frames the exchange with the ghost in such a way that it creates a sense of verisimilitude that resembles the narrative status of much ethnographic writing. I say *a sense* in order to indicate the way the poem creates the appearance of being true or real and simultaneously suggests to readers that it is only verisimilitude, the way the poem insists on its own reliability and believability even as it undermines both.

In order to emphasize the way ethnography has traditionally depended on this sort of delicately balanced truth claim (balanced between, on one hand, a realistic narrative that insists on the truth of the events it describes, and, on the other hand, a realization that ethnographic accounts are often vulnerable to charges of verisimilitude because they are often not supported by evidence other than the ethnographer's field notes), Gupta and Ferguson quote Foucault: "An experience is neither true nor false; it is always a fiction, something constructed, which exists only after it has been made, not before; it isn't something that is 'true' but it has been a reality."[38] Foucault's radical claim stands in for a number of claims (most of them considerably more cautious) about the inherently constructed status of all written accounts, claims that strike at the heart of traditional ethnographic practice by calling into question the core premise of the communicability and relevance of individual experience (that is, the idea that one's experience of a cultural group is an accurate representation of certain important facts about that group).

Anthropologist Marvin Harris observes that "postmodernists are quick to point out that there is little in the ethnographic literature that has been replicated by a second observer. Ethnographers have almost always worked alone; therefore, postmodernists claim, objectivity is a fiction." Harris responds to this reductive claim acidly and reminds postmodern theorists to consider the realities of ethnographic fieldwork: "I am not aware that anyone has shown that the reliability of ethnographic descriptions cannot be improved because there is some fatal warp in the universe that precludes two or more ethnographers from employing similar research protocols or from working at the same time in the same community. There are certainly plenty of planned ethnographic undertakings in which teams of ethnographers have worked together, although their final reports or dissertations only rarely have been issued as team products."[39] Harris's comments make it clear that ethnography's traditional reliance on truth claims that are difficult or impractical to verify is not grounds for disregarding its findings. Instead, he argues that "the limited reliability of ethnographic accounts is an aspect of the pauperization of the social sciences in combination with the highly individualized system of academic rewards that prevails almost everywhere."[40]

Gupta and Ferguson's citation and interpretation of Foucault may be helpful as readers consider the extent to which Heaney undermines his own implicit claims to ethnographic authority. Because Heaney does not present himself as a professional ethnographer constrained by the academic structures and disciplinary guidelines Harris identifies, Gupta and Ferguson's Foucauldian emphasis on ethnographic discourse (here again quoting from Foucault) relates more closely to Heaney's work: " 'Discourses are tactical elements or blocks operating in the field of force relations; there can exist different and even contradictory discourses within the same strategy; they can, on the contrary, circulate without changing their form from one strategy to another, opposing strategy.' Practices that are resistant to a particular strategy of power are thus never innocent of or outside power, for they are always capable of being tactically appropriated and redeployed within another strategy of power, always at risk of slipping from resistance against one strategy of power into complicity with another."[41] In many of the poems in which Heaney criticizes his own participant-observer approach to Northern Irish social conflict, it seems that the end result is the kind of redeployment or appropriation that Gupta and Ferguson describe. That is, Heaney's self-critiques often function in part to strengthen and legitimate his claims to ethnographic participant-observer status, particularly insider status or the halfie status described by Abu-Lughod.

In the memorably named "Making Strange," Heaney presents a halfie ethnographic self again, standing between an unnamed native informant (in reality, as Heaney has publicly explained, this character is modeled on his father) and an unnamed traveler or tourist (in reality the American poet and critic Louis Simpson, who was passing through the Bellaghy area with Heaney when they stopped at a pub and bumped into Heaney's father). In the poem, Heaney negotiates a balance between his role as native and his role as a cosmopolitan intellectual, positioning himself as ethnographer and tour guide by adopting a mode of speech that bridges the gap between his two worlds: "a cunning middle voice / came out of the field across the road / saying, 'be adept and be dialect . . .' " Soon after, Heaney appears fully involved in this role: "I found myself driving the stranger / Through my own country, adept at dialect, reciting my pride / In all that I knew, That began to make strange / At that same recitation."[42]

As is often the case in Heaney's poetry, it is difficult to know how much to make of seemingly simple word choices. In this instance, "I found myself" might or might not refer both to a sudden realization that one is doing something and to a deeper realization (akin to "finding oneself" in the terminology of pop psychology) about who or what one is as an individual. Regardless of whether readers grant both meanings, the poem's self-consciousness about the way discourse alienates the speaker from his home country reflects one of the major problematic aspects of halfie ethnography and perhaps of insider ethnography as well. Heaney's long-standing interest in etymology makes one strongly suspect that estrangement is very much on his mind here. Although "Making Strange" never mentions the word directly, the poem does show a slightly different aspect of the halfie ethnographic experience or the insider/native ethnographic experience: Here, ethnographic description leads to increasing estrangement from the culture, a possibility never mentioned by Abu-Lughod or Barrett.

With its odd ethnography-related linguistic instability, the short poem "Sweeney Redivivus" (part of a longer poetic sequence of the same name) apparently speaks to both sides of questions about the accuracy and verifiability of the ethnographic participant-observer's findings. After two stanzas that have little to do with this enterprise, the poem turns, in its last stanza, directly toward the issue:

> And there I was, incredible to myself,
> among people far too eager to believe me
> and my story, even if it happened to be true.[43]

Again, readers' interpretations of individual words and of the poem's syntactical arrangements effectively bring out multiple levels of meaning in the poem. The question of credibility is clear enough, in that it identifies Heaney's awareness of the fact that his narratives, no matter how accurate they might seem, are in some senses limited and incredible, not so much because of any intent to deceive as because of the inherent limits, editorial decisions, and selective exclusions that characterize any narrative, whether scientific or poetic, verbal or visual (via film, for instance). "[F]ar too eager to believe me/ and my story, even if it happened to be true" is something of an elusive passage because of its refusal to clarify itself entirely. It is unclear whether the people Heaney describes are too eager, and thus are unable or unwilling to believe him, or whether (more likely, I think) the speaker is disturbed by the people's eagerness to believe him and his story, disturbed because he senses that its truth or lack thereof has little to do with the people's reception of it. Insofar as it is difficult to interpret conclusively, this aspect of the poem perhaps represents and enacts the difficulty of interpreting Heaney's treatments of Northern Irish society. At the very least, it undercuts assumptions about clarity and believability and therefore undercuts assumptions about authority and the reception of authority.

Heaney returns to his family farm and to the subject of his brother Hugh in "Keeping Going," a poem that amplifies the sense of awkwardness and guilt found in "Making Strange." Heaney's work periodically deals with feelings of individual and social guilt on multiple levels: There is some general guilt about leaving home, which a number of people in a rural community such as the one in which Heaney lived would likely consider something of a betrayal of one's roots; guilt about being physically absent from scenes of social strife and sectarian violence; and a measure of discomfort—if not outright guilt, then at least an awkward self-consciousness—about the ethnographic elements of Heaney's ongoing literary project, an acute awareness of the relationship between his art and the ongoing social catastrophe of the Troubles. In "Keeping Going," an element of guilt is implicit in Heaney's praise of his brother, the farmer who did not leave the home, who inherited the family farm and remained in Northern Ireland despite the social turmoil:

> My dear brother, you have good stamina.
> You stay on where it happens. Your big tractor
> Pulls up at the Diamond, you wave at people,
> You shout and laugh above the revs, you keep
> Old roads open by driving on the new ones.[44]

Here, the praise for the brother's decision to live his life in rural County Derry seems heartfelt. It also has a function beyond simply expressing an older brother's approval of a younger brother. The poem's detailed description of aspects of the brother's day-to-day life as a farmer (juxtaposed with scenes of bloodshed on Bellaghy's Castle Street and a depiction of the young Heaney about to leave home for boarding school in Derry) works to establish and maintain Heaney's own insider or halfie credentials by demonstrating his connection to the place and implicitly identifying Heaney's brother as a native informant who is still in place.

"Two Lorries," the next poem in Heaney's expansive second volume of selected poems, *Opened Ground*, also works to establish and reinforce Heaney's credentials as an insider or a halfie, this time via an element of local specificity that reminds readers of Heaney's familiarity with rural County Derry. The poem imagines the events leading up to the truck bombing of the bus station at Magherafelt, a town a few miles from Bellaghy that (because it has a bus station) serves as a small hub for public transportation in the area. In describing the bus routes and the local scenes—"The Magherafelt (via Toomebridge) bus goes by,"[45] for instance—Heaney imbues the poem with an element of specificity that reinforces his implicit claims to ethnographic authority.

Heaney's remarks elsewhere reflect his deep interest in establishing and maintaining the sort of authority that makes possible his stance as an insider or halfie ethnographer, a spokesperson for Northern Irish culture whose native, intimate familiarity with the daily life thereof authorizes him to write and speak about Northern Ireland more directly and authentically than Yeats could speak for Ireland during his time. Despite their vastly different backgrounds (especially with regard to religion and social class identification), in an RTE radio conversation with Richard Ellmann Heaney looked to Yeats as an example of a poet who succeeded in establishing himself as a cultural spokesperson in the broadest sense: "In terms of the writer conducting himself in a politicized milieu, I think what is exemplary about him is that Yeats becomes important within that milieu not so much for what he says as for who he is. Now, what I mean is that within a culture the most important thing for the poet is to establish authority."[46] Years later, by the time of his Nobel Lecture "Crediting Poetry," Heaney's own authority as a poetic personage had been resoundingly confirmed; however, the lecture indicates that Heaney still apparently felt a need to reinforce his claim to a specific Northern Irish form of cultural authority: "This temperamental disposition towards an art that was earnest and devoted to things as they are was corroborated by the experience of having been born and brought up in Northern Ireland and of having lived with that place even though I have lived away from it for the past quarter of a century. No place prides itself more on its vigilance and realism, no place considers itself more qualified to censure any flourish of rhetoric or extravagance of aspiration."[47] Clearly, Heaney is aware that simple chronology and geography conspire against his credentials as a Northern Irish insider. Abu-Lughod's concept of the halfie seems inherently more durable, in that it does not insist on some mythical notion of purity with regard to an individual's cultural identity. The *half* in *halfie* is of course a rough estimate. Although Abu-Lughod does not deal directly with the notion, there is nothing in her theory to preclude the establishment of a "thirdie" or some such label for a person whose cultural influences are divided not between two countries or cultures but between three or more. Such a distinction might in fact apply more neatly to Heaney than the halfie label does.

Insofar as Northern Irish culture differs from Irish culture, it would make sense to attempt to distinguish between them in terms of Heaney's cultural influences. Northern Ireland—predominantly Protestant and still very much part of the United Kingdom (the police force, the Police Service of Northern

Ireland, was the Royal Ulster Constabulary until its renaming in November 2001, and Queen Elizabeth's likeness remains on every coin and every piece of paper money)—is to this day quite different from Ireland, which is of course predominantly Catholic and an independent nation. Heaney left Northern Ireland and moved to Ireland in 1972, and he has also lived for significant stretches of time in England, in California[48] (before 1975), and in Massachusetts. A sustained attempt to separate Northern Irish and Irish influences in Heaney's work is, however, best left at the theoretical level, for any attempt to carry out this idea would inevitably muddy the water greatly while producing a number of unanswerable questions about exactly how to identify Irish Protestants, Northern Irish Catholics, and the cultural influences at work when such people live and work (as many Northern Irish do) among people of both backgrounds. The salient point in this is that Heaney's cultural influences, if not his cultural loyalties, are complex and difficult to distinguish from one another.

When Heaney was to be included in the *Penguin Book of Contemporary British Poetry* in 1982, he sent the editors a verse epistle that reads, in part "Be advised, my passport's green. / No glass of ours was ever raised / To toast the Queen." This is about as close to a sectarian outburst as Heaney gets. Despite this strain of anti-British feeling, Heaney often manifests an awareness of his divided cultural position. He is a Northern Irish Catholic, part of the first generation of this group to see an end to institutionalized discrimination against Catholics in most aspects of Northern Irish life and a direct beneficiary of these social changes. (Previous generations of Northern Irish Catholics did not have the educational or employment opportunities made available to Heaney's generation.) He is also part of British literary culture (regardless of his feelings about his citizenship and his passport status), as well as a participant-observer who is studying his own culture. Heaney has spoken elsewhere about the double reality of being British and Irish—what he describes as "dwelling amphibiously in London literary life as well as Dublin literary life"—and says that he has had to live with "being more than a little bit British. I mean, I've lived total British culture for many years now. When I talked about the doubleness I was suggesting to the Unionist collective that they could live with two realities. Their Britishness is not threatened if they say, 'Oh, we're in Ireland too, damn it all.'"[49]

Henry Hart and Michael Parker point out a remarkable set of passport-related facts about Heaney's 2006 volume *District and Circle*, though neither relates those facts to Heaney's "my passport's green" verse epistle. Hart notes that the title "refers to the District and Circle lines in the London Underground that the twenty-three-year-old Heaney rode to a holiday job in 1962."[50] Parker says of the title poem, "Its origins lie in memories of a much earlier time, the summer of 1962 when the Queen's graduate [Heaney had graduated from Queen's University Belfast in 1961] was employed in London's Passport Office in Petty France and traveled regularly on the District Line."[51] On a related note, Jonathan O'Brien has pointed out that "[Heaney] revealed that he used to carry a British passport when visiting Lourdes in the 1960s."[52]

Given Heaney's complex matrix of cultural influences and identifications, it should come as no surprise that his negotiation of such issues in his poetry is not entirely consistent. What is somewhat surprising is that the inconsistency has less to do with cultural hybridity or identification with British culture than it has to do with different strategies by which Heaney effectively establishes and maintains his implicit claims to Northern Irishness and the insider or halfie ethnographic perspectives it makes possible. The Heaney who acknowledges his Britishness, however fractional that might be, exists only outside his poetry. There are two categories of poems by which Heaney demonstrates or establishes his credentials as an insider or halfie ethnographer: (1) Poems in which he does this through the use of specifically Northern Irish or Irish language such as idiomatic local usages, Irish-language words, and Irish place names; and (2) Poems in which he does this by way of his actions or thoughts within the text of the poem, poems in which the plot details sometimes identify him as an ethnographic participant-observer; sometimes, though, the poet becomes more participant than observer.

For readers unfamiliar with the Irish language, Heaney's use of Irish (or Irish-derived) words and place names is more or less impossible to overlook. Because Heaney's poetry is for the most part so reader friendly—so linear in its narrative progressions, so faithful to standard syntax and sentence structure, so apparently committed to a poetics of clarity and accuracy—such moments of nonstandard English usage or unfamiliar combinations of sounds stand out. Heaney's much-remarked-upon interest in etymology (that is, in the origins, the histories, and especially the submerged meanings of words) often manifests itself in ways that are specifically related to the Irish language or Northern Irish local usage and pronunciation, which at times differs markedly from pronunciation in some areas of Ireland, and sometimes varies significantly within the same area of Northern Ireland. In Northern Ireland, for example, the *gh* letter combination lives a double life in speech, often within the same word. Some Northern Irish people pronounce the *gh* as something like *ck* in words such as Bellaghy and Magherafelt, while others pronounce that letter combination in the same words with a soft *h* sound.

Heaney addresses this practical element of Northern Irish linguistic instability in the short early poem "Broagh." Readers unfamiliar with Irish pronunciation (which, as mentioned above, confounds even some native Irish and Northern Irish and is a source of amusement to others) must first confront the poem's title, which is a shibboleth of sorts. At first glance, such readers would identify the word as foreign and confusing; they would presumably guess at the pronunciation without much confidence. At the end of the poem, Heaney refers directly to the uncertainty the title word creates for such readers because of "that last / gh the strangers found / difficult to manage."[53] This description collapses Irish history (in which *strangers* is a traditional pejorative figure of speech used to identify the colonizing and occupying British as non-Irish) and the experience of contemporary readers who are unfamiliar with the Irish language (readers who are strangers in another sense) while demonstrating to audiences familiar with Irish and to linguistic strangers that Heaney is a cultural insider firmly in command of the shibboleth.

In the later poem "Alphabets" (presented as the Phi Beta Kappa poem at Harvard University in 1984), Heaney briefly addresses this variety of Northern Irish linguistic doubleness again in a depiction of a young boy who appears to be a version of Heaney himself. The boy, who is too young to attend school, learns about this linguistic instability as his father teaches him the letters of the alphabet: "Two rafters and a cross-tie on the slat / Are the letter some call *ah*, some call *ay*."[54] Whereas "Broagh" exposes Irish and Northern Irish linguistic instability at the level of the word or the phoneme, "Alphabets" takes things one step farther by insisting that this instability inheres in Irish English even at the level of the individual letter. Again, this is the type of observation that distinguishes Heaney from the vast majority of his readers, most of whom are likely unfamiliar with these elements of Irish and Northern Irish linguistic instability.

In "Whatever You Say Say Nothing," Heaney presents himself as both ethnographer and native informant, a literary embodiment of Abu-Lughod's theories about halfie ethnography, a participant-observer who both registers his own presence in the poem and identifies himself as the writer of the text: "I'm writing this just after an encounter / With an English journalist in search of 'views / On the Irish thing'." Heaney also indicates the extent to which media coverage of Northern Ireland's social violence has functioned as a sort of popular ethnography, a series of portrayals of Northern Irish society via journalists' summations of the situation:

> 'Backlash' and 'crack down', 'the provisional wing',
> 'Polarization' and 'long-standing hate'.
> Yet I live here, I live here too, I sing,
> Expertly civil-tongued with civil neighbours

A few lines later, Heaney moves from quoting the clichéd words of journalists reporting on Northern Ireland's sectarian violence to quoting the words of these "civil neighbours":

> 'Oh, it's disgraceful, surely, I agree.'
> 'Where's it going to end?' 'It's getting worse.'

'They're murderers.' 'Internment, understandably . . .'
The 'voice of sanity' is getting hoarse.

III

'Religion's never mentioned here,' of course.
'You know them by their eyes,' and hold your tongue.
'One side's as bad as the other,' never worse.
Christ, it's near time that some small leak was sprung

In the great dikes the Dutchman made
To dam the dangerous tide that followed Seamus.
Yet for all this art and sedentary trade
I am incapable. The famous

Northern reticence, the tight gag of place
And times: yes, yes. Of the 'wee six' I sing
Where to be saved you only must save face
And whatever you say, you say nothing.[55]

The poem is largely an ethnographic meditation on Yeatsian polite meaningless words, the kinds of politically safe platitudes that residents of Northern Ireland often use in order to speak about the ongoing sectarian conflict without clearly taking sides (or at least without making it clear which sides they take in private).

The insider or halfie element of Heaney's ethnography in this poem is especially evident to most American readers. The references to "the provisional wing" (the Provisional Irish Republican Army—also known as the Provos—the full name of the group that is usually identified simply as the IRA in American media), "the Dutchman" (William of Orange, the Dutch-born king of England whose victory over James II at the Battle of the Boyne in 1690 is generally recognized as the beginning of Protestant English rule over Ireland and the widespread oppression of the Catholic majority; *Seamus* is the Irish equivalent of James—a reference in this case to James II and his Catholic followers), and *the wee six* (the six counties of Northern Ireland) would likely baffle most readers who come from outside Northern Ireland or Ireland. Throughout the poem, Heaney acts as both an ethnographer and a bitterly ironic native commentator, juxtaposing his own assessments of Northern Irish society with quotations from other residents—quotations he stages carefully, comments on cuttingly, and undermines even as he asserts their status as representative views on the Irish thing.

Heaney sounded a more encouraging note in a 2009 interview with Marie-Louise Muir when Muir interviewed Heaney in Bellaghy and asked him about the outbreak of violence in Northern Ireland in March 2009 (two British soldiers and a police officer were shot to death in two separate incidents that served as reminders that the social conflict of the Troubles had not entirely disappeared): "For years . . . the word terrorism would have been a contested term . . . and for years . . . terrorist activity had a sneaking relationship to the secret middle class liberal persons on both sides . . . it's bad, bad, bad, but . . . there was some sanction . . . at a subtle underground unmentionable level . . . too bad . . . it's terrible . . . but . . . glory be to god . . . the but has gone out of the discourse."[56] This is an important quotation because of how it relates to Heaney's earlier statements about language use in Northern Ireland. Once again, Heaney's work pays close attention to significant words choices in Northern Irish discourse. Here Heaney indicates that the tacit endorsement of terrorism is no longer present in the general cultural conversation, an indication that stands as an optimistic counterpoint to any perceived sense that the sectarian conflict described in Heaney's poems is impossible to get beyond.

Lesser instances of Heaney's attention to language appear in early poems such as "Fodder," "Anahorish," and "The Stations of the West." The title and the first two lines of "Fodder" set up a cultural and linguistic contrast similar to the one in "Broagh." Readers first encounter the title, then the poem immediately corrects their pronunciation in its opening words: "Or, as we said, / fother."[57] "Anahorish" also opens with a sort of correction, a translation of the title word for the benefit of the uninitiated reader: "My 'place of clear water.' "[58]

A significantly more disturbing kind of cultural insider status appears in the later poem "The Flight Path." The poem's fourth section (which is the first section that Heaney included in *Opened Ground* and thus effectively functions there as the beginning of the poem) opens with a statement of its suitability for inclusion in the Heaney canon and perhaps in the arena of public debate about the situation in Northern Ireland: "The following for the record, in the light / Of everything before and since."[59] The poem then recounts a dream in which Heaney—at the behest of an unidentified acquaintance—takes part in some sort of unspecified cross-border smuggling that appears to be connected to republican nationalism, perhaps a shipment of weapons or explosives, although this too is unclear. The poem then returns to waking consciousness and the poet encounters the unidentified acquaintance, who confronts Heaney with a pointed question about the cultural loyalties of his poetry: "When, for fuck's sake, are you going to write / Something for us?"[60] The *us* is interesting, because it could refer to a group the poet does not belong to, or it could refer to a group that includes the poet.

Because of the ambiguity surrounding the illegal dream errand, and because Heaney has at times been attacked more or less simultaneously by critics from both sides of the Northern Irish social divide, this simple pronoun is less than clear. It is tempting to say that the *us* must refer to Catholics and therefore must include Heaney.[61] After all, a few lines later the poem mentions Long Kesh (a.k.a. Maze Prison—officially HM Prison Maze—the site of the fatal 1981 hunger strikes by

Bobby Sands and nine other Republican prisoners), and the next section of the poem acts as a reminder of the daily presence of the Troubles, as well as a reminder of Heaney's place in them as part of Northern Ireland's Catholic minority:

> When I answered that I came from 'far away',
> The policeman at the roadblock snapped, 'Where's that?'
> He'd only half-heard what I said and thought
> It was the name of some place up the country.
> And now it is—both where I have been living
> And where I left—a distance still to go
> Like starlight that is light years on the go
> From far away and takes light years arriving.[62]

Instead of clarifying the *us* and cementing Heaney's allegiance to place and social group, this section blurs these distinctions by emphasizing Heaney's suspension between points, a condition rendered that much more uncertain because of its rendering in terms of light.

Heaney offers no such impartial image of himself in "Punishment," offering instead an unsettling identification with sectarian violence beyond that of the dream in "The Flight Path." "Punishment" marks an important transition from the imaginative archaeological stance of Heaney's earlier bog poems to an engaged ethnographic participant-observer perspective. A return to Lloyd's complaints about "Punishment" will serve two purposes. First, it will serve as a reminder that one critic's trash is another critic's treasure by allowing me to highlight the work of another critic who praises the poem (and much of the rest of Heaney's work) because of some of the same elements Lloyd deplores. Second, it will obligate me to point out some of the salient differences between a literary perspective—no matter how ethnographic it may be in spirit—and the mode of ethnography traditionally recognized within professional and disciplinary boundaries.

Lloyd disapproves of "Punishment" on the grounds that it demonstrates insufficient engagement with the scene of social violence it describes and therefore aestheticizes the violence to the exclusion of more meaningful involvement. Paul Scott Stanfield sees in the poem an involvement of a different sort, one that is essentially an ethnographic participant-observer stance, although Stanfield does not identify it as such: "The crucial twist in 'Punishment' comes with the revelation that the poet half-participates as well in the other dimension of punishment, that of the crowd, the community that feels itself wronged . . . he had been one who 'would connive in civilized outrage,' civilized outrage being as much a tacit consent as disguised participation, as silence and inaction."[63] Unlike Lloyd, however, Stanfield considers this perspective to be among the poem's great strengths. He says of the conflicting sympathies inherent in the poem's participant-observer perspective, "They contend, but none finally dominates. This is the poem's peculiar virtue." Stanfield goes on to mention James Lafferty's discussion of the poem's "double perspective" and John Westlake's praise of the poem's "equivocal position" and "transparent honesty."[64]

Stanfield's next critical move draws an ethnography-minded reader's attention to what are perhaps the limits of ethnographic literary criticism, largely because Stanfield appears not to make the crucial distinction between an ethnographic poetics and the disciplinary practices of traditional professional ethnographers: "By concentrating on showing how these strands co-exist and interact rather than on making one or the other dominate, Heaney approaches the 'polyphony' Bakhtin ascribes to Dostoevsky's novels, in which no character, no voice among the contending voices, is granted ultimate authority." Stanfield quickly qualifies this statement:

> It may seem inappropriate to use the term "polyphony"—created to describe a kind of novel—in regard to a lyric poem which we think of as necessarily governed by a single voice. It may seem doubly inappropriate to use it of a poem by Heaney whose "*timbre*, a sound so familiar that it could border on self-parody, left little room for tone, the assumption of new voices or the adjustment of voice to audience," according to at least one perceptive critic, Dillon Johnston. I feel, however, that the deliberate symmetry of the juxtapositions in "Punishment," the clarity and immediacy with which it represents irreconcilable movements of thought, deserve to be called polyphonic rather than ambivalent.[65]

Stanfield's insistence on the applicability of the term *polyphony* to this poem (and, by extension, to much of Heaney's work) obscures some important points. The term *polyphony* does not in fact owe its origin to criticism of the novel; it has a long and separate life of its own in music and philology. This sort of hairsplitting is perhaps worthwhile at this point because it relates to another way in which Stanfield appears to overlook some of the simple implications of his claims. It is important to note, however, that Stanfield's ideas are not at odds with the ideas of some contemporary ethnographic theorists who emphasize the constructedness, the literariness, and the fictive elements of all ethnographic accounts.

Despite the similarities between Stanfield's claims and some contemporary ethnographic thought, Stanfield's readings of voices in Heaney's poems seem too often to take the ethnographic elements of Heaney's work at face value or too literally. In discussing the issue of voice in Heaney's work, for example, Stanfield writes, "In the later 'Station Island' sequence we see a plainer attempt at internalized drama and hear a host of voices other than Heaney's."[66] While examining Heaney's landmark 1975 volume *North*, Stanfield elaborates on his ideas about polyvocality in Heaney's work: "[*North*] refuses to privilege . . . the voice of the individual reason over that of the community's instinct, instead letting these two voices co-exist, interact, contend without declaring a victor. This is not to mythologize or explain away violence but merely to grant it the reality and immediacy that our newspapers daily witness and to let us know it to the bone as newspapers never possibly could. It is, in a word, *truthful*—truthful in a way it could never be did it not let the tribe's jealous all-demanding matrix of loyalties speak in its own unimpeded voice."[67] In his essay's conclusion, Stanfield says of Heaney's poetry, "Its truth lies in what I have called its polyphony."[68] It would be easy—and perhaps a bit unfair—to subject Stanfield's prose to the same type of scrutiny Heaney's work encounters. In doing so even briefly, it becomes evident that Stanfield's earnest declaration about where the truth lies resembles the sort of duplicitous or self-deconstructing wording often associated with Heaney—wording that seems innocent enough on the surface but conceals suggestions other than the ones it offers at first glance. Stanfield unwittingly suggests the problem with his argument in favor of what he identifies as polyphony in Heaney's work by way of his word choice: Heaney's polyphony lies insofar as it is not an accurate ethnographic record of conversations between the participant-observer and one or more informants.

By believing wholeheartedly that Heaney's poetry speaks authoritatively and comprehensively for an entire community, Stanfield takes things too literally, and in doing so he indirectly calls attention to the limits of an ethnographic approach to literature. He overlooks the simple fact that all the voices in the poems are mediated, if not created outright, by Heaney. In assigning Heaney's authorial voice ("the individual reason") the additional authority of the society's will at a sort of preconscious level ("the community's instinct"), Stanfield falls into the trap of essentialism not long after warning that Heaney's periodic explanations of Northern Irish social violence as a form of ongoing tribal warfare risk essentializing the Troubles and making the sectarian violence seem inevitable.

Gupta and Ferguson explain the effects of contemporary ethnographic theories that move from assertions of the inherently constructed status of written ethnographic accounts—assertions that minimize the above distinctions between creative ethnography and traditional professional ethnography—to assertions of the inherently constructed status of any described culture:

> The "polyphony" of ethnographic fieldwork—the many different "voices" present in the actual discussions and dialogues through which ethnographic understandings are constructed—is contrasted with the monophonic authorial voice of the conventional ethnographic monograph. [Many] critiques have implied that anthropology's "cultures" must be seen as less unitary and more fragmented, their boundedness more of a literary fiction—albeit a "serious fiction" [here Gupta and

Ferguson are quoting Clifford]—than as some sort of natural fact. If anthropologists working in this vein continue to speak of "culture," in spite of such concerns, it is with a clear awareness of just how problematic a concept this has become. "Culture," as James Clifford laments, remains "a deeply compromised idea I cannot yet do without."[69]

Although Heaney's work does not go so far as to question the existence or coherence of Northern Irish culture outright, it manifests an awareness of the element of constructedness that Gupta and Ferguson describe. Heaney both perpetuates the fiction of a bounded, coherent Northern Irish culture and exposes it as a fiction by positioning himself as an insider/halfie in some poems and as an outsider/ethnographer in other poems, particularly his Gaeltacht poems, in which he appears as a would-be participant-observer who is largely unable to participate because of the language barrier. He also subverts notions of boundedness and coherence in his repeated assertions of cultural portability—his claims to have lived with Northern Irish culture despite living physically removed from it for a quarter of a century—and his contradictory remarks about living British culture and being more than a little bit British.

The prose poem "The Stations of the West" is the first poem of Heaney's that portrays Heaney in the Gaeltacht, the Irish-speaking areas in the west of Ireland. (Most people in these regions can speak English if necessary, but they often prefer not to.) One can best understand Heaney's familiarity with the Irish language by situating the young Heaney in terms of the politics of Irish language study in Northern Ireland and Ireland: Heaney learned Irish at St. Columb's College in Derry, where he attended boarding school. This would have involved a strict daily regimen of Irish language study taught by a priest who was also a teacher. He would have had a smattering of Irish from his childhood and primary school, but the formal study was required at secondary school only. In Ireland, Irish language study was legally compulsory, but not of course in Northern Ireland, where it was and still is taught mostly in Catholic secondary schools.[70]

"The Stations of the West" dramatizes the difference between English-speaking Ireland and the Gaeltacht regions by portraying the young Heaney's sense of isolation in this area of Irish-language supremacy and presumably authentic Irishness:

> On my first night in the Gaeltacht the old woman spoke to me
> in English: 'You will be all right.' I sat on a twilit bedside
> listening through the wall to fluent Irish, homesick for a speech
> I was to extirpate.[71]

The use of *extirpate* indicates the extent to which the younger Heaney (like a number of Catholic Northern Irish) regarded the English language as inherently undesirable because of its historical association with England's colonial hold on Ireland and Northern Ireland, a sentiment that is historically associated with the Celtic Revival of Yeats's era and the decision of the newly independent Irish Free State to encourage and support the Irish language through school programs and government agencies. Although the poem makes it clear that the younger Heaney was somewhat at sea in the spoken Irish of the Gaeltacht, he emerges with a heightened appreciation of the sounds (and, presumably, of the shibboleth-like qualities) of the Irish place names he has encountered, names that the poem presents almost as touchstones of Irishness: "Rannafast and Errigal, / Annaghry and Kincasslagh: names portable as altar stones, un- / leavened elements."[72]

In his 2001 collection *Electric Light*, Heaney's Gaeltacht poetry makes visible the double nature of his ethnographic literary project. In "The Little Canticles of Asturias," Heaney refers again to his time in the Gaeltacht in a way that makes clear his inability to blend in and achieve either halfie or insider status:

> I was a pilgrim new upon the scene
> Yet entering it as if it were home ground,
> The Gaeltacht, say, in the nineteen fifties,
> Where I was welcome, but of small concern
> To families at work in the roadside fields
> Who'd watch and wave at me from their other world . . .[73]

The Gaeltacht poems, when considered in relation to the rest of Heaney's oeuvre, emphasize the partiality and constructedness of Heaney's ethnographic representations of Northern Irish culture by reminding readers of a core of alternative Irishness that exists in the west of Ireland, a site of culture to which the poet has limited access and of which the poet can ultimately claim only the limited knowledge of the cultural outsider.

The poem "Casualty" shows Heaney moving in Northern Irish society as an ethnographic participant-observer and concentrates on one particular relationship with a native informant, a fisherman who (in real life) regularly drank at the pub owned by Heaney's father-in-law. The poem describes Northern Irish Catholics as "our tribe" but once again presents Heaney struggling to blend in among his native informants:

> Incomprehensible
> To him, my other life.
> Sometimes, on his high stool,

> Too busy with his knife
> At a tobacco plug
> And not meeting my eye,
> In the pause after a slug
> He mentioned poetry.
> We would be on our own
> And, always politic
> And shy of condescension,
> I would manage by some trick
> To switch the talk to eels
> Or lore of the horse and cart
> Or the Provisionals.[74]

When a conversation turns toward poetry—that is, when someone brings up Heaney's field of expertise and his ongoing intellectual work—he quickly steers the conversation back toward subject matter more in line with his ethnographic project.

This visible estrangement of the halfie or native ethnographic consciousness from the home culture shows up again, and more poignantly, in a poetic sequence called "Clearances." Here, Heaney the ethnographic participant-observer describes the awkwardness of dealing with his home culture in the person of his mother. As is often the case in Heaney's poetry, accent and diction are of great importance in terms of establishing where one fits in the social pattern. Heaney says of his adult interactions with his mother, "I governed my tongue / In front of her, a genuinely well- / Adjusted betrayal / Of what I knew better. I'd *naw* and *aye* / And decently relapse into the wrong / Grammar which kept us allied and at bay."[75]

"I governed my tongue" is an echo of the title of Heaney's essay "The Government of the Tongue" and his eponymous essay collection. In the essay, Heaney makes it clear that the title refers not only to disciplining and controlling one's speech but to being disciplined or controlled by it, particularly with regard to Irish Catholics speaking and writing in English, but also with regard to social class divisions. Both the poem and the essay demonstrate Heaney's immersion in multiple environments that fairly demand what Hans Osterwalder identifies as diglossia in Heaney's writing: "Diglossia is defined as the use of two varieties (normally a standard and a non-standard one) of the same language, depending on the function, that is the social context."[76]

Despite the apparent differences between poetry and standard ethnographic texts, claiming a measure of ethnographic authority for poems such as Heaney's is not necessarily at odds with recent ethnographic theory. The explanations of postmodern ethnographic theory provided above make this clear in a general sense. I want to move toward a conclusion by revisiting a critical passage I have cited above (in the Warren chapter) and thereby focusing now on a more specific aspect of ethnographic writing: In "Textual Play, Power, and Cultural Critique: An Orientation to Modernist Anthropology," Manganaro explains Geertz's account of the inherent creative textuality of ethnographic writing in a way that highlights commonalities between ethnography and creative work such as Heaney's: "Geertz's recent book, *Works and Lives: The Anthropologist as Author*, affirms an essentially textual approach to ethnography, claiming that the anthropologist's ability to convince is based primarily not upon the suitability or solidity of fieldwork, but upon the very writerly task of convincing us 'that what they say is a result of having actually penetrated . . . another form of life, of having, one way or another, truly 'been there.' "[77] This recalls an aforementioned remark from Heaney's RTE radio conversation with Richard Ellmann: "Within a culture, the most important thing for the poet is to establish authority." In his Nobel Lecture, Heaney makes it clear that the way a poet may do this is through specificity and accurate representation of local details in poetry: "Its trustworthiness and its travel-worthiness have to do with its local setting."[78]

Clifford asks, rhetorically, "If ethnography produces cultural interpretations through intense research experiences, how is unruly experience transformed into an authoritative written account?" His answer: "The process is complicated by the action of multiple subjectivities and political constraints beyond the control of the writer. In response to these forces ethnographic writing enacts a specific strategy of authority. This strategy has classically involved an unquestioned claim to appear as the purveyor of truth in the text. A complex cultural experience is enumerated by an individual."[79] As contemporary ethnographic theory increasingly indicates and Heaney strongly suggests, ethnographic accounts are always already partial and creative. Heaney is the author of his poems, a persona, a participant-observer, a native informant, and a constant reminder that although his poems may present ongoing polyphonic exchange, the governing intellect behind it all is that of Heaney himself. Because of the multilayered presence of the persona of Heaney moving within the poems as a participant-observer and the existence of the actual Heaney standing outside the poems as the controlling consciousness behind the words, Heaney's poetry (much like Warren's *Brother to Dragons*) self-consciously dramatizes and enacts the problems of perspective, voice, and interpretation that surround ethnographic texts.

Although the first-person participant-observer perspective on Northern Irish culture is not as prominent in *District and Circle* as it is in much of Heaney's previous work, in this collection the ethnographic impulse or the rhetorical strategy of ethnographic authority is arguably even stronger: In its use of full-poem quotation (in the poem "Anahorish 1944"), found poetry (the poem "Poet to Blacksmith," translated from the Irish), and found prose (the three-part sequence entitled "Found Prose") as poems within a collection of Heaney's work, *District and Circle* implicitly indicates that such texts are accurate, important representations of Northern Irish culture and that when presented in such a context such materials are, in themselves, worthy of consideration as poetry.

District and Circle in this sense brings Heaney's ethnographic perspective full circle and thus renders the connections between his work and archaeology described by Stallworthy, McHale, Finn, and Russell more useful in an ethnographic literary context. Heaney's career-long project has emphasized giving voice to his home culture more than examining artifacts per se, an emphasis that makes sense given poetry's necessary emphasis (whether intentional or unavoidable) on words rather than physical objects. Numerous critics have remarked on Heaney's characteristic attention to etymologies. That habit is particularly intriguing when considered in light of anthropology, because Heaney tends to treat individual words as artifacts. This tendency shows clearly in earlier poems such as "Broagh" and "Anahorish."

District and Circle extends this habit of mind in that its found poems and found prose are presented as artifacts themselves. The poem "Anahorish 1944" (the title of which clearly gestures back toward "Anahorish"), for example, is entirely a quotation, as if it were much like the "found prose" that appears later in *District and Circle*, something that is not the product of the poet's imagination so much as the poet's fancy in the Coleridgean sense. In other words, this poem and the found prose pieces in *District and Circle* are presented not as literary creations of the poet's imagination but as authentic moments of almost-unmediated engagement with the words, thoughts, and lives of local people (*almost* unmediated because Heaney has in fact silently selected and presented these pieces as poems, framing them as objects of aesthetic contemplation and selecting them from innumerable native sources).

The unidentified narrator of "Anahorish 1944" is clearly too old to be Heaney himself (who was born in 1939). The narrator recalls that he and unidentified others were slaughtering pigs (I say *he* because it is unlikely that women would have been working in a slaughterhouse in rural County Antrim in the 1940s) when American troops arrived in the area as U.S. forces massed in preparation for D-Day, " 'Not that we knew then / Where they were headed, standing there like youngsters / As they tossed us gum and tubes of coloured sweets.' "[80] Though the syntax of the final sentence draws attention to the fact that many of the soldiers would have been quite young, the primary meaning is that the adult locals stood like children as soldiers distributed candy to them (a basic military public-relations practice that is in use to this day as an attempt to win hearts and minds via stomachs).

Unlike "Anahorish 1944," "The Nod" (a sonnet that also appears in *District and Circle*) employs a narrative voice familiar to Heaney's readers, a voice that seems to be Heaney himself remembering incidents from his youth. The poem's final lines describe recurring moments of sectarian tension from an insider's perspective:

> Saturday evenings too the local B-Men,
> Unbuttoned but on duty, thronged the town,
> Neighbours with guns, parading up and down,
> Some nodding at my father almost past him
> As if deliberately they'd aimed and missed him
> Or couldn't seem to place him, not just then.[81]

The B-Men are of course the notorious B-Specials, and *parading* is a particularly loaded term in Northern Ireland: The issue of regulating parades has been a major sticking point in negotiations over the power-sharing government of Northern Ireland, in part because sectarian parades are major events in Northern Ireland and have often been flashpoints for violence and in part because since 1998 the Northern Ireland Parades Commission has had the power to restrict or prohibit any parades it decides are "contentious." Most parades are organized by Protestant unionist/loyalist groups, and many routes pass through Catholic neighborhoods, but Catholic nationalist/republican groups also organize separate parades, as do some nonpolitical groups. (A section of Heaney's "Singing School" called "Orange Drums, Tyrone, 1966" deals directly with a Protestant parade.) The choice of the word *aimed* in describing the nods the armed Protestants directed toward their Catholic neighbor in "The Nod" is also an important part of the poem given the climate of tension the poem establishes via describing the B-Specials and their guns.

Perhaps the most remarkable thing about the three-part prose poem "Found Prose" is not even visible in the poem itself. As Dennis O'Driscoll explains in the introduction to his *Stepping Stones: Interviews with Seamus Heaney*, Heaney wrote almost all the poems in *District and Circle* during the years when he sat for that series of interviews with O'Driscoll: "Some poems ('Anahorish 1944' 'Tate's Avenue' and 'Home Help', for instance) drew their initial inspiration from the ongoing interviews; others were excerpted directly from Chapter 8 as the opening sections of 'Found Prose' and 'Out of This World.'"[82]

In effect, O'Driscoll's remarks show how in *District and Circle* Heaney both builds upon and employs his already-established ethnographic/poetic status, the status of a truth-telling participant-observer that is so inextricably linked with his renderings of the political and social elements that pervade his work. Heaney continues to act as his own ethnographic native informant and in "Found Prose" does so even more than usual by treating transcripts of his own remarks as raw material that shows significant truths about Northern Irish culture and simultaneously deserves consideration as a prose poem.

Stephen James has written about the sense of poetic authority that pervades Heaney's work: "By poetic authority I mean the rights and weight which accrue to a voice not only because of a sustained history of truth-telling but by virtue also of its tonality, the sway it gains over the deep ear and, through that, over other parts of our mind and nature." Although James does not approach the ethnographic elements of Heaney's work, his description of poetic authority is, if anything, even more useful in an ethnographic literary context because it draws attention to the "rights and weight which accrues to a voice . . . because of a sustained history of truth-telling." James also refers to "a larger narrative (some might say a mythology) of rootedness in Heaney's work, an authenticating of cultural identity through remembered childhood experience."[83]

Heaney's 2010 collection *Human Chain* continues this authentication of cultural poetic authority via full-poem quotations, translations from medieval Irish texts, and the inclusion of Irish words in the section titles of a poem sequence that blends medieval Irish elements with Latin (a language strongly associated with Catholicism and thus a significant cultural marker in Ireland and Northern Ireland). The title of the poem sequence "Sweeney Out-Takes" gestures back toward Heaney's 1983 *Sweeney Astray: A Version from the Irish* (a translation of the *Buile Shuibhne* or *Buile Suibhne*) as well as the "Sweeney Redivivus" section of Heaney's 1984 collection *Station Island*. "Sweeney Out-Takes" presents each of its three 12-line sections entirely as quotations, thereby positioning them as something like artifacts in a process similar to the presentation of found prose and the quotation poems in *District and Circle*. The poem sequence "Colum Cille Cecinit" further strengthens the sense of Heaney's cultural poetic authority by way of multiple levels of necessary interpretation. "Cecinit" is Latin for "sang" and "has sung"; "Colum Cille" means "dove of the church" and is the Irish name of St. Columba or St. Colmcille (for whom Heaney's boarding school and a cathedral in Derry were named), who appears in "Lick the Pencil," another poem in *Human Chain*. Northern Irish and Irish Catholics (like Catholics anywhere) are far more likely than Protestants or other non-Catholics to have some familiarity with Latin, thus the Latin title stands as a reminder of Heaney's cultural background.

The individual sections add to the implicit cultural significance of "Colum Cille Cecinit" by presenting readers with section titles in Irish. The sections are translations of early Irish lyrics attributed to St. Colmcille, complete with Irish titles that confront readers with the original version of the first line of each translated section: "Is scíth mo chrob ón scríbainn" (translated by Heaney as "My hand is cramped from penwork."); "Is aire charaim Doire" (translated by Heaney as "Derry I cherish ever."); and "Fil súil nglais" (translated by Heaney as "a grey eye will look back," though this line has been translated by others as "a blue eye looks back"). Heaney includes a brief note—"11th/12th CENTURY"—at the end of the sequence. Although these elements are not ethnographic in any direct way, they—like salient parts of *District and Circle*—buttress Heaney's ethnographic/ poetic authority by contributing to the sense of anthropological awareness and overall cultural expertise inherent in so much of his work.[84]

District and Circle and *Human Chain* extend the sense of poetic authority in Heaney's work, in part by treating translations and entire quotations as ethnographic resources and in part by presenting them as both poetry and more or less unmediated truth. These elements are presented not as imaginative quotations from ghostly figures such as the bombing victim of "Casualty" or the ghost of Heaney's murdered cousin Colum McCartney and the other local spirits in "Station Island" (quotations that are generally understood to be primarily products of Heaney's imagination) but as both artifacts and facts, quotations in which Heaney fulfills a complex ethnographic role: staging, controlling, and even creating quotations, thereby governing the text and the tongue as and so the subject culture seemingly speaks for itself.

The question all this prompts is germane to much of Heaney's work and is crucial to ethnographic literary criticism: What is being authenticated, the portrayal of culture in Heaney's poetry or the portrayer of culture, Heaney himself? Ethnographic approaches to literature provoke readers to think about the extent to which it is possible to answer such questions about Heaney; the extent to which the cases of Heaney, Warren, Frost, and Yeats suggest useful ethnographic approaches to the works of other authors; and even the extent to which the question above could upon closer inspection prove to be a false dichotomy.

Notes

Introduction

1. James Clifford, *The Predicament of Culture: Twentieth-Century Ethnography, Literature, and Art* (Cambridge: Harvard University Press, 1988), 9.

2. Arjun Appadurai, "Global Ethnoscapes: Notes and Queries for a Transnational Anthropology," in *Recapturing Anthropology: Working in the Present*, ed. Richard G. Fox (Santa Fe, NM: School of American Research Press, 1991), 195–96.

3. Ibid., 196.

4. Clifford Geertz, *After the Fact: Two Countries, Four Decades, One Anthropologist* (Cambridge, MA: Harvard University Press, 1995), 62.

5. Lila Abu-Lughod, "Writing against Culture," in *Recapturing Anthropology: Working in the Present*, ed. Richard G. Fox (Santa Fe, NM: School of American Research Press, 1991), 138.

6. Luke Eric Lassiter, "Authoritative Texts, Collaborative Ethnography, and Native American Studies," *The American Indian Quarterly* 24, no. 4 (2000): 605. Lassiter's use of *evolving* presumes/constructs a fiction of organic development. The use of *consultant* rather than *informant* is not uncommon in recent ethnography, though it is not yet standard practice. I favor the traditional term throughout this book primarily to minimize confusion.

7. E. Valentine Daniel, "The Coolie," *Cultural Anthropology* 23, no. 2 (2008): 254–55. Like Lassiter's word choices, Daniel's make it sound—not entirely coherently or consistently—as if there were

some organic form to the piece of writing. This leaves a reader unsure whether, if pressed, Daniel would ultimately say that he chose the verse form, as he says later in the passage, or that it somehow chose itself, as he says earlier in the passage.

8. "Editors' Overview," *Cultural Anthropology*, accessed July 8, 2011, http://www .culanth.org/?q=node/144. This website contains the editors' statement.

9. Lassiter, "Authoritative Texts," 610.

10. Quetzil E. Castañeda, "The Invisible Theatre of Ethnography: Performative Principles of Fieldwork," *Anthropological Quarterly* 79, no. 1 (2006): 79–80.

11. George Marcus, "The Passion of Anthropology in the U.S., Circa 2004," *Anthropological Quarterly* 78, no. 3 (2005): 678. Malinowski's posthumously published diaries generated considerable controversy because they revealed Malinowski's racist views regarding the purported inferiority of the Trobriand Island people he studied, his frequent use of insulting terms to describe them, and his own sexual thoughts about them.

12. Ibid., 686–88.

13. Eric Aronoff, "Anthropologists, Indians, and New Critics: Culture and/as Poetic Form in Regional Modernism," *Modern Fiction Studies* 55, no. 1 (Spring 2009): 93.

14. Marc Manganaro, "Textual Play, Power, and Cultural Critique: An Orientation to Modernist Anthropology," in *Modernist Anthropology: From Fieldwork to Text*, ed. Marc Manganaro (Princeton, NJ: Princeton University Press, 1990), 5.

15. Jahan Ramazani, "A Transnational Poetics," *American Literary History* 18, no. 2 (2006): 332–33.

16. Richard van Oort, "The Critic as Ethnographer," *New Literary History* 35, no. 4 (2004): 622.

17. Ibid., 624.

18. Ibid., 638.

19. Yiorgos Anagnostou, "Metaethnography in the Age of 'Popular Folklore,'" *Journal of American Folklore* 119, no. 4 (2006): 382–83.

20. Geertz, *After the Fact*, 133.

Chapter 1

1. Edward M. Bruner, "The Ethnographic Self and the Personal Self," in *Anthropology and Literature*, ed. Paul Benson (Urbana: University of Illinois Press, 1993), 14.

2. Robin Ridington, "A Tree That Stands Burning: Reclaiming a Point of View as from the Center," in *Anthropology and Literature*, ed. Paul Benson (Urbana: University of Illinois Press, 1993), 48.

3. Derek Hand, "Breaking Boundaries, Creating Spaces: W. B. Yeats's *The Words upon the Window-Pane* as a Postcolonial Text," in *W. B. Yeats and Postcolonialism*, ed. Deborah Fleming (West Cornwall, CT: Locust Hill, 2001), 188.

4. Brian Phillips, "Everything and Nothing in Yeats," *Hudson Review* 57, no. 1 (2004): 144.

5. Seamus Deane, *Celtic Revivals: Essays in Modern Irish Literature, 1880–1980* (London: Faber & Faber, 1985), 40.

6. George W. Stocking, *Victorian Anthropology* (New York: Free Press, 1987), 189.

7. Ibid., 191.

8. Ibid., 287.

9. Michael Valdez Moses, "The Rebirth of Tragedy: Yeats, Nietzsche, the Irish National Theatre, and the Anti-Modern Cult of Cuchulain," *Modernism/modernity* 11, no. 3 (2004): 565.

10. Russell McDonald, "The Reception of W. B. Yeats in Europe," *Comparative Literature Studies* 45, no. 3 (2008): 415.

11. Jonathan Allison, "Magical Nationalism, Lyric Poetry, and the Marvellous: W. B. Yeats and Seamus Heaney," in *A Companion to Magical Realism*, ed. Stephen M. Hart and Wen-ching Ouyang (London: Tamesis, 2005), 228–30.

12. Yiorgos Anagnostou, "Metaethnography in the Age of 'Popular Folklore,'" *Journal of American Folklore* 119, no. 4 (2006): 384.

13. Arnold Krupat, *Ethnocriticism: Ethnography, History, Literature* (Berkeley: University of California Press, 1992), 69.

14. Ibid., 64.

15. Ibid., 90.

16. Ibid., 92.

17. Ibid., 93.

18. R. F. Foster, *W. B. Yeats: A Life. Volume I: The Apprentice Mage, 1865–1914* (Oxford: Oxford University Press, 1999), 130.

19. Deborah Fleming, "'Sing whatever is well made': W. B. Yeats and Postcolonialism," in *W. B. Yeats and Postcolonialism*, ed. Deborah Fleming (West Cornwall, CT: Locust Hill, 2001), xiv.

20. Declan Kiberd, *Inventing Ireland: The Literature of the Modern Nation* (London: Jonathan Cape, 1995), 30.

21. Ibid., 32.

22. Rached Khalifa, "W. B. Yeats: Theorizing the Irish Nation," in *W. B. Yeats and Postcolonialism*, ed. Deborah Fleming. (West Cornwall, CT: Locust Hill Press, 2001), 281.

23. Deane, *Celtic Revivals*, 22.

24. Ibid., 25.

25. Ibid., 34.

26. David Krause, "The De-Yeatsification Cabal," in *Yeats's Political Identities: Selected Essays*, ed. Jonathan Allison (Ann Arbor: University of Michigan Press, 1996), 293.

27. Jahan Ramazani, "A Transnational Poetics," *American Literary History* 18, no. 2 (2006): 340.

28. W. B. Yeats, *Uncollected Prose: Early Reviews and Articles, 1897–1939, Vol. 1*, ed. John P. Frayne. (New York: Columbia University Press, 1970–76), 369.

29. W. B. Yeats, "Irish Wonders," National Library of Ireland Yeats Collection, MS #12147, 17.

30. Ibid., 18.

31. Ibid., 20.

32. W. B. Yeats, *Essays and Introductions* (New York: Macmillan, 1961), 42.

33. Ibid., 44–45.

34. Ibid., 46–47.

35. Ibid., 46–48.

36. Ibid., 522.

37. Ibid., 31.

38. Ibid., 34.

39. W. B. Yeats, *The Celtic Twilight: and a Selection of Early Poems* (New York: New American Library, 1962), 88–89.

40. Yeats, *Essays and Introductions*, 32.

41. R. B. Kershner, "Yeats/Bakhtin/Orality/Dyslexia," in *Yeats and Postmodernism*, ed. Leonard Orr (Syracuse, NY: Syracuse University Press, 1991), 170.

42. Ibid., 176. In emphasizing Yeats's dyslexia, Kershner effectively argues that the subject of Yeats's well-known poem "The Fascination

of What's Difficult" is at least in part the basic acts of reading and writing.

43. Edith Turner, "Poetics and Experience in Anthropological Writing," in *Anthropology and Literature*, ed. Paul Benson (Urbana: University of Illinois Press, 1993), 33.

44. Kershner, "Yeats/Bakhtin/Orality/Dyslexia," 185.

45. Augusta Gregory, *Visions and Beliefs in the West of Ireland Collected and Arranged by Lady Gregory: With Two Essays and Notes by W. B. Yeats*, The Coole Edition of Lady Gregory's Works, vol. 1 (London: Colin Smythe, 1992), 278.

46. George W. Stocking, *Victorian Anthropology* (New York: Free Press, 1987), 65.

47. Gregory, *Visions and Beliefs*, 279.

48. Ibid., 281.

49. R. F. Foster, "Protestant Magic: W. B. Yeats and the Spell of Irish History," in *Yeats's Political Identities: Selected Essays*, ed. Jonathan Allison (Ann Arbor: University of Michigan Press, 1996), 171.

50. Innismurray or Innishmurray is a few miles north of Sligo Bay off the west coast of Ireland.

51. W. B. Yeats, "Tales from the Twilight," National Library of Ireland Yeats Collection, Notebook #25.

52. W. B. Yeats, "The Irish Dramatic Movement: A Letter to the Students at a California School" (typescript draft version), National Library of Ireland Yeats Collection, MS #461.

53. Bruner, "The Ethnographic Self and the Personal Self," 5–6.

54. W. B. Yeats, *Essays and Introductions*, 314.

55. Ibid., 173.

56. Ibid., 181.

57. W. B. Yeats, *Later Essays*, ed. William H. O'Donnell (New York: Scribner, 1994), 221–22.

58. Ibid., 222.

59. Ibid., 223.

60. Ibid., 224–5.

61. National Library of Ireland Yeats Collection, MS #5918.

62. Yeats, *Later Essays*, 228.

63. Ronald Schliefer, "Yeats's Postmodern Rhetoric," in *Yeats and Postmodernism*, ed. Leonard Orr (Syracuse, NY: Syracuse University Press, 1991), 25.

64. Adam Trexler, "Veiled Theory: The Transmutation of Anthropology in T. S. Eliot's Critical Method," *Paragraph* 29, no, 3 (2006): 83.

65. Ibid., 79.

66. Kershner, "Yeats/Bakhtin/Orality/Dyslexia," 177.

67. Yeats, *Essays and Introductions*, 154.

68. Kiberd, *Inventing Ireland*, 119.

69. Paul Muldoon, "7, Middagh Street," in *Selected Poems 1968–1986* (New York: Farrar, Strauss, and Giroux, 1993), 134.

70. Richard Rankin Russell, "W. B. Yeats and Eavan Boland: Postcolonial Poets," in *W. B. Yeats and Postcolonialism*, ed. Deborah Fleming (West Cornwall, CT: Locust Hill, 2001), 115.

71. Akhil Gupta, "The Song of the Nonaligned World: Transnational Identities and the Reinscription of Space in Late Capitalism," in *Culture, Power, Place: Explorations in Critical Anthropology*, ed. Akhil Gupta and James Ferguson (Durham, NC: Duke University Press, 1997), 196.

72. Khalifa, "W. B. Yeats: Theorizing the Irish Nation," 285.

73. Gupta, "The Song of the Nonaligned World," 189–91.

74. Foster, "Protestant Magic," 86.

75. Ibid., 92.

76. Seamus Heaney, *Opened Ground: Poems, 1966–1996* (London: Faber & Faber, 1998), 126.

77. W. B. Yeats, *Senate Speeches*, ed. Donald R. Pearce (New York: Macmillan, 1961), 99.

78. W. B. Yeats, *The Collected Works of W. B. Yeats Volume I: The Poems*, ed. Richard Finneran (New York: Scribner, 1996), 108.

79. Ibid., 109.

80. Ibid., 180.

81. Ibid., 207.

82. Ibid., 461.

83. Gregory, *Visions and Beliefs*, 282.

84. Ibid., 283.

85. John Paul Riquelme, "The Negativity of Modernist Authenticity/ The Authenticity of Modernist Negativity: 'No Direction Home' in Yeats, Dylan, and Wilde," *Modernism/modernity* 14, no. 3 (2007): 541n6.

86. Trexler, "Veiled Theory," 89.

87. Moses, "The Rebirth of Tragedy," 565.

88. Ibid., 568.

89. Foster, "Protestant Magic," 97.

90. Ibid., 98.

91. Ibid., 104n43.

92. Yeats, *Later Essays*, 456–57n68.

93. Kiberd notes that modern Ireland has done the same, effectively inventing and promoting purportedly authentic national cultural forms, including Gaelic football.

Chapter 2

1. R. Clifton Spargo mentions the misperception (widespread in certain literary circles) that "Frost was a poet for readers who didn't much care for poetry, not to mention critical thought or conceptual difficulty." Spargo, "Robert Frost and the Allure of Consensus," *Raritan* 28, no. 3 (2009): 39.

2. James Clifford, *The Predicament of Culture: Twentieth-Century Ethnography, Literature, and Art* (Cambridge, MA: Harvard University Press, 1988), 4.

3. Akhil Gupta and James Ferguson, "Culture, Power, Place: Ethnography at the End of an Era," in *Culture, Power, Place: Explorations in Critical Anthropology,* ed. Akhil Gupta and James Ferguson (Durham, NC: Duke University Press, 1997), 8.

4. John C. Kemp, *Robert Frost and New England: The Poet as Regionalist* (Princeton, NJ: Princeton University Press, 1979), 170.

5. Jeffrey S. Cramer, *Robert Frost Among His Poems: A Literary Companion to the Poet's Own Biographical Contexts and Associations* (Jefferson, NC: McFarland & Company, 1996), 63.

6. Maria Farland, "Modernist Versions of Pastoral: Poetic Inspiration, Scientific Expertise, and the 'Degenerate' Farmer," *American Literary History* 19, no. 4 (2007): 907. Farland examines *North of Boston* rather than Frost's work as a whole. She focuses on Frost's "Mending Wall" because of the narrator's comparison of the neighbor to a savage but does not generally position Frost as an ethnographer or describe his work as ethnographic.

7. Ibid., 907–8.

8. Andrew Lakritz, "Frost in Transition," in *Roads Not Taken: Rereading Robert Frost,* ed. Earl J. Wilcox and Jonathan N. Barron (Columbia: University of Missouri Press, 2000), 211.

9. Gupta and Ferguson, "Culture, Power, Place," 9.

10. Robert Frost, *Robert Frost: Collected Poems, Prose, and Plays,* ed. Richard Poirier and Mark Richardson (New York: Library of America, 1995), 684.

11. Ibid., 685.

12. David Sanders, "Frost's *North of Boston*, Its Language, Its People, and Its Poet." *Journal of Modern Literature* 27, no. 1/2 (2003), 73–74.

13. Ibid., 75–76.

14. Clifford, *Predicament of Culture*, 9.

15. Ibid., 28.

16. Kemp, *Robert Frost*, 27.

17. Ibid., 103.

18. Ibid., 105.

19. Jeffrey N. Wasserstrom, "Anti-Americanisms, Thick Description, and Collective Action," Social Science Research Council, http://www.ssrc.org/sept11/essays/wasserstrom_text_only.htm.

20. Kemp, *Robert Frost*, 49–50.

21. Ibid., 153.

22. Spargo, "Frost and Allure," 48.

23. Robert Frost, *The Notebooks of Robert Frost*, ed. Robert Faggen (Cambridge, MA: Belknap Press of Harvard University Press, 2006), 122.

24. Amy Lowell, *A Critical Fable* (Cambridge, MA: Riverside Press/Houghton Mifflin, 1922), 21.

25. Robert Frost, *Selected Letters of Robert Frost* (New York: Holt, Rinehart, and Winston, 1964), 226.

26. Wendy Griswold and Nathan Wright, "Cowbirds, Locals, and the Dynamic Endurance of Regionalism," *American Journal of Sociology* 109, no. 6 (2004): 1438.

27. Ibid., 1454.

28. Robert Frost, *Robert Frost: Farm-Poultryman; The Story of Robert Frost's Career as a Breeder and Fancier of Hens and the texts of eleven long-forgotten prose contributions by the poet, which appeared in two New England poultry journals in 1903–05, during his years of farming at Derry, New Hampshire,* ed. Edward Connery Lathem and Lawrance Thompson (Hanover: Dartmouth Publications, 1963), 18–19.

29. Ibid., 20.

30. Frost, *Selected Letters*, 67.

31. Ibid., 245.

32. Kemp, *Robert Frost*, 77.

33. Clifford, *Predicament of Culture*, 10.

34. Kemp, *Robert Frost*, 71.

35. Siobhan Phillips, "The Daily Living of Robert Frost," *PMLA* 123, no. 3 (2008): 610n2.

36. Frost, *Robert Frost: Collected Poems, Prose, and Plays*, 759.

37. Kemp, *Robert Frost*, 43.

38. Ibid., 65.

39. Frost, *Robert Frost: Collected Poems, Prose, and Plays*, 760.

40. Robert Frost, *Frost: A Time to Talk: Conversations & Indiscretions Recorded by Robert Francis,* ed. Robert Francis (Amherst: University of Massachusetts Press, 1972), 108.

41. Frost, *Robert Frost: Collected Poems, Prose, and Plays*, 96.

42. Ibid., 93.

43. Ibid., 96.

44. Clifford, *Predicament of Culture*, 46.

45. Frost, *Robert Frost: Collected Poems, Prose, and Plays*, 95.

46. Ibid., 100.

47. Ibid., 248.

48. Clifford, *Predicament of Culture*, 44.

49. Frost, *Robert Frost: Collected Poems, Prose, and Plays*, 131.

50. Ibid., 131.

51. Clifford, *Predicament of Culture*, 6.

52. Frost, *Robert Frost: Collected Poems, Prose, and Plays*, 131.

53. Kemp, *Robert Frost*, 213.

54. Scott Romine quotes Frost commenting wryly on the authentic origins of one of his most famous lines ("Good fences make good neighbors"): "'I didn't get that up. It goes back to something B.C. It is on one of the pyramids.'" Scott Romine's "Frost on Frost: Marginalia from Lynda Moore's Copies of his Poetry," *ANQ* 8, no. 4 (1995): 35. Of Frost's famous "Good fences make good neighbors," Kenneth Lincoln says, "Consider the real gap: fences have holes and are not walls. Folk sayings may be riddled with mischief. In rebellious America a father's strictures should never be completed by blind obedience." Kenneth Lincoln, "Quarreling Frost, Northeast of Eden," *Southwest Review* 93, no. 1 (2008): 96.

55. Clifford, *Predicament of Culture*, 22.

56. Ibid., 41.

57. Ibid., 33.

58. Frost, *Robert Frost: Collected Poems, Prose, and Plays*, 136.

59. Clifford, *Predicament of Culture*, 39.

60. Frost, *Robert Frost: Collected Poems, Prose, and Plays*, 136.

61. Clifford, *Predicament of Culture*, 53.

62. Frost, *Robert Frost: Collected Poems, Prose, and Plays*, 151.

63. Ibid., 152.

64. Ibid., 154.

65. Ibid., 156.

66. Ibid., 157.

67. Ibid., 162.

68. Clifford, *Predicament of Culture*, 104.

69. Frost, *Robert Frost: Collected Poems, Prose, and Plays*, 72.

70. Ibid., 73.

71. Ibid., 74.

72. Ibid., 71.

73. Clifford, *Predicament of Culture*, 106.

74. Frost, *Robert Frost: Collected Poems, Prose, and Plays*, 139.

75. Ibid., 140.

76. Ibid., 144.

77. Ibid., 144.

78. Ibid., 51.

79. Ibid., 52.

80. Clifford, *Predicament of Culture*, 110.

81. Frost, *Robert Frost: Collected Poems, Prose, and Plays*, 42.

82. Ibid., 43.

83. Ibid., 83.

84. Ibid., 742.

85. Ibid., 903.

86. Ibid., 252.

87. Clifford, *Predicament of Culture*, 113.

Chapter 3

1. This chapter will deal most extensively with the 1979 edition of *Brother to Dragons* but will draw upon the 1953 edition to clarify certain points and identify significant differences between the two versions. Citations from the 1979 edition will appear as *BTD79*, page number, and citations from the 1953 edition will appear as *BTD53*, page number.

2. Michael Kreyling, *Inventing Southern Literature* (Jackson: University Press of Mississippi, 1998), xi.

3. Stuart Wright, "Hunches, Itches, and Intimations," *Sewanee Review* 117, no. 1 (Winter 2009): iii.

4. Sullivan made this remark in a lecture at the Millennial Gathering of Southern Writers, a conference at Vanderbilt University from April 6–8, 2000.

5. Robert Penn Warren, *Brother to Dragons* (Baton Rouge: Louisiana State University Press, 1979), xii.

6. Marc Manganaro, "Textual Play, Power, and Cultural Critique: An Orientation to Modernist Anthropology," in *Modernist Anthropology: From Fieldwork to Text*, ed. Marc Manganaro (Princeton, NJ: Princeton University Press, 1990), 16.

7. James Clifford, *The Predicament of Culture: Twentieth-Century Ethnography, Literature, and Art* (Cambridge, MA: Harvard University Press, 1988), 1.

8. Warren, *BTD79*, xv.

9. Clifford, *Predicament of Culture*, 4.

10. Ibid.

11. Ibid., 46.

12. Ibid., 47.

13. Warren, *BTD79*, 2.

14. Ibid., 31.

15. Manganaro, "Textual Play," 19.

16. Clifford, *Predicament of Culture*, 9.

17. Ibid., 30.

18. Warren, *BTD79*, 14.

19. Ibid., 23.

20. Ibid., 25.

21. Ibid., 32.

22. Ibid., 130.

23. Michael Kreyling, "Robert Penn Warren: The Real Southerner and the 'Hypothetical Negro,'" *American Literary History* 21, no. 2 (Summer 2009): 268–70. Kreyling examines Warren texts that deal directly with racial issues and in some sense attempt to or could be said to "speak for the Negro," especially *John Brown: The Making of a Martyr* (1929), "The Briar Patch" (1930), and *Who Speaks for the Negro?* (1965), though not from an ethnographic perspective.

24. Clifford, *Predicament of Culture*, 30.

25. Ibid., 28.

26. Manganaro, "Textual Play," 5.

27. Warren, *BTD79*, 15.

28. Ibid., 58.

29. Kreyling, "Robert Penn Warren," 106.

30. Warren, *BTD79*, 70.

31. Stanley R. Barrett, "Forecasting Theory: Problems and Exemplars in the Twenty-First Century," in *Anthropological Theory in North America*, ed. E. L. Cerroni-Long (Westport, CT: Bergin and Garvey, 1999), 271.

32. Ibid., 272.

33. Ibid.

34. Manganaro, "Textual Play," 29.

35. Warren, *BTD79*, 58.

36. Ibid., 70.

37. Larry J. Griffin's excellent essay "Southern Distinctiveness, Yet Again, or, Why America Still Needs the South" (*Southern Cultures* [Fall 2000]) points out the surprising persistence of this idea at what we might identify as conscious and unconscious levels in thinking done by and about Southerners. Griffin specifically deals with C. Vann Woodward's famous identification of guilt, poverty, and defeat as the inherent traits of the South.

38. Barrett, "Forecasting Theory," 266.

39. Clifford, *Predicament of Culture*, 25.

40. Warren, *BTD79*, 2.

41. Barrett notes that "Harding's (1992) argument about the obligation of men to produce feminist scholarship applies equally to racism. Only people of color can write *as* people of color. But white scholars can meaningfully write *about* people of color; and in some

areas they may even have an advantage: studying victimizers rather than victims, especially those located in the corridors of power." Barrett, "Forecasting Theory," 271.

42. Warren, *BTD79*, xii.

43. Warren, *BTD53*, 148.

44. Manganaro, "Textual Play," 33.

45. Clifford, *Predicament of Culture*, 25.

46. Ibid., 26.

47. Warren, *BTD79*, xii, 31, 85.

48. Ibid., 133–41.

49. Ibid., 108.

50. Ibid., 89.

51. Ibid., 40, 46.

52. Ibid., 57, 68.

53. Clifford, *Predicament of Culture*, 47.

54. Ibid., 24.

55. Ibid., 7.

56. Ibid., 28.

57. Warren, *BTD79*, 68.

58. Ibid., 69.

59. Clifford, *Predicament of Culture*, 49.

60. Ibid., 51.

61. Warren, *BTD79*, xiii.

62. Qtd. in E. L. Cerroni-Long, "Anthropology at Century's End," in *Anthropological Theory in North America*, ed. E. L. Cerroni-Long (Westport, CT: Bergin and Garvey, 1999) 14.

63. Clifford, *Predicament of Culture*, 39.

64. Ibid.

65. Ibid., 53.

66. Warren, *BTD79*, 2.

67. Clifford, *Predicament of Culture*, 31.

68. Warren, *BTD79*, 9.

69. Ibid., 10.

70. Ibid., 67.

71. Ibid., 93.

72. Ibid., 141.

73. Ibid., 99.

74. Ibid., 83.

75. Ibid., 68.

76. Warren, *BTD53*, 125–26.

77. Warren, *BTD79*, 103.

78. Ibid., 7.

79. Ibid., 87.

80. Ibid.

81. Ibid., 57.

82. Ibid., 58.

83. Ibid., 92.

84. Ibid., 58.

85. Ibid., 41, 47.

86. Ibid., 52.

87. Ibid., 73.

88. Ibid., 75.

89. Ibid., 82.

90. Ibid., 83.

91. Ibid., 89.

92. Ibid., 111.

93. Ibid., 92. The purposeful confusion of John's scream with an owl's cry relates to the poem's title, which demonstrates Warren's skill with modernist poetic techniques. In the King James Bible, Job 30:28–31 reads, "I stood up, and I cried in the congregation. I am a brother to dragons, and a companion to owls. My skin is black upon me, and my bones are burned with heat. My harp also is turned to mourning, and my organ into the voice of them that weep." This highly indirect complex of literary and religious references evinces Warren's mastery of modernist discourse. My thanks to Mark Jarman for this information.

94. Ibid., 36.

95. Clifford, *Predicament of Culture*, 5.

96. Warren, *BTD79*, 40.

97. Ibid., 43.

98. Ibid., 68.

99. Ibid., 85.

100. Ibid., 86.

101. Warren's long poem "Chief Joseph of the Nez Perce" demonstrates a similar concern with the fate of colonized and displaced Native Americans and also deals with Thomas Jefferson, Meriwether Lewis, and American national complicity.

102. Ibid., 120–21.

103. Muriel Dimen-Schein, *The Anthropological Imagination* (New York: McGraw-Hill, 1977), 95.

104. Ibid., 111.

105. Warren, *Segregation: The Inner Conflict in the South.* (London: Eyre and Spottiswoode, 1956), 14.

106. Ibid., 12.

107. Ibid., 13.

108. Dimen-Schein, *Anthropological Imagination*, 49.

109. Warren, *Talking with Robert Penn Warren*, ed. Floyd C. Watkins, John T. Hiers, and Mary Louise Weaks (Athens: University of Georgia Press, 1990), xvii.

110. Ibid., 110.

111. Ibid., 136.

112. Ibid., 231.

113. Warren frequently remarked that he tended to identify with Tennessee even though he actually grew up a few miles across the state line in Guthrie, Kentucky.

114. Warren, *Talking*, 149.

115. Warren, *Segregation*, 18.

116. Warren, *Talking*, 383.

117. Warren, *Segregation*, 15.

118. Ibid., 16–17.

119. Ibid., 16.

120. Ibid., 56.

121. Ibid., 27.

122. Ibid., 64.

123. Ibid., 66.

124. Karen Ramsay Johnson, "'Voices in My Own Blood': The Dialogic Impulse in Warren's Nonfiction Writings about Race," *Mississippi Quarterly* 52 (Winter 1998/1999): 34.

125. Warren, *Segregation*, 3.

126. Johnson, "Voices," 35.

127. Anthony E. Szczesiul, "The Immolation of Influence: Aesthetic Conflict in Robert Penn Warren's Poetry," *Mississippi Quarterly* 52 (Winter 1998/1999): 65–66.

128. Kristina Morris Baumli, email to the author, February 20, 2002.

129. Warren, *Who Speaks for the Negro?* (New York: Random House, 1965), 230.

130. Ibid., 217.

131. Ibid., 221.

132. Ibid., 265–66.

133. Ibid., 423.

Chapter 4

1. Abdul JanMohamed makes a related point about this issue by saying that the term *postcolonial* is itself something of an evasion: "To be post-whatever is to be morally on the good side of everything." JanMohamed believes that the word *postcolonial* lets people avoid thinking about continuing forms or issues of colonialism. (Rheney Lecture, Vanderbilt University, March 18, 2000).

2. In his 2009 essay "Heaney's Ghosts," William Logan says, "Heaney was surrounded by politics of the most violent sort (friends, a cousin, and a pub owner who lived down the street in Belfast were all murdered)." "Heaney's Ghosts," *The New Criterion*, April 2009, 62.

3. Dennis O'Driscoll, "An Ear to the Line: An Interview." *Poetry* 193, no. 3 (December 2008): 260.

4. Seamus Heaney, *Opened Ground: Selected Poems, 1966–1996* (London: Faber and Faber, 1998), 3–4.

5. Ibid., 417.

6. Seamus Heaney, *The Place of Writing*, introduction by Ronald Schuchard (Atlanta: Scholars Press, 1989), 35.

7. Ibid., 37.

8. Ibid., 48.

9. Akhil Gupta and James Ferguson, "Culture, Power, Place: Ethnography at the End of an Era," in *Culture, Power, Place: Explorations in Critical Anthropology*, ed. Akhil Gupta and James Ferguson (Durham, NC: Duke University Press, 1997), 2.

10. Gupta and Ferguson, "Beyond 'Culture': Space, Identity, and the Politics of Difference," in *Culture, Power, Place: Explorations in Critical Anthropology*, ed. Akhil Gupta and James Ferguson (Durham, NC: Duke University Press, 1997), 34.

11. Abdul JanMohamed, "The Specular Border Intellectual," in *Edward Said: A Critical Reader*, ed. Michael Sprinker (Oxford: Blackwell, 1992), 112.

12. Heaney, *Place of Writing*, 46.

13. Qtd. in Jonathan Allison's "The Erotics of Heaney's Joyce," *Colby Quarterly* 30, no. 1 (March 1994): 25.

14. Seamus Heaney, *The Government of the Tongue: Selected Prose, 1978–1987* (New York: Farrar, Straus and Giroux, 1989), 40. The hill of Tara was the ceremonial seat of Irish kings from the third century until 1022. Holyhead (in Wales) is the port at other end of a major ferry route crossing the Irish Sea from Dublin.

15. Ibid., 102.

16. Ibid., 105.

17. Arnold Krupat, *Ethnocriticism: Ethnography, History, Literature* (Berkeley: University of California Press, 1992), 75.

18. Ibid., 54.

19. David Lloyd, "'Pap for the Dispossessed': Seamus Heaney and the Poetics of Identity," in *Seamus Heaney*, ed. Michael Allen (New York: St. Martin's Press, 1997), 135.

20. Ibid., 136. Lloyd's reading is all the more perplexing because he was born in Ireland and is a respected critic of Irish literature and culture.

21. Ibid., 133.

22. Jonathan Allison, "Magical Nationalism, Lyric Poetry, and the Marvellous: W. B. Yeats and Seamus Heaney," in *A Companion to Magical Realism*, ed. Stephen M. Hart and Wen-ching Ouyang (London: Tamesis Books, 2005), 235–36.

23. John Carey, "Aerial Ships and Underwater Monasteries: The Evolution of a Monastic Marvel," *Proceedings of the Harvard Celtic Colloquium* 12 (1992): 16.

24. Allison, "Magical Nationalism," 236.

25. Lloyd, "Pap for the Dispossessed," 127.

26. Ibid., 131.

27. Seamus Heaney, *Place and Displacement: Recent Poetry of Northern Ireland* (Grasmere: Trustees of Dove Cottage, 1985), 15.

28. Helen Vendler, *Seamus Heaney* (Cambridge, MA: Harvard University Press, 1998), 9.

29. Ibid., 2.

30. Ibid., 68.

31. Ibid., 69.

32. Ibid., 69.

33. Heaney, *Opened Ground*, 113.

34. Ibid., 132.

35. Ibid., 237.

36. Station Island, also known as St. Patrick's Purgatory, has been the site of annual pilgrimages (each of which involves three days of penitential exercises) since at least the thirteenth century. The island is in Lough Derg, County Donegal, Ireland.

37. Ibid., 239.

38. Gupta and Ferguson, "Culture, Power, Place," 19.

39. Marvin Harris, *Theories of Culture in Postmodern Times* (Walnut Creek: Alta Mira Press, 1998), 159.

40. Ibid.

41. Gupta and Ferguson, "Culture, Power, Place," 19.

42. Heaney, *Opened Ground*, 208.

43. Ibid., 248.

44. Ibid., 377.

45. Ibid., 378.

46. RTE program, "Joyce, Yeats, and Wilde: Seamus Heaney and Richard Ellmann in Conversation," broadcast November 20, 1982.

47. Heaney, *Opened Ground*, 418.

48. Hence Heaney's singularly incongruously titled poem "Farewell to Malibu."

49. Heaney makes these remarks on an undated tape of a *BBC Newsnight* program that is housed in Bellaghy Bawn's Media Archive. The broadcast must date from the mid to late nineties because of references to the cease-fire.

50. Henry Hart, "Seamus Heaney: Circling Back." *Sewanee Review* 114, no. 3 (2006): 457.

51. Michael Parker, "Fallout from the Thunder: Poetry and Politics in Seamus Heaney's *District and Circle*," *Irish Studies Review* 16, no. 4 (November 2008): 375.

52. Jonathan O'Brien, "Heaney Now and Heaney Then," *Sunday Business Post* (Cork, Ireland), April 19, 2009.

53. Heaney, *Opened Ground*, 55.

54. Ibid., 269.

55. Ibid. 123–24.

56. Mary-Louise Muir, "District and Full Circle," *Verbal*, April 2009, 15.

57. Heaney, *Opened Ground*, 41.

58. Ibid., 47.

59. Ibid., 385.

60. Ibid., 385.

61. Timothy O'Leary explains an important detail about the background of "The Flight Path": "In 1979, Seamus Heaney was traveling by train from Dublin to Belfast when an old school friend, who had just been released from Long Kesh prison, and who therefore was presumably a member of the IRA, entered the carriage." O'Leary, "Governing the Tongue: Heaney among the Philosophers" *Textual Practice* 22, no. 4 (December 2008): 657.

62. Heaney, *Opened Ground*, 386.

63. Paul Scott Stanfield, "Facing North Again: Polyphony, Contention," *Eire-Ireland* 23, no. 4 (Winter 1988): 136.

64. Ibid., 138.

65. Ibid., 139.

66. Ibid., 139.

67. Ibid., 143.

68. Ibid., 144.

69. Gupta and Ferguson, "Culture, Power, Place," 3.

70. My thanks to Jonathan Allison for this information.

71. Heaney, *Opened Ground*, 88.

72. Ibid., 88.

73. Seamus Heaney, *Electric Light* (London: Faber and Faber, 2001), 29.

74. Heaney, *Opened Ground*, 147–48.

75. Ibid., 286.

76. Hans Osterwalder, "The Divided Self's Struggle for Identity in a Diglossic Culture: Heaney, Harrison, Frisch, and Dürrenmatt," *English Studies* 89, no. 6 (December 2008): 697.

77. Marc Manganaro, "Textual Play, Power, and Cultural Critique: An Orientation to Modernist Anthropology," in *Modernist Anthropology: From Fieldwork to Text,* ed. Marc Manganaro (Princeton, NJ: Princeton University Press, 1990), 16.

78. Heaney, *Opened Ground*, 424.

79. James Clifford, *The Predicament of Culture: Twentieth-Century Ethnography, Literature, and Art* (Cambridge, MA: Harvard University Press, 1988), 25.

80. Seamus Heaney, *District and Circle* (London: Faber and Faber, 2006), 7.

81. Heaney, *District and Circle*, p. 33.

82. Dennis O'Driscoll, *Stepping Stones: Interviews with Seamus Heaney* (London: Faber and Faber, 2008), viii. The opening section of the three-part poem "Out of This World" deals with Catholicism, receiving Communion, and the enduring power of terms associated

with Communion. Despite the relevance of the cultural details to Catholics in general, the poem does not deal with Northern Ireland or with ethnographic issues.

83. Stephen James, "Seamus Heaney's Sway," *Twentieth Century Literature* 51, no. 3 (Fall 2005): 264.

84. Seamus Heaney, *Human Chain* (London: Faber and Faber, 2010), 69–70.

Index